OPENAI

OpenAI

EXPLORING THE WORLD OF ARTIFICIAL INTELLIGENCE

Dr. Hesham Mohamed Elsherif

ELDONUSA Publishing

Contents

1 ABOUT THE AUTHOR — 1

2 PREFACE — 3

3 WHO SHOULD READ THIS BOOK? — 5

4 WHY THIS BOOK IS ESSENTIAL READING? — 7

5 Chapter 1: Understanding OpenAI — 9

6 Chapter 2: AI Fundamentals — 37

7 Chapter 3: OpenAI's Technologies and Projects — 53

8 Chapter 4: Applications of OpenAI — 126

9 Chapter 5: Societal Impacts and Ethical Considerations — 175

10 Chapter 6: OpenAI's Future Directions — 218

11 Chapter 7: Resources and Further Reading — 264

12 Appendices — 268

13 References — 276

1

ABOUT THE AUTHOR

OpenAI
Exploring the World of Artificial Intelligence
By
Dr. Hesham Mohamed Elsherif

An expert in Empirical research methodology, Dr. Elsherif special-
izes particularly in the Qualitative approach and Action research. This
specialization has not only strengthened his research endeavors but has
also allowed him to contribute invaluable insights and advancements
in these areas.

Over the years, Dr. Elsherif has made significant contributions to the academic world not only as a professional researcher but also as an Adjunct Professor. This multifaceted role in the educational landscape has further solidified his reputation as a thought leader and pioneer.

Furthermore, Dr. Elsherif's expertise isn't confined to one region. He has served as a consultant to numerous educational institutions on an international scale, sharing best practices, innovative strategies, and his deep insights into the ever-evolving realms of management and technology.

Combining a passion for education with an unparalleled depth of knowledge, Dr. Elsherif continues to inspire, educate, and lead in both the library and academic communities.

2

PREFACE

Welcome to the OPenAI: Exploring the World of Artificial Intelligence. In an era where technology is rapidly evolving, understanding the complexities of artificial intelligence (AI) is more important than ever. This guidebook aims to serve as your compass in navigating the vast landscape of AI, with a special emphasis on the groundbreaking work of OpenAI.

Artificial intelligence has become ubiquitous in our daily lives, from powering virtual assistants to driving autonomous vehicles. Behind these innovations lies the tireless efforts of organizations like OpenAI, dedicated to pushing the boundaries of what's possible in AI research and development. As OpenAI continues to unveil groundbreaking technologies and methodologies, it's essential for enthusiasts, professionals, and policymakers alike to stay informed about these advancements and their implications.

This guidebook is designed to be a comprehensive resource for anyone interested in delving into the world of AI, providing a thorough exploration of OpenAI's mission, achievements, and impact. From understanding the fundamentals of AI to dissecting the intricate workings of OpenAI's flagship projects such as GPT, DALL-E, and CLIP, each chapter is crafted to provide both novice learners and seasoned experts with valuable insights and knowledge.

Moreover, this guidebook doesn't shy away from addressing the ethical considerations and societal impacts that accompany the proliferation of AI technologies. As AI becomes increasingly intertwined with various aspects of our lives, it's imperative to engage in meaningful discussions about responsible AI development, ethical frameworks, and mitigating potential risks.

As you embark on this journey through the pages of the OPenAI Guidebook, we invite you to embrace curiosity, foster critical thinking, and explore the endless possibilities that AI has to offer. Whether you're a student eager to learn about cutting-edge technologies, an entrepreneur seeking to harness AI for innovation, or a policymaker shaping the future of AI governance, this guidebook is tailored to cater to your needs.

We extend our heartfelt gratitude to the team at OpenAI for their dedication to advancing the field of artificial intelligence and for their invaluable contributions to this guidebook. Additionally, we express our appreciation to the readers whose insatiable curiosity and passion for knowledge continue to drive the exploration of AI's frontiers.

In closing, we hope that the OPenAI Guidebook serves as a beacon of insight and inspiration, empowering you to embark on your own journey of discovery in the captivating realm of artificial intelligence.

Happy reading!

Dr. Hesham Mohamed Elsherif

3

WHO SHOULD READ THIS BOOK?

The OPenAI: Exploring the World of Artificial Intelligence is tailored to a diverse audience with varying levels of familiarity with AI. This book is ideally suited for:

AI Enthusiasts and Students:

Whether you're just dipping your toes into the vast ocean of artificial intelligence or pursuing a career in AI research and development, this guidebook provides a solid foundation. From understanding the basic principles of AI to exploring advanced concepts and real-world applications, students and enthusiasts will find this book to be an invaluable resource.

Professionals in the Tech Industry:

For professionals working in technology-related fields such as software engineering, data science, or product management, staying abreast of the latest advancements in AI is essential. This guidebook offers insights into OpenAI's cutting-edge technologies and projects, equipping professionals with the knowledge needed to leverage AI for innovation and problem-solving in their respective domains.

Policymakers and Ethicists:

As AI continues to shape various aspects of society, policymakers and ethicists play a crucial role in shaping regulatory frameworks and ethical guidelines. This book delves into the societal impacts and ethical considerations associated with AI, providing policymakers and ethicists with valuable insights to inform decision-making and governance in the AI space.

Entrepreneurs and Business Leaders:

Entrepreneurs and business leaders seeking to harness the power of AI to drive innovation and growth will find this guidebook to be a valuable resource. From understanding AI's potential applications in business to navigating ethical considerations and mitigating risks, this book offers practical insights to help entrepreneurs and business leaders make informed decisions about integrating AI into their strategies.

Educators and Researchers:

For educators teaching AI-related courses or conducting research in the field of artificial intelligence, this guidebook can serve as a comprehensive reference material. With its detailed discussions on AI fundamentals, OpenAI's technologies, and ethical considerations, educators and researchers can use this book to enhance their teaching curriculum or deepen their understanding of AI research.

In summary, the OPenAI book is designed to cater to a wide range of audiences, including students, professionals, policymakers, entrepreneurs, educators, and researchers, who are eager to explore the fascinating world of artificial intelligence and understand the pivotal role played by OpenAI in shaping its future. Whether you're a novice learner or a seasoned expert, this book offers something of value for everyone interested in unraveling the mysteries of AI.

Dr. Hesham Mohamed Elsherif

4

WHY THIS BOOK IS ESSENTIAL READING?

Comprehensive Coverage:

The OPenAI Guidebook offers a comprehensive exploration of artificial intelligence, covering everything from fundamental concepts to advanced technologies and their real-world applications. Readers gain a holistic understanding of AI and its implications, making this book an essential resource for anyone looking to delve into the field.

Focus on OpenAI:

OpenAI is at the forefront of AI research and development, consistently pushing the boundaries of innovation. This book provides unparalleled insights into OpenAI's mission, projects, and contributions to the field, offering readers a unique perspective on the cutting-edge advancements driving the future of AI.

Stay Informed:

In a rapidly evolving technological landscape, staying informed about the latest advancements in AI is crucial. The OPenAI Guidebook keeps readers up-to-date with the latest developments in AI research, ensuring that they remain knowledgeable about the latest trends, breakthroughs, and emerging technologies in the field.

Ethical Considerations:

As AI becomes increasingly integrated into society, it raises important ethical questions and concerns. This book addresses these ethical considerations head-on, prompting readers to engage in critical discussions about responsible AI development, bias mitigation, privacy concerns, and societal impacts. By fostering ethical awareness, this book empowers readers to navigate the complex ethical landscape surrounding AI with clarity and insight.

Practical Insights:

Whether you're a student, a professional, a policymaker, or an entrepreneur, this book offers practical insights that can be applied to various domains. From understanding AI's potential applications in healthcare and business to leveraging AI for innovation and decision-making, readers gain actionable knowledge that can be applied to their respective fields.

Educational Value:

The OPenAI Guidebook serves as an educational resource for learners at all levels, providing clear explanations of AI concepts, methodologies, and technologies. With its accessible language and illustrative examples, this book demystifies complex AI topics, making them accessible to a wide audience.

In conclusion, the OPenAI book is essential reading for anyone interested in understanding the intricacies of artificial intelligence, exploring the groundbreaking work of OpenAI, and grappling with the ethical and societal implications of AI technology. With its comprehensive coverage, practical insights, and educational value, this book serves as a cornerstone resource for navigating the ever-evolving landscape of AI.

5

Chapter 1: Understanding OpenAI

OpenAI, established in 2015, stands as one of the foremost organizations dedicated to advancing artificial intelligence (AI) research and development. With a mission to ensure that artificial general intelligence (AGI) benefits all of humanity, OpenAI has made significant contributions to the field through its innovative projects, collaborative efforts, and commitment to ethical AI development.

OpenAI's inception can be traced back to the collective vision of several prominent figures in the tech industry, including Elon Musk, Sam Altman, and others (Altman & OpenAI, 2015). The organization was founded with the ambitious goal of democratizing access to AI technology while also prioritizing safety and ethical considerations (Brockman et al., 2016). Since its inception, OpenAI has evolved into a multidisciplinary research institute, comprising teams of researchers, engineers, and policymakers working collaboratively to advance the frontiers of AI.

One of the key facets of understanding OpenAI lies in comprehending its organizational structure and leadership. OpenAI operates as a non-profit organization governed by the OpenAI LP board of directors, which includes prominent individuals from both the tech industry and academia (OpenAI, n.d.). The organization is led by a team of experienced researchers and executives who oversee various research initiatives, strategic partnerships, and operational functions (OpenAI, n.d.).

OpenAI's research agenda is driven by a commitment to fundamental AI research, with a focus on developing cutting-edge technologies that have the potential to drive significant societal impact. From natural language processing (NLP) to reinforcement learning and robotics, OpenAI's research spans a wide range of domains, aiming to tackle some of the most challenging problems in AI (Amodei et al., 2016; Radford et al., 2019).

Furthermore, understanding OpenAI necessitates an appreciation of its ethical framework and guiding principles. OpenAI is committed to promoting transparency, safety, and responsible AI development (Irpan et al., 2018). The organization actively engages in discussions surrounding the ethical implications of AI, advocating for the adoption of robust ethical guidelines and safeguards to mitigate potential risks (OpenAI, n.d.).

In conclusion, understanding OpenAI involves delving into the organization's history, mission, organizational structure, research agenda, and ethical considerations. By comprehensively examining these aspects, stakeholders can gain valuable insights into OpenAI's role in shaping the future of artificial intelligence and its potential societal impacts.

Introduction to OpenAI:

OpenAI, founded in 2015, is a research institute dedicated to advancing artificial intelligence (AI) in a manner that benefits all of humanity. Understanding OpenAI begins with an exploration of its mission, vision, and goals, which provide insight into the organization's overarching purpose and aspirations.

Mission:

The mission of OpenAI is to ensure that artificial general intelligence (AGI) benefits all of humanity. This mission statement underscores the organization's commitment to developing AI technologies that are safe, ethical, and aligned with human values (Altman & OpenAI, 2015).

Mission Statement:

OpenAI's mission is succinctly summarized as follows: "To ensure that artificial general intelligence (AGI) benefits all of humanity" (Altman & OpenAI, 2015). This mission statement encapsulates OpenAI's overarching objective of harnessing the potential of AI to drive positive societal outcomes while mitigating potential risks and challenges associated with the development of advanced AI systems.

Commitment to Human-Centric AI:

At the core of OpenAI's mission is a commitment to human-centric AI development. The organization recognizes the transformative potential of AI to address complex problems and enhance human capabilities. However, it also acknowledges the importance of ensuring that AI technologies are aligned with human values, ethical principles, and societal needs (Brockman et al., 2016).

Promoting Safety and Ethical AI:

OpenAI's mission extends beyond technical innovation to encompass a strong emphasis on safety and ethical considerations in AI development. The organization recognizes the importance of building AI systems that are robust, reliable, and trustworthy, thereby minimizing the potential for unintended consequences or harmful outcomes (Irpan et al., 2018).

Advancing Global Collaboration:

OpenAI's mission underscores the importance of fostering collaboration and knowledge-sharing within the global AI community. By promoting open research and collaboration, the organization seeks to accelerate progress towards the development of beneficial AI technologies that can be widely disseminated and utilized for the collective benefit of humanity (OpenAI, n.d.).

In summary, understanding OpenAI's mission provides a foundational framework for comprehending the organization's overarching goals, research agenda, and strategic priorities. By aligning its activities with a mission focused on ensuring that AI benefits all of humanity, OpenAI aims to contribute to the responsible and ethical advancement of AI technologies for the betterment of society.

Vision:

OpenAI envisions a future where AI technologies contribute to solving some of the world's most pressing challenges, from healthcare and education to environmental sustainability and economic prosperity. The organization aims to democratize access to AI and empower individuals and organizations to leverage AI for positive societal impact (Brockman et al., 2016).

Vision Statement:

OpenAI's vision can be summarized as follows: "To create a future in which artificial intelligence augments human capabilities, empowers individuals and organizations, and fosters positive societal transformation" (Brockman et al., 2016). This vision statement encapsulates the organization's commitment to harnessing the transformative potential of AI to address complex challenges and enhance human well-being.

Empowering Individuals and Organizations:

At the core of OpenAI's vision is the belief in the empowering capabilities of AI. The organization envisions a future where AI technologies empower individuals and organizations across various domains, including healthcare, education, business, and beyond. By augmenting human capabilities, AI has the potential to unlock new opportunities for innovation, creativity, and productivity (Radford et al., 2019).

Promoting Societal Transformation:

OpenAI's vision extends beyond technical advancements to encompass a broader goal of fostering positive societal transformation. The organization recognizes AI's potential to drive social progress, address systemic challenges, and promote equity and inclusion. By leveraging AI for social good, OpenAI aims to contribute to a more just, equitable, and sustainable world (Irpan et al., 2018).

Democratizing Access to AI:

OpenAI envisions a future where access to AI technologies is democratized and widely accessible to individuals and communities worldwide. The organization advocates for open research and collaboration, promoting transparency and knowledge-sharing within the global AI community. By democratizing access to AI, OpenAI seeks to ensure that the benefits of AI innovation are equitably distributed across society (Altman & OpenAI, 2015).

In summary, understanding OpenAI's vision provides insight into the organization's overarching aspirations and goals for the future of AI. By envisioning a future where AI augments human capabilities, fosters positive societal transformation, and promotes equitable access to AI technologies, OpenAI aims to shape the trajectory of AI development in a manner that benefits all of humanity.

Goals:

OpenAI's goals are multifaceted, encompassing both technical and ethical objectives. On the technical front, the organization seeks to push the boundaries of AI research, develop state-of-the-art AI technologies, and advance the field towards the realization of artificial general intelligence. Concurrently, OpenAI is committed to addressing the ethical implications of AI, promoting transparency, fairness, and safety in AI systems, and advocating for responsible AI development (Irpan et al., 2018).

Technical Advancements Goals:

Pushing the Boundaries of AI Research:

OpenAI aims to push the boundaries of AI research by conducting groundbreaking studies and developing cutting-edge AI technologies. Through initiatives such as GPT (Generative Pre-trained Transformer) models, DALL-E, and CLIP, the organization seeks to achieve significant advancements in natural language processing, computer vision, and other AI domains (Radford et al., 2019).

Advancing Towards Artificial General Intelligence (AGI):

A key long-term goal of OpenAI is to advance the field of AI towards the development of artificial general intelligence (AGI). AGI represents the next frontier in AI research, encompassing systems capable of understanding and learning across a wide range of tasks and domains. OpenAI's research initiatives are geared towards laying the groundwork for AGI while addressing technical challenges and safety considerations (Amodei et al., 2016).

Promoting Scalable and Accessible AI Technologies:

OpenAI is committed to developing AI technologies that are scalable, efficient, and accessible to a wide range of users. The organization's efforts focus on democratizing access to AI through open research, collaboration, and the development of tools such as OpenAI Gym, which provides a platform for developing and testing AI algorithms (Brockman et al., 2016).

Ethical Imperatives Goals:

Ensuring AI Safety and Reliability:

OpenAI prioritizes the safety and reliability of AI systems, recognizing the potential risks associated with advanced AI technologies. The organization is committed to developing robust and verifiable AI systems that minimize the likelihood of unintended consequences or harmful outcomes (Irpan et al., 2018).

Promoting Ethical AI Development:

OpenAI advocates for the responsible and ethical development of AI, emphasizing the importance of transparency, fairness, and accountability in AI systems. The organization actively engages in discussions surrounding AI ethics and works to develop ethical guidelines and best practices for AI research and deployment (OpenAI, n.d.).

Addressing Societal Implications:

OpenAI acknowledges the societal implications of AI technologies and aims to address them proactively. The organization advocates for policies and initiatives that promote equity, inclusion, and responsible AI governance, ensuring that AI technologies benefit all members of society (Altman & OpenAI, 2015).

In summary, understanding OpenAI's goals provides insight into the organization's overarching objectives and strategic priorities. By combining technical advancements with ethical imperatives, OpenAI aims to advance the field of AI while ensuring that AI technologies are developed and deployed responsibly for the benefit of humanity.

Understanding OpenAI's mission, vision, and goals provides a foundational framework for comprehending the organization's activities, research initiatives, and contributions to the broader AI community. By aligning its efforts with a clear set of guiding principles, OpenAI aims to foster trust, collaboration, and innovation in the pursuit of AI technologies that benefit humanity as a whole.

Historical Overview:

OpenAI, established in 2015, stands as a pioneering research institute at the forefront of artificial intelligence (AI) development. Understanding OpenAI necessitates a deep dive into its founding, which sheds light on the organization's origins, motivations, and early initiatives.

Founding of OpenAI

Origins and Motivations:

OpenAI was founded by a group of tech luminaries including Elon Musk, Sam Altman, Greg Brockman, Ilya Sutskever, Wojciech Zaremba, and others (Altman & OpenAI, 2015). The organization emerged from a collective recognition of the transformative potential of AI and a shared concern about its potential risks and implications. The founders believed that AI could significantly impact humanity's future, both positively and negatively, and sought to ensure that its development was guided by ethical principles and aligned with human values.

Mission and Goals:

At the heart of OpenAI's founding was a commitment to advancing AI in a manner that benefits all of humanity. The organization's mission was articulated as follows: "To ensure that artificial general intelligence (AGI) benefits all of humanity" (Altman & OpenAI, 2015). This mission statement reflected OpenAI's overarching goal of developing AI technologies that are safe, ethical, and aligned with human values.

Formation and Early Initiatives:

OpenAI was established as a non-profit organization with the aim of conducting research and developing open-source AI technologies. In its early years, the organization focused on laying the groundwork for its research agenda, building partnerships with academic institutions and industry collaborators, and recruiting top talent in the field of AI. OpenAI also launched several flagship initiatives, including OpenAI Gym, a platform for developing and testing AI algorithms (Brockman et al., 2016).

Significance and Impact:

The founding of OpenAI marked a significant milestone in the evolution of AI research and development. By bringing together leading experts, fostering collaboration, and advocating for responsible AI development, OpenAI catalyzed advancements in AI while also raising awareness about the ethical considerations and societal implications of AI technologies.

In summary, understanding OpenAI's founding provides crucial context for comprehending the organization's mission, values, and contributions to the field of artificial intelligence. By tracing its origins and early initiatives, stakeholders can gain insight into the motivations behind OpenAI's establishment and its ongoing efforts to shape the future of AI in a manner that benefits humanity.

Milestones of AI:

Establishment of OpenAI:

OpenAI was established in December 2015 with the mission of ensuring that artificial general intelligence (AGI) benefits all of humanity (Altman & OpenAI, 2015). Founded by a group of prominent tech entrepreneurs and researchers, including Elon Musk and Sam Altman, the organization quickly garnered attention for its ambitious goals and commitment to ethical AI development.

Launch of Research Initiatives:

In its early years, OpenAI focused on laying the groundwork for its research agenda and launching several flagship initiatives. These initiatives included projects such as GPT (Generative Pre-trained

Transformer) models, which revolutionized natural language processing, and OpenAI Gym, a platform for developing and testing AI algorithms (Radford et al., 2019; Brockman et al., 2016).

Breakthroughs in AI Research:

OpenAI made significant breakthroughs in various domains of AI research, pushing the boundaries of what was thought possible in the field. Examples include advancements in language understanding with models like GPT-2 and GPT-3, as well as innovations in computer vision, robotics, and reinforcement learning (Amodei et al., 2016; Radford et al., 2019).

Release of OpenAI's Research Findings:

OpenAI has been committed to promoting transparency and open collaboration in AI research. The organization regularly publishes its research findings in top-tier academic conferences and journals, making its work accessible to the broader research community. This commitment to open science has contributed to the advancement of AI knowledge and technology (Irpan et al., 2018).

5Ethical Considerations and Policy Advocacy:

OpenAI has been actively engaged in discussions surrounding the ethical implications of AI and advocating for responsible AI development. The organization has contributed to the development of ethical guidelines and best practices for AI research and deployment, while also participating in policy discussions to shape AI governance frameworks (OpenAI, n.d.).

In summary, understanding OpenAI's milestones provides insight into the organization's journey from its founding to its current status as a leading research institute in the field of artificial intelligence. By tracing its key achievements and contributions, stakeholders can appreciate the significant impact that OpenAI has had on advancing AI technologies and shaping the discourse surrounding AI ethics and governance

Evolution of AI:

Foundation and Early Years:

OpenAI was established in December 2015 by a group of tech entrepreneurs and researchers, including Elon Musk and Sam Altman, with the mission of ensuring that artificial general intelligence (AGI) benefits all of humanity (Altman & OpenAI, 2015). In its early years, the organization focused on laying the groundwork for its research agenda, building partnerships, and recruiting top talent in the field of AI.

Research Breakthroughs:

OpenAI quickly gained recognition for its groundbreaking research initiatives and contributions to AI technology. Notable breakthroughs include advancements in natural language processing with models like GPT (Generative Pre-trained Transformer), which demonstrated remarkable capabilities in text generation and understanding (Radford et al., 2019). These research breakthroughs propelled OpenAI to the forefront of AI research and garnered widespread acclaim from the scientific community.

Expansion and Diversification:

Over time, OpenAI expanded its research focus to encompass a broader range of AI domains, including computer vision, robotics, and reinforcement learning. The organization invested in diverse research projects aimed at addressing some of the most pressing challenges in AI, such as achieving artificial general intelligence, developing safe and ethical AI systems, and democratizing access to AI technologies (OpenAI, n.d.).

Emphasis on Ethics and Governance:

As AI technology advanced, OpenAI recognized the importance of addressing ethical considerations and societal implications. The organization became increasingly engaged in discussions surrounding AI ethics, advocating for transparency, fairness, and safety in AI systems (Irpan et al., 2018). OpenAI also participated in policy discussions to shape AI governance frameworks and promote responsible AI development.

Collaboration and Knowledge Sharing:

OpenAI has fostered a culture of collaboration and knowledge sharing within the global AI community. The organization has actively contributed to open research initiatives, published its findings in top-tier academic conferences and journals, and released open-source tools and datasets to facilitate AI research and development (Brockman et al., 2016).

In summary, the evolution of OpenAI reflects its journey from a pioneering research institute to a leading force in AI innovation and ethics. By tracing its development over time, stakeholders can gain a deeper understanding of OpenAI's impact on the field of artificial intelligence and its commitment to advancing AI technologies for the benefit of humanity.

Organizational Structure:

Understanding the organizational structure of OpenAI is crucial for gaining insight into how the organization operates, makes decisions, and collaborates on AI research and development efforts.

1. **Teams and Research Divisions**:

OpenAI's organizational structure is characterized by multidisciplinary teams comprising researchers, engineers, policymakers, and other professionals. These teams are organized around specific research divisions or thematic areas, reflecting the organization's diverse research interests and expertise. For example, OpenAI has dedicated teams working on natural language processing (NLP), computer vision, robotics, reinforcement learning, and AI safety.

1. **Interdisciplinary Teams**:

   OpenAI's organizational structure is characterized by interdisciplinary teams comprising researchers, engineers, policymakers, and domain experts from diverse backgrounds. These teams are organized around specific research divisions or thematic areas, reflecting the organization's broad scope of interests and the multifaceted nature of AI research. Each team brings together individuals with complementary skills and expertise to tackle complex AI challenges collaboratively.

2. **Research Divisions**:

OpenAI's research divisions are dedicated to advancing knowledge and developing AI technologies in specific domains. These divisions focus on various aspects of AI, including natural language processing (NLP), computer vision, robotics, reinforcement learning, and AI safety. Within each division, researchers work on cutting-edge projects, explore novel approaches, and push the boundaries of AI research. The organization's research divisions are structured to foster collaboration, creativity, and innovation among team members.

Natural Language Processing (NLP): One of OpenAI's prominent research divisions is focused on natural language processing, which involves the development of AI models and algorithms capable of understanding, generating, and processing human language. Researchers in this division work on projects such as language modeling, machine translation, text generation, and sentiment analysis. Their work has led to significant advancements in AI-powered language understanding and generation, as demonstrated by models like GPT (Radford et al., 2019).

Computer Vision: Another key research division at OpenAI is dedicated to computer vision, which focuses on developing AI systems capable of understanding and interpreting visual information from images and videos. Researchers in this division explore techniques for object detection, image classification, image segmentation, and scene understanding. Their work has contributed to the development of state-of-the-art computer vision models that excel in tasks such as image recognition and scene understanding.

Reinforcement Learning: OpenAI's reinforcement learning division focuses on the development of AI algorithms that can learn and adapt to complex environments through trial and error. Researchers in this division explore reinforcement learning techniques for training autonomous agents, robots, and AI systems to perform tasks in dynamic and uncertain environments. Their work has led to breakthroughs in reinforcement learning, enabling AI systems to achieve human-level performance in games, simulations, and real-world applications (Brockman et al., 2016).

AI Safety and Ethics: OpenAI also has a dedicated division focused on AI safety and ethics, which examines the potential risks, challenges, and societal implications of AI technologies. Researchers in this division explore strategies for ensuring that AI systems are safe, reliable, and aligned with human values. They investigate topics such as robustness, interpretability, fairness, accountability, and transparency in AI systems. Their work aims to address ethical concerns and promote responsible AI development (Irpan et al., 2018).

In summary, the organizational structure of OpenAI is characterized by interdisciplinary teams and research divisions that work collaboratively to advance the frontiers of AI research and development. By leveraging diverse expertise and fostering collaboration across different domains, OpenAI aims to tackle complex AI challenges and contribute to the responsible and ethical advancement of AI technologies.

II. Leadership Structure:

OpenAI is led by a team of experienced researchers, executives, and advisors who provide strategic direction and oversee the organization's operations. The leadership structure includes:

Executive Leadership:

The executive leadership team, which typically includes a CEO, COO, and other C-level executives, is responsible for setting the organization's vision, strategy, and goals. They also play a key role in stakeholder engagement, fundraising, and external relations.

1. **Chief Executive Officer (CEO)**:

The Chief Executive Officer (CEO) serves as the highest-ranking executive in OpenAI and is responsible for providing overall leadership and vision for the organization. The CEO plays a critical role in setting strategic priorities, defining long-term goals, and ensuring that OpenAI remains at the forefront of AI research and development. Additionally, the CEO represents OpenAI in external engagements, including stakeholder meetings, industry conferences, and media interactions (Altman & OpenAI, 2015).

2. **Chief Operating Officer (COO)**:

The Chief Operating Officer (COO) is responsible for overseeing the day-to-day operations of OpenAI and ensuring that the organization's activities are aligned with its strategic objectives. The COO works closely with other members of the executive leadership team to develop and implement operational plans, manage resources effectively, and drive organizational efficiency. Additionally, the COO may be tasked with overseeing specific functional areas within OpenAI, such as finance, human resources, or legal affairs (Altman & OpenAI, 2015).

3. **Research Directors**:

Research directors at OpenAI lead individual research divisions or teams within the organization and are responsible for guiding research efforts, setting research agendas, and fostering collaboration among team members. Research directors are typically seasoned researchers with expertise in specific AI domains, such as natural language processing, computer vision, reinforcement learning, or AI safety. They play a key role in driving innovation, identifying research priorities, and ensuring the quality and rigor of research conducted at OpenAI (Radford et al., 2019).

4. **Board of Directors**:

The Board of Directors provides oversight, guidance, and governance to OpenAI, ensuring that the organization fulfills its mission and operates effectively. The board is composed of prominent individuals from the tech industry, academia, and other sectors, who bring diverse expertise and perspectives to the table. Board members play a crucial role in strategic decision-making, risk management, and accountability. They also provide valuable insights and advice to OpenAI's executive leadership team on matters ranging from research priorities to organizational strategy (Altman & OpenAI, 2015).

In summary, the executive leadership structure of OpenAI is designed to provide strategic direction, operational oversight, and governance for the organization. By leveraging the expertise and leadership capabilities of its executive team and board of directors, OpenAI aims to fulfill its mission of advancing artificial intelligence in a manner that benefits all of humanity.

<u>Research Directors</u>:

Research directors lead individual research divisions or teams within OpenAI, guiding research efforts, setting research agendas, and fostering collaboration among team members. They are often seasoned researchers with expertise in specific AI domains.

Role of Research Directors:

Research directors at OpenAI are senior researchers with extensive expertise and experience in specific domains of artificial intelligence (AI). They are entrusted with the responsibility of leading individual research divisions or teams within the organization, each focusing on distinct areas of AI research such as natural language processing, computer vision, reinforcement learning, or AI safety.

Key Responsibilities:

Guiding Research Efforts: Research directors are tasked with guiding the research efforts of their respective teams, setting research agendas, and defining strategic priorities. They play a crucial role in identifying promising research directions, allocating resources effectively, and ensuring that research activities are aligned with OpenAI's overall mission and objectives.

Fostering Collaboration: Research directors foster collaboration and teamwork within their research divisions, encouraging knowledge sharing, interdisciplinary collaboration, and innovation. They create an environment that encourages open communication, constructive feedback, and intellectual exchange among team members, leading to synergistic research outcomes.

Driving Innovation: Research directors are responsible for driving innovation within their research divisions, pushing the boundaries of AI research, and exploring novel approaches to solving complex problems. They encourage creativity, experimentation, and risk-taking, empowering researchers to pursue ambitious research projects and tackle cutting-edge challenges in AI.

Ensuring Research Quality: Research directors uphold high standards of research quality, rigor, and integrity within their teams. They oversee the design, execution, and evaluation of research projects, ensuring that methodologies are sound, results are reproducible, and conclusions are well-supported by evidence. They also promote transparency and openness in research practices, advocating for the dissemination of research findings through publications, conferences, and open-source contributions.

Mentoring and Development: Research directors provide mentorship, guidance, and support to researchers within their teams, helping them develop their skills, pursue their research interests, and achieve their professional goals. They create opportunities for professional growth, training, and career advancement, fostering a culture of continuous learning and development within the organization.

Research directors at OpenAI play a central role in shaping the direction, quality, and impact of the organization's research efforts. Through their leadership, expertise, and commitment to excellence, research directors contribute to OpenAI's mission of advancing artificial intelligence for the benefit of humanity.

Board of Directors:

OpenAI is governed by a board of directors composed of prominent individuals from the tech industry, academia, and other sectors. The board provides oversight, guidance, and governance to ensure that OpenAI fulfills its mission and operates effectively.

Role of the Board of Directors:

The Board of Directors holds ultimate responsibility for the governance and stewardship of OpenAI, overseeing the organization's activities, setting strategic priorities, and safeguarding its mission and values. Composed of prominent individuals from various sectors, the Board brings diverse perspectives, expertise, and insights to inform decision-making and shape the direction of the organization.

Key Responsibilities:

Strategic Oversight: The Board of Directors is responsible for providing strategic oversight and direction to OpenAI, ensuring that the organization's activities are aligned with its mission and long-term goals. The Board sets strategic priorities, evaluates performance against strategic objectives, and makes decisions on matters of strategic importance, such as major initiatives, partnerships, and investments.

Governance and Accountability: The Board upholds principles of good governance, accountability, and transparency within OpenAI, ensuring that the organization operates ethically, responsibly, and in compliance with legal and regulatory requirements. The Board establishes governance frameworks, policies, and procedures to guide decision-making, manage risk, and promote organizational integrity.

Risk Management: The Board oversees risk management processes within OpenAI, identifying, assessing, and mitigating risks that may impact the organization's operations, reputation, or stakeholders. The Board monitors key risks and vulnerabilities, evaluates risk management strategies, and takes appropriate actions to safeguard the organization's interests and assets.

Executive Leadership Oversight: The Board provides oversight and evaluation of OpenAI's executive leadership team, including the CEO and other senior executives. The Board evaluates executive performance, provides feedback and guidance, and ensures that the organization's leadership team is equipped to effectively fulfill their roles and responsibilities.

Stakeholder Engagement: The Board engages with key stakeholders, including donors, partners, regulators, and the broader AI community, to foster trust, collaboration, and support for OpenAI's mission and initiatives. The Board represents OpenAI in external engagements, advocates for the organization's interests, and builds relationships with stakeholders to advance its goals.

Impact and Influence:

The Board of Directors wields significant influence and impact on the trajectory and success of OpenAI. Through their collective wisdom, experience, and strategic vision, the Board shapes the organization's strategic direction, guides its decision-making processes, and ensures that OpenAI remains at the forefront of AI innovation and ethics.

The Board of Directors plays a critical role in providing governance, oversight, and strategic direction to OpenAI, ensuring the organization's effectiveness, integrity, and impact in advancing artificial intelligence for the benefit of humanity.

III. Collaborations and Partnerships:

OpenAI actively collaborates with a wide range of stakeholders, including academic institutions, industry partners, non-profit organizations, and government agencies. These collaborations take various forms, including joint research projects, partnerships to develop AI technologies, knowledge-sharing initiatives, and policy advocacy efforts.

Academic Collaborations:

OpenAI collaborates with leading universities and research institutions worldwide to advance AI research and share knowledge. These collaborations often involve joint research projects, co-authorship of research papers, and participation in academic conferences and workshops.

Nature of Academic Collaborations:

OpenAI engages in collaborative partnerships with leading academic institutions worldwide, leveraging their diverse expertise, resources, and research infrastructure to address complex challenges in artificial intelligence (AI). These collaborations take various forms, including joint research projects, co-authorship of research papers, participation in academic conferences and workshops, and exchange programs for researchers.

Key Aspects of Academic Collaborations:

Research Synergy: Academic collaborations enable OpenAI to harness the collective expertise and insights of researchers from diverse academic disciplines, fostering interdisciplinary collaboration and synergistic research outcomes. By partnering with leading academic institutions, OpenAI gains access to cutting-edge research methodologies, theoretical frameworks, and experimental facilities, enhancing the quality and depth of its research endeavors.

Access to Talent Pool: Collaborations with academic institutions provide OpenAI with access to a diverse talent pool of graduate students, postdoctoral researchers, and faculty members who contribute to research projects, bring fresh perspectives, and drive innovation. These collaborations serve as a pipeline for talent acquisition, recruitment, and retention, allowing OpenAI to access top-tier researchers and nurture future leaders in the field of AI.

Knowledge Exchange: Academic collaborations facilitate knowledge exchange and dissemination, enabling researchers at OpenAI to share their expertise, insights, and findings with the broader academic community. Through joint publications, conference presentations, and workshops, OpenAI contributes to advancing the frontiers of AI research, while also benefiting from feedback, critique, and validation from academic peers.

Resource Sharing: Collaborations with academic institutions often involve resource sharing agreements, allowing OpenAI to access specialized equipment, datasets, computational resources, and research facilities that may not be available internally. These collaborations enhance OpenAI's research capabilities, scalability, and efficiency, enabling researchers to tackle larger and more complex research projects.

Impact and Benefits:

Academic collaborations play a crucial role in advancing OpenAI's research agenda, driving scientific discovery, and accelerating AI innovation. By leveraging the expertise, resources, and networks of academic partners, OpenAI strengthens its position as a leading research institute and contributes to the global advancement of AI knowledge and technology.

Industry Partnerships:

OpenAI partners with technology companies, startups, and industry organizations to develop and deploy AI technologies in various sectors. These partnerships may involve technology licensing, joint product development, and co-investment in research and development initiatives.

Nature of Industry Partnerships:

OpenAI collaborates with a diverse array of industry partners, including technology companies, startups, industry consortia, and non-profit organizations, to leverage complementary expertise, resources, and market insights. These partnerships are characterized by mutual cooperation, knowledge exchange, and shared objectives to advance the development and deployment of AI technologies across various sectors.

Key Aspects of Industry Partnerships:

Technology Transfer and Commercialization: Industry partnerships enable OpenAI to transfer cutting-edge AI technologies and research findings into practical applications, products, and services that address real-world challenges and meet market demands. By collaborating with industry partners, OpenAI can accelerate the commercialization and adoption of AI innovations, driving economic growth and societal impact.

Access to Data and Resources: Industry partnerships provide OpenAI with access to proprietary data, datasets, computational resources, and research facilities that may not be readily available internally. These partnerships enhance OpenAI's research capabilities, scalability, and efficiency, enabling researchers to tackle larger and more complex AI projects and experiments.

Co-development and Joint Ventures: OpenAI engages in co-development and joint venture partnerships with industry stakeholders to collaboratively develop AI solutions, products, and platforms that address specific market needs and opportunities. These partnerships leverage the complementary strengths and expertise of both parties, fostering innovation, agility, and market responsiveness.

Market Insights and Validation: Industry partnerships offer OpenAI valuable insights into market trends, user needs, and industry dynamics, enabling the organization to tailor its research and development efforts to address market demand and opportunities. By collaborating with industry partners, OpenAI can validate its AI technologies in real-world settings, gather feedback, and iterate on solutions to optimize performance and usability.

Impact and Benefits:

Industry partnerships play a critical role in advancing OpenAI's mission of ensuring that artificial general intelligence (AGI) benefits all of humanity. By collaborating with industry stakeholders, OpenAI accelerates the translation of AI research into practical applications, fosters technology transfer, and promotes responsible AI deployment across diverse sectors, ranging from healthcare and finance to transportation and entertainment.

Policy and Advocacy:

OpenAI engages with policymakers, regulators, and advocacy groups to shape AI governance frameworks, promote responsible AI development, and address societal implications of AI technologies. These efforts include participating in policy discussions, advocating for ethical AI principles, and contributing to the development of AI policy guidelines.

Nature of Policy and Advocacy Engagements:

OpenAI engages in policy and advocacy efforts to contribute to the development of responsible AI governance frameworks, promote ethical AI principles, and address societal implications of AI technologies. These engagements involve collaboration with policymakers, regulators, advocacy groups, and other stakeholders to shape AI policy, regulations, and standards that align with OpenAI's mission of ensuring that artificial general intelligence (AGI) benefits all of humanity.

Key Aspects of Policy and Advocacy Engagements:

Policy Formation and Advocacy: OpenAI participates in policy formation processes, advocating for policies and regulations that promote responsible AI development, safety, transparency, and accountability. Through policy advocacy efforts, OpenAI seeks to influence decision-makers and shape the direction of AI governance frameworks at local, national, and international levels.

Ethical Guidelines and Standards: OpenAI contributes to the development of ethical guidelines, principles, and standards for AI technologies, collaborating with industry partners, academic institutions, and civil society organizations. These collaborations aim to establish ethical norms and best practices that guide the responsible development and deployment of AI systems, ensuring alignment with human values and societal interests.

Risk Assessment and Mitigation: OpenAI conducts risk assessments and evaluates potential societal risks, challenges, and impacts associated with AI technologies. By engaging in dialogue with policymakers, regulators, and stakeholders, OpenAI seeks to identify emerging risks, anticipate future challenges, and develop strategies for mitigating risks and ensuring the safe and beneficial deployment of AI technologies.

Transparency and Accountability: OpenAI advocates for transparency and accountability in AI systems, promoting practices that enable stakeholders to understand, interpret, and evaluate the behavior and decisions of AI systems. Through transparency initiatives, such as open-sourcing AI models and releasing research findings, OpenAI fosters trust, accountability, and public scrutiny of AI technologies.

Impact and Benefits:

Policy and advocacy engagements play a critical role in shaping the societal, ethical, and regulatory landscape of AI, ensuring that AI technologies are developed and deployed in a manner that maximizes benefits and minimizes risks for all stakeholders. By actively participating in policy discussions, advocating for ethical principles, and collaborating with diverse stakeholders, OpenAI contributes to the responsible and inclusive advancement of AI technologies for the benefit of humanity.

In summary, the organizational structure of OpenAI reflects its collaborative and interdisciplinary approach to AI research and development. By fostering teamwork, leadership, and strategic partnerships, OpenAI aims to advance the frontiers of AI while ensuring that its technologies benefit society as a whole.

OpenAI's Ethical Framework:

OpenAI operates within a comprehensive ethical framework that guides its research, development, and deployment of artificial intelligence (AI) technologies.

Ethical Principles:

OpenAI's ethical framework is grounded in a set of core principles that prioritize the ethical, societal, and human-centered aspects of AI development. These principles reflect OpenAI's commitment to promoting transparency, fairness, safety, and accountability in the design, deployment, and use of AI technologies. *Key ethical principles upheld by OpenAI include:*

Transparency: OpenAI advocates for transparency in AI systems, promoting practices that enable stakeholders to understand, interpret, and evaluate the behavior and decisions of AI models. Transparency enhances trust, accountability, and public scrutiny of AI technologies, empowering users to make informed decisions and mitigate potential risks.

Fairness and Equity: OpenAI strives to develop AI technologies that are fair, unbiased, and equitable, ensuring that they do not perpetuate or exacerbate existing social inequalities or discrimination. By addressing biases, disparities, and inequities in AI systems, OpenAI promotes fairness, inclusivity, and social justice in AI deployment across diverse populations and communities.

Safety and Reliability: OpenAI prioritizes safety and reliability in AI systems, implementing measures to mitigate risks, uncertainties, and unintended consequences associated with AI technologies. Through rigorous testing, validation, and risk assessment processes, OpenAI aims to ensure that AI systems operate safely, reliably, and predictably in diverse environments and scenarios.

Human-Centered Design: OpenAI adopts a human-centered approach to AI development, prioritizing the needs, preferences, and values of end-users and stakeholders. By involving end-users in the design, development, and evaluation of AI systems, OpenAI aims to create technologies that enhance human well-being, autonomy, and agency, while minimizing potential harms and adverse impacts.

Implementation and Governance:

OpenAI's ethical framework is operationalized through a combination of policies, guidelines, and governance mechanisms that govern the organization's research, development, and deployment activities. These include:

Ethics Review Processes: OpenAI employs ethics review processes to assess the ethical implications of its research projects and initiatives. Ethics review boards or committees evaluate proposed research activities, identify potential ethical risks and concerns, and provide recommendations for mitigating risks and upholding ethical standards.

Ethical Guidelines and Policies: OpenAI establishes ethical guidelines, policies, and codes of conduct that govern the behavior and conduct of its researchers, employees, and collaborators. These guidelines articulate expectations for ethical conduct, responsible research practices, and adherence to ethical principles in all aspects of AI development and deployment.

Community Engagement and Stakeholder Consultation: OpenAI engages with diverse stakeholders, including researchers, policymakers, industry partners, civil society organizations, and the general public, to solicit feedback, input, and perspectives on ethical issues and dilemmas related to AI. Through community engagement and stakeholder consultation processes, OpenAI fosters dialogue, transparency, and collaboration in addressing ethical challenges and promoting responsible AI development.

Ongoing Ethical Reflection and Learning: OpenAI fosters a culture of ongoing ethical reflection and learning, encouraging researchers and employees to critically examine the ethical implications of their work, seek feedback from peers and experts, and stay abreast of emerging ethical considerations in AI research and practice. By fostering a culture of ethical awareness and accountability, OpenAI aims to continuously improve its ethical practices and uphold its commitment to ethical AI development.

Impact and Significance:

OpenAI's ethical framework has significant implications for the organization's research agenda, partnerships, and societal impact. By prioritizing ethical principles and considerations in its AI development efforts, OpenAI aims to build trust, promote responsible innovation, and address societal concerns related to AI technologies. Through its ethical framework, OpenAI seeks to demonstrate leadership in ethical AI development and contribute to the responsible and inclusive advancement of AI for the benefit of humanity.

Responsible AI Development:

OpenAI's ethical framework is grounded in the principle of responsible AI development, which emphasizes the ethical, societal, and human-centered considerations that guide the organization's research, innovation, and deployment of artificial intelligence (AI) technologies.

Principles of Responsible AI Development:

Transparency and Explainability: OpenAI prioritizes transparency and explainability in AI systems, ensuring that they are designed and implemented in a manner that enables users to understand, interpret, and trust their behavior and decisions. Transparent AI systems enhance accountability, facilitate error diagnosis, and enable stakeholders to assess the reliability and fairness of AI algorithms and outcomes.

Fairness and Equity: OpenAI is committed to developing AI technologies that are fair, unbiased, and equitable, ensuring that they do not perpetuate or exacerbate existing social inequalities, biases, or discrimination. Responsible AI development involves mitigating algorithmic biases, ensuring equitable access to AI technologies, and promoting inclusive design practices that address the diverse needs and perspectives of all users and stakeholders.

Safety and Reliability: OpenAI prioritizes safety and reliability in AI systems, implementing measures to mitigate risks, uncertainties, and unintended consequences associated with AI technologies. Responsible AI development involves rigorous testing, validation, and risk assessment processes to ensure that AI systems operate safely, reliably, and predictably across diverse environments and scenarios.

Privacy and Data Protection: OpenAI respects individuals' privacy and data protection rights, adhering to ethical principles and legal regulations governing the collection, use, and storage of personal data in AI systems. Responsible AI development involves implementing privacy-preserving technologies, data anonymization techniques, and robust data governance practices to safeguard sensitive information and protect individuals' privacy rights.

Human-Centered Design: OpenAI adopts a human-centered approach to AI development, prioritizing the needs, preferences, and values of end-users and stakeholders. Responsible AI development involves actively involving end-users in the design, development, and evaluation of AI systems, soliciting feedback, and incorporating user perspectives to ensure that AI technologies enhance human well-being, autonomy, and agency.

Strategies for Responsible AI Development:

Ethics by Design: OpenAI integrates ethical considerations into the design and development process of AI technologies from the outset, embedding ethical principles, guidelines, and best practices into the development lifecycle. By incorporating ethics by design principles, OpenAI aims to proactively identify and address ethical challenges, promote responsible decision-making, and minimize ethical risks throughout the AI development process.

Ethics Review and Governance: OpenAI establishes ethics review processes and governance mechanisms to assess the ethical implications of its research projects, initiatives, and partnerships. Ethics review boards or committees evaluate proposed research activities, identify potential ethical risks and concerns, and provide recommendations for mitigating risks and upholding ethical standards in AI development and deployment.

Stakeholder Engagement and Collaboration: OpenAI engages with diverse stakeholders, including researchers, policymakers, industry partners, civil society organizations, and the general public, to solicit feedback, input, and perspectives on ethical issues and dilemmas related to AI. Through stakeholder engagement and collaboration, OpenAI fosters dialogue, transparency, and mutual understanding, enabling stakeholders to contribute to the responsible development and governance of AI technologies.

Continuous Monitoring and Evaluation: OpenAI conducts continuous monitoring and evaluation of AI systems' ethical impact and performance, assessing their compliance with ethical principles, legal regulations, and organizational policies. Responsible AI development involves implementing mechanisms for tracking and evaluating AI systems' behavior, identifying potential ethical concerns or biases, and taking corrective actions to address them in a timely and transparent manner.

Implications and Significance:

Responsible AI development is foundational to OpenAI's mission of ensuring that artificial general intelligence (AGI) benefits all of humanity. By prioritizing ethical considerations, promoting transparency, fairness, and safety in AI development, OpenAI aims to build trust, foster public confidence, and mitigate potential risks and harms associated with AI technologies. Through its commitment to responsible AI development, OpenAI seeks to lead by example and contribute to the ethical and inclusive advancement of AI for the betterment of society.

6

Chapter 2: AI Fundamentals

The exploration of Artificial Intelligence (AI) fundamentals, as discussed in the hypothetical book "OpenAI: Exploring the World of Artificial Intelligence," encompasses a broad spectrum of foundational principles that serve as the bedrock upon which the field of AI is constructed. This detailed exploration sheds light on various pivotal aspects, including the history of AI, machine learning algorithms, neural networks, AI ethics, and the future implications of AI technologies.

History and Evolution of AI

The journey of AI from its inception to its current state is a testament to the rapid advancements in technology and the persistent quest for creating machines that can mimic human intelligence. The book likely delves into the early days of AI, highlighting key milestones such as the Turing Test, introduced by Alan Turing in 1950, which proposed a criterion for determining machine intelligence (Turing, 1950). Further exploration might include the Dartmouth Conference of 1956, often considered the birthplace of AI as a field, where the term "Artificial Intelligence" was first coined (McCarthy et al., 1956).

Machine Learning Algorithms

A substantial portion of the book would be dedicated to machine learning algorithms, which are at the heart of AI's ability to learn from and make predictions or decisions based on data. The text likely covers various types of machine learning, including supervised learning, unsupervised learning, and reinforcement learning, each with distinct methodologies and applications (Russell & Norvig, 2016). For instance, supervised learning algorithms, which learn from labeled training data, could be exemplified by the support vector machines (SVM) and decision trees.

Neural Networks and Deep Learning

Neural networks and deep learning represent a significant leap in the AI domain, enabling advancements in processing large volumes of complex data. The book might explore the basic structure of neural networks, comprising layers of interconnected nodes or neurons that mimic the human brain's structure and function (LeCun, Bengio, & Hinton, 2015). Deep learning, a subset of machine learning involving neural networks with many layers, has been pivotal in achieving remarkable success in fields such as image and speech recognition.

AI Ethics and Societal Impact

The ethical considerations and societal impact of AI are critical components of AI fundamentals. The text would likely address concerns related to privacy, bias, accountability, and the future of employment in the wake of AI advancements (Bostrom & Yudkowsky, 2014). Discussions might include the importance of developing AI in a manner that is ethical and aligns with human values, as well as the role of regulations and policies in ensuring responsible AI deployment.

Future Implications of AI Technologies

The exploration of AI's future implications offers insights into the potential transformative impact of AI on society, the economy, and the global landscape. Speculative discussions in the book could cover emerging technologies, such as generative AI, quantum computing's role in AI, and the prospects of achieving artificial general intelligence

(AGI) — an AI with the ability to understand, learn, and apply knowledge across a wide range of tasks (Kurzweil, 2005).

What is Artificial Intelligence?

This question is foundational to understanding the entire field of AI, as it delves into the essence, objectives, and scope of AI technologies. This academic discussion will articulate the concept of AI as it might be presented in such a book, drawing on hypothetical APA in-text citations and references to offer a comprehensive understanding of AI's definition and its multifaceted nature.

Defining Artificial Intelligence

Artificial Intelligence, at its core, is the branch of computer science that is concerned with the development of algorithms, systems, or applications that exhibit human-like intelligence and cognitive functions, such as learning, reasoning, problem-solving, perception, and language understanding (Russell & Norvig, 2016). The book likely emphasizes that AI is not a monolith but a collection of methodologies and technologies aimed at mimicking or surpassing human cognitive abilities in specific or general tasks.

The Objectives of AI

The objectives of AI are twofold: to create machines that can perform tasks that, when performed by humans, require intelligence; and to understand human intelligence from a computational perspective (McCarthy et al., 1956). This dual purpose underscores the interdisciplinary nature of AI, bridging computer science, cognitive science, psychology, and more, to not only advance technological capabilities but also to gain insights into human intelligence itself.

Scope and Subfields of AI

AI encompasses a broad range of subfields, each focusing on specific aspects or capabilities of intelligence. These include:

Machine Learning (ML): The study and development of algorithms that improve their performance at some tasks through experience or data (LeCun, Bengio, & Hinton, 2015).

Natural Language Processing (NLP): Enabling computers to understand, interpret, and generate human language (Hirschberg & Manning, 2015).

Robotics: The design and creation of robots that can perform tasks autonomously or semi-autonomously.

Computer Vision: Giving machines the ability to 'see' and interpret visual information from the world (Szeliski, 2010).

Theoretical Foundations and Practical Applications

The theoretical foundations of AI involve concepts from mathematics, logic, economics, neuroscience, and psychology, providing a broad base for various AI applications in real-world scenarios. Applications range from simple tasks like spam filtering to complex systems such as autonomous vehicles, healthcare diagnostics, and intelligent recommendation systems.

Ethical and Societal Implications

As AI technologies advance, ethical and societal implications become increasingly significant. The book likely addresses the importance of ethical AI development, focusing on fairness, transparency, accountability, and the impact on employment and privacy (Bostrom & Yudkowsky, 2014).

Machine Learning vs. Deep Learning:

A crucial discussion is dedicated to distinguishing between Machine Learning (ML) and Deep Learning (DL), two fundamental aspects of AI that have propelled the field into new frontiers of innovation and application. This distinction is vital for understanding the breadth and depth of AI's capabilities, methodologies, and the specific challenges each approach addresses.

Machine Learning: An Overview

Machine Learning, a subset of AI, involves the development of algorithms that enable computers to learn from and make predictions or decisions based on data. ML is grounded in the idea that systems can learn from data, identify patterns, and make decisions with minimal human intervention (Russell & Norvig, 2016). It encompasses a range of techniques and algorithms, from linear regression and decision trees to more complex ensemble methods like random forests and gradient boosting machines.

Core Principles and Techniques

At the heart of machine learning are its core principles and techniques, which include supervised learning, unsupervised learning, and reinforcement learning. Supervised learning involves training models on a labeled dataset, which means that each training example is paired with an output label. Algorithms such as linear regression for continuous outputs and logistic regression for categorical outputs are foundational to this type of learning. Unsupervised learning, on the other hand, deals with data that has no labels, focusing instead on discovering the inherent structure within the data using algorithms like k-means clustering and principal component analysis. Reinforcement learning is characterized by agents that learn to make decisions by performing actions in an environment to achieve some goal, optimizing their behavior based on the rewards received for their actions (Sutton & Barto, 2018).

Importance of Data

Machine learning's effectiveness is deeply tied to the quantity and quality of data available for training. The models' ability to learn and generalize well to new, unseen data depends on having a diverse and representative dataset. This underscores the critical role of data preprocessing and feature engineering in ML, where raw data is cleaned, selected, and transformed into a format that is more suitable for the specific ML algorithms being used (Goodfellow, Bengio, & Courville, 2016).

Applications of Machine Learning

Machine Learning has found applications across numerous fields and industries, revolutionizing the way tasks are performed and decisions are made. In healthcare, ML algorithms assist in diagnosing diseases and predicting patient outcomes. In finance, they are used for credit scoring and algorithmic trading. ML also powers many of the technologies we use daily, from search engines and recommendation systems to voice assistants and personalized marketing (Jordan & Mitchell, 2015).

Challenges and Limitations

Despite its significant advancements and applications, machine learning is not without its challenges and limitations. Issues such as overfitting, where a model performs well on training data but poorly on new data, and underfitting, where a model is too simple to capture the underlying structure of the data, are critical concerns. Moreover, the transparency and interpretability of ML models, particularly those that become complex, pose ethical and operational challenges, necessitating ongoing research into explainable AI (XAI) (Doshi-Velez & Kim, 2017).

Deep Learning: A Specialized Subset of ML

Deep Learning, a specialized subset of machine learning, involves neural networks with many layers. These deep neural networks are capable of learning high-level features from data in a hierarchical manner, which makes DL particularly effective for tasks involving large amounts of unstructured data, such as image and speech recognition (LeCun, Bengio, & Hinton, 2015). DL models, through their deep architecture, can automatically discover the representations needed for feature detection or classification, bypassing the manual feature extraction process that is often necessary in traditional ML approaches.

Key Differences Between ML and DL

Data Dependency: DL algorithms require a significantly larger amount of data to learn effectively compared to traditional ML algorithms. This is because DL models learn more complex patterns and need more examples to generalize well.

Computational Resources: DL models, due to their complexity and depth, typically require more computational power and resources, such as high-performance GPUs, for training and inference compared to ML models (Goodfellow, Bengio, & Courville, 2016).

Feature Engineering: In ML, feature engineering is a critical step where domain knowledge is used to create features that help models learn better. In DL, the need for manual feature engineering is greatly reduced as deep neural networks are capable of automatically learning features from raw data.

Interpretability: ML models, especially those with simpler structures, tend to be more interpretable than DL models. The complexity and 'black box' nature of deep neural networks make them less transparent, posing challenges for understanding and interpreting model decisions (Castelvecchi, 2016).

Applications and Implications

The applications of ML and DL span across various domains, from healthcare diagnostics and financial modeling to autonomous vehicles and natural language processing systems. While ML has been instrumental in developing systems that improve efficiency and decision-making, DL has pushed the boundaries further, enabling the development of systems with near or surpassing human-level performance in tasks like image recognition and language translation.

Applications of Machine Learning

Machine Learning, with its diverse algorithms and approaches, finds utility in a vast array of applications across various sectors:

Finance: ML algorithms are employed for credit scoring, fraud detection, and algorithmic trading, significantly enhancing accuracy and efficiency in financial services (Jordan & Mitchell, 2015).

Healthcare: In the medical field, ML contributes to disease diagnosis, personalized treatment recommendations, and patient outcome prediction, revolutionizing patient care (Esteva et al., 2019).

E-commerce and Marketing: Recommendation systems powered by ML personalize user experiences by suggesting products, services, and content, driving sales and customer engagement (Koren & Bell, 2015).

Natural Language Processing (NLP): ML is pivotal in translating languages, sentiment analysis, and chatbots, improving communication and information accessibility (Young et al., 2018).

Applications of Deep Learning

Deep Learning, a subset of ML with capabilities to learn from vast amounts of unstructured data, has enabled breakthroughs in several areas:

Image and Speech Recognition: DL models, particularly Convolutional Neural Networks (CNNs) and Recurrent Neural Networks (RNNs), have achieved state-of-the-art performance in recognizing images and speech, used in applications from smartphone cameras to virtual assistants (LeCun, Bengio, & Hinton, 2015).

Autonomous Vehicles: DL algorithms process and interpret the complex visual environment around vehicles to enable safe autonomous navigation (Bojarski et al., 2016).

Drug Discovery and Genomics: DL techniques accelerate the identification of potential therapeutic drug molecules and the analysis of genetic sequences, contributing to advances in personalized medicine (Senior et al., 2020).

Implications

The widespread adoption of ML and DL technologies brings profound implications:

Economic Impact: Automation and optimization enabled by ML and DL have the potential to significantly increase productivity, but also pose challenges to employment in sectors susceptible to automation (Acemoglu & Restrepo, 2020).

Ethical and Societal Considerations: The deployment of AI technologies raises ethical concerns regarding privacy, surveillance, bias, and fairness. The capability of DL models to generate realistic media, for example, has implications for misinformation and digital trust (Bostrom & Yudkowsky, 2014).

Scientific Research: AI, particularly DL, is transforming scientific research by enabling the analysis of complex data sets beyond human capability, opening new avenues for discovery in fields such as climate science, astrophysics, and materials science.

Reinforcement Learning:

The comprehensive examination of Reinforcement Learning, underscores RL's significance within the AI landscape, from its foundational principles to its transformative applications across various domains. It highlights the complexity and potential of RL in advancing intelligent systems that can learn and adapt through interaction with their environments, while also acknowledging the critical ethical and societal implications of deploying such technologies.

Reinforcement Learning: Basics

Reinforcement Learning is a type of machine learning where an agent learns to make decisions by performing actions and receiving feedback in the form of rewards or penalties. This learning process is modeled as a Markov Decision Process (MDP), where the agent interacts with its environment over discrete time steps, aiming to maximize its total future reward. The fundamental components of any RL problem include the environment, the agent, states, actions, and rewards (Sutton & Barto, 2018).

The agent learns a policy, which is a strategy for choosing actions based on the current state, that maximizes the cumulative reward over time. Learning can be achieved through various methods, including value-based approaches, policy-based approaches, and model-based approaches. Value-based learning focuses on estimating the value of being in a state or taking an action in a state, whereas policy-based methods directly learn the policy without requiring a value function. Model-based approaches involve building a model of the environment to improve the learning efficiency of the agent.

Exploration vs. Exploitation

A key challenge in reinforcement learning is the trade-off between exploration and exploitation. Exploration involves taking actions that might not have the highest immediate reward but could lead to higher long-term rewards by discovering better strategies. Exploitation involves taking actions that the agent currently believes will yield the highest reward based on its existing knowledge. Balancing these two aspects is crucial for the success of RL algorithms (Tokic, 2010).

Theoretical Foundations

Exploration involves the agent trying out actions that it has not sufficiently tried in the past, which is essential for acquiring new knowledge about the environment. Without adequate exploration, an agent might miss out on discovering optimal actions. Exploitation, on the other hand, leverages the agent's existing knowledge to maximize immediate rewards based on actions that have previously resulted in high rewards. The challenge lies in optimally balancing these two strategies to ensure that the agent neither gets stuck in a suboptimal policy due to insufficient exploration nor fails to maximize rewards due to excessive exploration (Tokic, 2010).

Several strategies have been proposed to address this dilemma, including ε-greedy, where the agent explores with a probability ε and exploits with a probability $1-\varepsilon$; softmax selection, which chooses actions based on a distribution that favors higher-valued actions but still allows for exploration; and Upper Confidence Bound (UCB), which selects actions based on both the average reward and the uncertainty or variance in the estimate of that action's value, naturally balancing exploration and exploitation by favoring actions with high uncertainty (Auer et al., 2002).

Applications of Reinforcement Learning

Reinforcement Learning has found applications in a wide array of fields, showcasing its versatility and power:

Gaming: One of the most publicized applications of RL is in playing games, where agents learn to achieve superhuman performance in complex games like Go, Chess, and various video games (Silver et al., 2016).

Robotics: In robotics, RL is used to teach robots to perform tasks that require fine motor skills and adaptation to the environment, such as manipulation and locomotion (Gu et al., 2017).

Autonomous Vehicles: RL algorithms are instrumental in developing decision-making systems for autonomous driving, optimizing actions based on real-time traffic conditions and sensor data (Shalev-Shwartz et al., 2016).

Personalized Recommendations: RL techniques optimize recommendation systems by continuously learning from user interactions to improve the relevance and personalization of content (Zheng et al., 2018).

Ethical and Societal Implications

The deployment of RL in real-world applications also raises ethical and societal considerations. The autonomous nature of RL agents, particularly in sensitive areas like healthcare and autonomous vehicles, necessitates careful consideration of safety, privacy, and accountability. Ensuring that RL systems act in ways that are aligned with human values and ethical standards is an ongoing challenge in the field.

The exploration vs. exploitation concept also brings ethical considerations, especially in applications affecting human decisions, such as healthcare or finance. Ensuring that the exploration of new strategies does not adversely affect individuals' well-being or financial security is essential. This necessitates the development of RL algorithms that can responsibly balance exploration with exploitation, prioritizing safety and ethical considerations in their decision-making processes.

Natural Language Processing (NLP):

This comprehensive examination of Natural Language Processing, underscores NLP's foundational role in bridging human language and computational understanding. Highlighting core tasks, technological advances, applications, and future challenges, this discussion reflects the dynamic and impactful nature of NLP within the AI domain, demonstrating its critical importance in achieving more sophisticated and effective human-computer interactions.

Natural Language Processing: Foundations and Evolution

Natural Language Processing combines computational linguistics—concerning with the rules and structures of language—with statistical, machine learning, and deep learning models to process and understand natural language data. The evolution of NLP from rule-based systems to machine learning and deep learning approaches has significantly enhanced its capabilities, enabling more sophisticated and nuanced language understanding and generation (Jurafsky & Martin, 2019).

Core NLP Tasks

NLP encompasses a wide range of tasks, each aimed at bridging the gap between human communication and computer understanding:

Syntax and Parsing: Analyzing the grammatical structure of sentences to understand the relationship between words.

Semantic Analysis: Understanding the meaning conveyed in a text, including word sense disambiguation and the representation of meaning.

Discourse Processing: Understanding how sentences in a text relate to each other, managing context, and coherence across sentences.

Pragmatic Understanding: Interpreting language in context, including indirect speech acts, irony, and sarcasm.

Machine Translation: Automatically translating text from one language to another, considering grammatical structure and context.

Information Retrieval: Finding documents or content within documents that meet a user's query, often used in search engines.

Sentiment Analysis: Determining the sentiment expressed in a piece of text, such as positive, negative, or neutral opinions.

Question Answering and Chatbots: Building systems that can answer questions posed by humans in a natural language or engage in conversation.

Advances in NLP Technologies

Recent advancements in NLP have been driven by deep learning models, particularly Transformer-based models like BERT (Bidirectional Encoder Representations from Transformers) and GPT (Generative Pre-trained Transformer), which have set new benchmarks in language understanding and generation tasks (Devlin et al., 2018; Brown et al., 2020). These models leverage vast amounts of text data to learn complex patterns in language, enabling them to perform a wide range of NLP tasks with high accuracy.

Deep Learning in NLP

The integration of Deep Learning (DL) techniques has been a pivotal advancement in NLP, enabling significant improvements in language understanding and generation. Neural networks, particularly Recurrent Neural Networks (RNNs) and Transformers, have been at the forefront of this revolution. Transformers, introduced by Vaswani et al. (2017), for example, have become the backbone of modern NLP, enabling models to handle sequences of data, such as text, more effectively than their predecessors. This architecture facilitates the handling of long-range dependencies in text, making it better suited for understanding the context and nuances of language.

Pre-trained Language Models

Another significant advancement has been the development of pre-trained language models such as BERT (Bidirectional Encoder Representations from Transformers), GPT (Generative Pretrained Transformer), and their successors. These models are trained on vast amounts of text data and then fine-tuned for specific NLP tasks, such as question answering, text summarization, and sentiment analysis. The pre-training process allows these models to understand the complexities and subtleties of language, leading to unprecedented performance across a wide range of NLP tasks (Devlin et al., 2018; Brown et al., 2020).

Transfer Learning and Few-shot Learning

Transfer learning and few-shot learning have emerged as powerful strategies in NLP, allowing models to adapt to new tasks with minimal additional training. This approach is particularly beneficial in scenarios where labeled data is scarce. By leveraging knowledge gained from related tasks, NLP models can achieve high performance on new tasks with only a few examples (Brown et al., 2020). This advancement has democratized NLP applications, making state-of-the-art results more accessible across various languages and domains.

Multilingual and Cross-lingual Models

The development of multilingual and cross-lingual models has expanded the reach of NLP technologies to a global scale. Models like mBERT (Multilingual BERT) and XLM-R (Cross-lingual Language Model-RoBERTa) are trained on text from multiple languages, enabling them to understand and generate text across different linguistic boundaries. This progress has been crucial for applications in non-English languages, facilitating more inclusive and accessible AI technologies worldwide (Conneau et al., 2020).

Ethical Considerations and Challenges

With these advancements, NLP technologies face new ethical considerations and challenges. Issues such as bias in language models, privacy concerns with data used for training, and the environmental impact of training large models have come to the forefront. Addressing these challenges requires ongoing research and thoughtful consideration of the societal impacts of NLP technologies.

Applications of NLP

The applications of NLP are vast and varied, impacting numerous industries and domains:

Content Summarization: Automatically generating concise summaries of long documents or articles.

Customer Service Automation: Using chatbots and virtual assistants to handle customer queries efficiently.

Social Media Monitoring: Analyzing social media content for trends, sentiment, and public opinion.

Legal and Medical Document Analysis: Extracting relevant information from legal contracts or medical records for review or decision-making processes.

Challenges and Future Directions

Despite significant progress, NLP faces challenges such as understanding language nuances, sarcasm, cultural references, and managing ambiguity in human language. Future directions in NLP research aim to address these challenges by developing more sophisticated models that can understand context better, manage multimodal inputs (combining text with visual or auditory data), and improve the efficiency and interpretability of NLP systems (Hirschberg & Manning, 2015).

Challenges in NLP

Handling Ambiguity and Context

One of the foremost challenges in NLP is the inherent ambiguity and context-dependency of natural language. Words and phrases can have multiple meanings, and the correct interpretation often depends on complex contextual cues or world knowledge, which are challenging for algorithms to grasp (Jurafsky & Martin, 2019). Moreover, sarcasm, irony, and humor add additional layers of complexity that models often struggle to understand and generate appropriately.

Data and Resource Limitations

Although large-scale language models have demonstrated remarkable capabilities, their performance is deeply tied to the quantity and quality of the training data. For languages and dialects with limited available data, developing high-performing NLP systems remains a significant challenge. Furthermore, the creation and maintenance of large annotated datasets for training and evaluation are resource-intensive tasks (Bender & Friedman, 2018).

Bias and Fairness

The issue of bias in NLP models has gained considerable attention. Since models learn from existing data, they can inadvertently perpetuate and amplify biases present in that data. This raises concerns about fairness and the ethical implications of NLP applications, particularly in sensitive areas such as hiring, law enforcement, and loan approval processes (Blodgett et al., 2020).

Future Directions in NLP

Improved Contextual Understanding

Future research in NLP aims to develop models with a deeper understanding of context and the ability to integrate world knowledge more effectively. This includes advancing models that can better handle long-range dependencies and nuanced language use, as well as incorporating external knowledge bases and reasoning capabilities into language models (Bisk et al., 2020).

Cross-lingual and Low-resource Language Support

Enhancing the capabilities of NLP systems to support cross-lingual understanding and low-resource languages is a critical area of future work. This involves not only creating more robust multilingual models but also developing techniques for efficient transfer learning and data augmentation to improve performance in languages with limited available data (Ruder et al., 2019).

Addressing Bias and Ensuring Ethical Use

Addressing bias and ensuring the ethical use of NLP technologies are paramount for the future development of the field. This includes developing methodologies for identifying and mitigating bias in training data and models, as well as establishing ethical guidelines for the development and deployment of NLP systems (Hovy & Spruit, 2016).

Interactive and Multimodal NLP

The integration of NLP with other AI domains, such as computer vision and speech processing, to develop interactive and multimodal systems represents an exciting direction for future research. This could enable more sophisticated human-computer interaction systems that understand and generate natural language in conjunction with visual and auditory information (Baltrušaitis et al., 2018).

7

Chapter 3: OpenAI's Technologies and Projects

OpenAI, a leading AI research lab, has been at the forefront of advancing artificial intelligence technologies with a focus on ensuring that such advancements benefit all of humanity.

Generative Pretrained Transformer (GPT) Series

One of the most groundbreaking technologies developed by OpenAI is the Generative Pretrained Transformer series, including GPT-3, the third iteration. These models have set new benchmarks in the field of natural language processing (NLP) and understanding, demonstrating remarkable capabilities in generating human-like text, answering questions, translating languages, and more. The GPT series utilizes deep learning techniques and is trained on vast datasets, enabling it to generate coherent and contextually relevant text based on input prompts (Brown et al., 2020).

DALL·E and Image Generation

OpenAI has also ventured into the domain of AI-driven art and image generation with DALL·E, a model capable of creating images from textual descriptions. This project illustrates the potential of AI in understanding and generating visual content, showcasing the ability to produce novel, creative images based on complex, abstract concepts described in natural language. DALL·E's advancements highlight the intersection of AI with creativity and design, opening new pathways for artistic expression and visual communication (Ramesh et al., 2021).

Robotics and Autonomous Systems

In the realm of robotics, OpenAI has made significant contributions through projects focused on developing autonomous systems capable of learning complex tasks through techniques such as reinforcement learning. One notable project involved training a robotic hand to solve a Rubik's Cube, demonstrating the potential of AI to master dexterity and problem-solving in physical tasks. These advancements in robotics emphasize the potential of AI to augment and automate physical operations across various industries (Akkaya et al., 2019).

Ethics and Safety in AI

OpenAI places a strong emphasis on the ethical development and deployment of AI technologies. The lab has engaged in research and discussions aimed at ensuring AI's safety and aligning AI systems with human values. This includes work on AI policy and governance, the societal impacts of AI, and strategies to prevent malicious use of AI technologies. OpenAI's commitment to ethical AI underscores the importance of responsible innovation in the field (Leike et al., 2017).

GPT (Generative Pre-trained Transformer) Models:

The GPT series represents a monumental leap in the field of natural language processing (NLP) and understanding, demonstrating OpenAI's leading role in AI research and development. This academic discussion aims to detail the progression of GPT models, from their inception to their latest iterations, and to explore their wide-ranging applications, supported by hypothetical APA in-text citations and references.

Evolution of GPT Models

GPT-1: The Foundation

The journey began with the introduction of the original GPT model by Radford et al. (2018), which laid the foundation for subsequent advancements. GPT-1 was notable for its unified approach to NLP tasks, utilizing a transformer architecture that was pre-trained on a large corpus of text and then fine-tuned for specific tasks. This model demonstrated the potential of transfer learning in NLP, showing that a single model could achieve competitive results across various language tasks without task-specific model architectures (Radford et al., 2018).

Development of GPT-1

GPT-1 emerged from OpenAI's research into improving language understanding by generative pre-training of a transformer-based model followed by discriminative fine-tuning on specific tasks. The model was innovative in its approach to learning: it was first pre-trained on a large corpus of text data in an unsupervised manner to learn a general understanding of language. This pre-training involved predicting the next word in sentences, allowing the model to capture a wide range of linguistic patterns and contexts. The pre-trained model was then fine-tuned on smaller, task-specific datasets, adapting its generalized language understanding to perform well on specific NLP tasks (Radford et al., 2018).

Architecture and Features

GPT-1's architecture was based on the transformer model introduced by Vaswani et al. (2017), which was a departure from previous RNN and LSTM-based approaches to language tasks. The transformer model utilizes self-attention mechanisms to process sequences of words, allowing it to weigh the importance of different words within a sentence or document regardless of their positional distance from each other. This ability to capture long-range dependencies in text was a significant factor in GPT-1's success in understanding and generating coherent and contextually relevant language.

Impact on NLP and AI Research

GPT-1's introduction marked a significant milestone in NLP research, demonstrating the potential of transformer-based models pre-trained on large text corpora for a wide range of language tasks. Its success paved the way for further research into scaling up transformer models and exploring the limits of unsupervised pre-training followed by task-specific fine-tuning. GPT-1 showed that a single model architecture, when pre-trained on a sufficient amount of data, could achieve competitive or even state-of-the-art performance across diverse NLP tasks, including translation, question-answering, and text classification. This approach significantly reduced the need for task-specific model architectures and extensive task-specific training data, which had been major challenges in NLP.

Applications and Legacy

Although GPT-1 itself was primarily a research breakthrough, its methodology and architecture laid the foundation for its successors, GPT-2 and GPT-3, which have found numerous practical applications. GPT-1 demonstrated the feasibility and effectiveness of leveraging large-scale unsupervised data to pre-train models that could then be fine-tuned for specific tasks, a paradigm that has since been adopted and refined in subsequent GPT models and other transformer-based architectures.

GPT-2: Scaling Up

GPT-2, introduced by Radford et al. (2019), marked a significant leap forward, featuring a much larger model with 1.5 billion parameters trained on an expanded dataset. GPT-2 showcased remarkable improvements in language generation, capable of producing coherent and contextually relevant text passages that often-resembled human writing. Its ability to understand context and generate text across a wide array of domains without task-specific training underscored the model's versatility and advanced capabilities in language understanding (Radford et al., 2019).

Architecture and Training

GPT-2 was a direct response to the limitations observed in GPT-1, particularly regarding model capacity and training data. With 1.5 billion parameters, GPT-2 was significantly larger than its predecessor, which allowed for more complex and nuanced understanding and generation of text. Unlike GPT-1, which was already impressive in its capabilities, GPT-2 utilized an expanded dataset for pre-training, encompassing a diverse range of internet text. This extensive training enabled the model to capture a wide variety of linguistic patterns, styles, and knowledge, making it far more versatile and capable (Radford et al., 2019).

Breakthroughs in Language Understanding and Generation

GPT-2's enhanced capacity facilitated breakthroughs in several areas of NLP. It demonstrated an unparalleled ability to generate coherent and contextually relevant text over extended passages, complete stories, and even simulate dialogue. Furthermore, GPT-2 showed a remarkable understanding of language nuances, including humor, irony, and cultural references, which were challenging for previous models. Its performance across various NLP tasks—without task-specific training—underscored the potential of large-scale transformer models for generalizable language understanding and generation.

Ethical Considerations and OpenAI's Approach

The release of GPT-2 was accompanied by unprecedented ethical considerations. OpenAI initially withheld the full model, citing concerns about potential misuse, including the generation of misleading news articles, impersonation, and other forms of misinformation. This cautious approach sparked a significant discussion within the AI community about the responsibilities of AI researchers and developers in mitigating potential negative impacts of powerful AI technologies (Radford et al., 2019).

Applications of GPT-2

Content Creation and Augmentation

GPT-2 found applications in content creation, where it was used to assist in writing tasks, generate creative fiction, and even produce poetry. Its ability to understand context and generate relevant content made it a valuable tool for augmenting human creativity, offering new possibilities for writers and content creators.

Educational Tools

In education, GPT-2 served as a basis for developing tutoring systems and educational aids capable of providing explanations, generating practice questions, and offering feedback on written assignments. Its adaptability made it an effective tool for personalized learning experiences.

Data Analysis and Summarization

GPT-2's capabilities were also leveraged in data analysis, particularly in summarizing large volumes of text. Its ability to distill complex information into concise summaries proved useful in fields ranging from legal document review to academic research, where quick understanding of vast datasets is invaluable.

GPT-2's development represented a significant milestone in the evolution of GPT models, showcasing the immense potential of scaling up AI systems. Its capabilities in understanding and generating human-like text paved the way for subsequent innovations in NLP and demonstrated the critical importance of considering ethical implications in AI research and development. As detailed in "OpenAI: Exploring the World of Artificial Intelligence," GPT-2 not only advanced the technical capabilities of AI models but also set new standards for responsible AI development and deployment.

GPT-3: A New Benchmark

The release of GPT-3 by Brown et al. (2020) set a new benchmark in the AI community, with its unprecedented scale of 175 billion parameters. GPT-3's capabilities extended far beyond text generation; it demonstrated an ability to perform a variety of language-based tasks directly from natural language instructions, showcasing few-shot learning. This iteration highlighted the potential of scaling up model size and training data to achieve significant improvements in performance across a broad spectrum of NLP tasks, including translation, question-answering, and summarization, without the need for extensive task-specific data or fine-tuning (Brown et al., 2020).

Architectural Innovations and Scale

GPT-3, introduced by Brown et al. (2020), represents a significant leap in AI model architecture and capacity, featuring an unprecedented

175 billion parameters. This scale, orders of magnitude larger than its predecessor GPT-2, enables GPT-3 to demonstrate advanced understanding and generation of natural language, far surpassing previous models in complexity and versatility. GPT-3's architecture builds upon the transformer model, optimizing it for efficiency and performance across a broad spectrum of NLP tasks without task-specific tuning.

Training and Knowledge Acquisition

The training regime for GPT-3 involved processing diverse and extensive datasets, enabling the model to acquire a vast reservoir of knowledge. This comprehensive training allows GPT-3 to generate text that is not only coherent and contextually relevant but also rich in information and nuance. The model's ability to perform "few-shot" learning, where it can understand and execute tasks given just a few examples, underscores its remarkable adaptability and intelligence (Brown et al., 2020).

Applications of GPT-3

Content Creation and Language Tasks

GPT-3's prowess in generating human-like text has seen it being applied to a wide array of content creation tasks, including writing articles, composing poetry, and generating code. Its capacity for understanding and generating multiple languages has further broadened its applicability, enabling more global and accessible AI solutions.

Conversational Agents and Customer Service

The enhanced natural language understanding capabilities of GPT-3 have significantly improved conversational agents, making interactions with chatbots and virtual assistants more natural and informative. This has profound implications for customer service, education, and accessibility, where conversational agents can provide assistance, answer queries, and even tutor users in various subjects.

Application Development and Automation

GPT-3 has also been instrumental in application development, particularly in automating coding tasks and generating software components from natural language descriptions. Its ability to interpret user intent and generate functional code has the potential to streamline software development processes, making technology creation more accessible to those without formal programming expertise.

Ethical Considerations and Future Directions

The release of GPT-3 has not been without its ethical considerations, including concerns about misinformation, privacy, and bias. OpenAI has been at the forefront of addressing these issues, implementing usage policies and research initiatives aimed at mitigating potential negative impacts. The ongoing development of GPT-3 and future iterations will likely continue to emphasize ethical AI use, ensuring that advancements in AI technology are aligned with societal values and norms.

GPT-3 represents a monumental achievement in AI, setting a new benchmark for natural language understanding and generation. Its capabilities extend beyond mere text processing, offering transformative potential across various sectors, including education, customer service, and software development. As detailed in "OpenAI: Exploring the World of Artificial Intelligence," GPT-3 not only showcases the technical prowess of OpenAI but also exemplifies the broader aspirations and challenges of AI research and application in the modern era.

Applications of GPT Models

Content Creation

GPT models have revolutionized content creation, offering tools for generating articles, stories, poetry, and more. Their ability to produce coherent, context-aware text has been utilized by writers, marketers, and content creators to augment human creativity and efficiency.

Technological Underpinnings

The GPT series, developed by OpenAI, leverages deep learning techniques and transformer architecture to process and generate human-like text. These models are pre-trained on vast datasets from diverse sources, enabling them to understand context, mimic writing styles, and generate coherent, creative content across a wide range of formats and genres (Brown et al., 2020). The capability of GPT models, especially GPT-3, to engage in "few-shot" learning allows them to perform tasks with minimal additional input, adapting to specific content creation requirements with unprecedented flexibility.

Applications in Content Creation

Writing Assistance and Automation

GPT models have been instrumental in providing writing assistance, enabling writers to generate ideas, outlines, and even full drafts of articles, stories, and reports. The models can produce content that aligns with the given tone, style, and subject matter, significantly reducing the time and effort involved in content creation processes.

Creative Writing and Literary Works

In the realm of creative writing, GPT models have pushed the boundaries of AI-assisted literature, poetry, and other forms of creative expression. These models have been used to compose novels, poems, and short stories, often in collaboration with human authors. The ability of GPT models to generate narrative structures, develop characters, and evoke emotions has opened new avenues for exploring the intersection of technology and art (Brown et al., 2020).

Marketing and Advertising Content

In marketing and advertising, GPT models have been applied to generate engaging and persuasive content, including product descriptions, ad copy, and content for social media campaigns. The models' ability to tailor content to specific audiences and optimize for engagement metrics has made them a valuable tool for digital marketing strategies.

Educational and Instructional Material

GPT models have also been used to create educational and instructional materials, such as textbook content, study guides, and online course materials. Their capacity to simplify complex concepts and present information in an accessible manner has been leveraged to enhance learning experiences and educational outcomes.

Ethical Considerations and Challenges

While GPT models offer significant advantages in content creation, their use also raises ethical considerations, including the potential for generating misleading information, copyright issues, and the dilution of human creativity. Addressing these concerns requires careful management and oversight, ensuring that AI-generated content is used responsibly and in ways that enhance, rather than diminish, human creativity and intellectual property rights.

The application of GPT models in content creation represents a significant milestone in the use of AI technologies to augment and automate the generation of written content. As detailed in "OpenAI: Exploring the World of Artificial Intelligence," these models have not only enhanced productivity and creativity in various writing tasks but also posed new questions about the role of AI in creative processes. The continued evolution of GPT models and their applications in content creation will likely remain a key area of interest and development within the field of artificial intelligence.

Conversational Agents

The advancements in GPT models have significantly enhanced the development of conversational agents, enabling more natural, contextually relevant interactions. Chatbots and virtual assistants powered by GPT technology can engage in more meaningful dialogues, providing users with information, assistance, and even companionship in a manner that closely mimics human conversation.

Technological Foundations of GPT in Conversational Agents

The integration of GPT models into conversational agents is predicated on their advanced natural language processing (NLP) capabilities. Leveraging the transformer architecture, GPT models, especially GPT-3, have demonstrated an unparalleled ability to generate human-like text based on a given prompt, understand context over extended conversations, and provide relevant and coherent responses (Brown et al., 2020). This is facilitated by their extensive pre-training on diverse internet text, enabling them to grasp a wide array of topics, conversational nuances, and language styles.

Applications in Conversational Agents

Enhancing User Interaction

GPT-powered conversational agents have significantly enhanced user interaction experiences across various platforms, including customer service chatbots, virtual personal assistants, and social bots. By generating more natural and contextually appropriate responses, these agents can maintain engaging and meaningful dialogues with users, improving satisfaction and efficiency in information retrieval and task execution.

Personalization and Contextual Awareness

One of the key strengths of GPT models in conversational AI is their ability to personalize interactions and maintain context over the course of a conversation. This allows for a more seamless and intuitive user experience, as the model can recall previous exchanges and adapt its responses accordingly, making conversations feel more natural and less fragmented.

Multilingual Support

The adaptability of GPT models extends to multilingual capabilities, enabling conversational agents to interact with users in multiple languages. This broadens the accessibility and applicability of conversational AI across different linguistic and cultural contexts, facilitating global communication and support.

Educational and Therapeutic Applications

GPT-powered conversational agents have also found applications in education and therapy, where they can provide tutoring, language learning support, and mental health counseling. Their ability to generate informative, empathetic, and contextually relevant responses makes them valuable tools in these domains, offering personalized and accessible assistance.

Challenges and Ethical Considerations

Despite their advancements, the deployment of GPT models in conversational agents presents challenges, including the potential for generating inappropriate or biased responses. Ensuring the ethical use of these technologies involves ongoing efforts to detect and mitigate biases in training data, develop safeguards against misuse, and maintain transparency in AI-generated communications.

The future of GPT-powered conversational agents lies in further enhancing their contextual understanding, personalization, and ethical governance. Advances in AI and NLP will likely focus on improving the models' ability to understand and generate increasingly nuanced and complex interactions, while also addressing ethical and societal implications of conversational AI.

The application of GPT models in conversational agents represents a significant advancement in artificial intelligence, offering the potential to transform how humans interact with machines. As chronicled in "OpenAI: Exploring the World of Artificial Intelligence," these technologies have not only enhanced the functionality and user experience of conversational agents but also set new benchmarks for the development of intelligent, responsive, and ethically responsible AI systems.

Educational Tools

GPT models have been applied in educational contexts, facilitating personalized learning experiences. They assist in generating practice problems, explaining complex concepts in simpler terms, and providing instant feedback on assignments, thereby supporting a wide range of learning activities.

Leveraging GPT Models for Educational Tools

Personalized Learning Experiences

GPT models have significantly contributed to the development of personalized learning platforms. By analyzing students' responses, learning styles, and progress, these AI-driven systems can tailor educational content to meet individual learners' needs, optimizing learning outcomes. GPT's ability to generate dynamic content and provide instant feedback enables a more adaptive learning environment, catering to diverse learning preferences and abilities (Brown et al., 2020).

Automated Content Generation

Educational content creation, traditionally a time-consuming task, has been revolutionized by GPT models. Teachers and educational content creators can leverage these models to generate instructional materials, quizzes, and practice exercises in a fraction of the time it would take manually. This not only enhances the efficiency of content production but also enriches the pool of educational resources available, covering a wider range of topics and catering to various learning stages.

Language Learning and Literacy Improvement

GPT models have been applied in language learning applications, offering learners interactive and engaging ways to practice language skills. These models can simulate conversations, correct language use, and provide explanations, making language learning more accessible and effective. Additionally, GPT-driven tools assist in literacy improvement by offering reading practice and comprehension exercises tailored to the learner's proficiency level.

Tutoring and Homework Assistance

AI-powered tutoring systems built on GPT technology offer students on-demand access to educational support. These systems can assist with homework, explain complex concepts in understandable terms, and provide practice problems across subjects like mathematics, science, and humanities. By mimicking one-on-one tutoring, GPT models help bridge educational gaps, making high-quality educational support more widely accessible.

Challenges and Ethical Considerations

While GPT models offer promising advancements in educational technologies, their deployment is not without challenges. Concerns over data privacy, the accuracy of generated content, and the potential for reinforcing biases present in training data necessitate careful consideration. Ensuring that these models are used ethically and responsibly, with appropriate safeguards and oversight, is paramount to leveraging their benefits while minimizing potential harms.

Future Directions in Educational Technologies

The ongoing development of GPT models and their applications in education suggests a future where AI-driven tools play a central role in educational delivery. Future iterations of GPT models could offer even more personalized learning experiences, greater interactivity, and enhanced accessibility, potentially transforming global education landscapes. Continued research and development in this area, particularly in improving model reliability and addressing ethical concerns, will be crucial for realizing the full potential of AI in education.

The application of GPT models in educational tools represents a significant stride toward enhancing and personalizing the learning experience. As detailed in "OpenAI: Exploring the World of Artificial Intelligence," these models have the potential to revolutionize educational practices by making learning more accessible, engaging, and tailored to individual needs. The continued evolution of GPT models promises further advancements in educational technologies, heralding a new era of AI-assisted learning.

Code Generation and Assistance

With the advent of GPT-3, the ability to generate and understand code has seen remarkable applications. Automated code generation, code review, and even the creation of entire applications from natural language descriptions have become increasingly feasible, aiding developers in their work and lowering the barrier to entry for programming.

The Advent of AI in Code Generation

The intersection of artificial intelligence and software development through the advent of GPT models has opened new frontiers in code generation and assistance. With their ability to understand and generate human-like text, GPT models have been extended to comprehend programming languages, thereby assisting developers in writing code, debugging, and even generating code snippets from natural language descriptions (Brown et al., 2020).

GPT-3: A Milestone in Programming Assistance

GPT-3, with its 175 billion parameters, has been particularly instrumental in advancing the capabilities of AI-assisted code generation. Its profound understanding of multiple programming languages, combined with its ability to process natural language inputs, allows GPT-3 to interpret programming tasks described in plain English and generate syntactically correct and functional code. This not only accelerates the coding process but also makes software development more accessible to individuals without extensive programming experience.

Applications in Software Development

Automated Code Generation: GPT models have been utilized to automatically generate code snippets, functions, and even entire applications based on high-level requirements described in natural language. This capability significantly reduces development time and helps developers focus on more complex and creative aspects of software development.

Debugging and Code Review: Leveraging GPT models for debugging and code review has transformed the way developers approach error detection and correction. By analyzing code, GPT models can identify errors, suggest fixes, and improve code quality, contributing to more efficient and reliable software development processes.

Learning and Documentation: GPT models assist in generating documentation and tutorials tailored to specific coding tasks or projects. This application is particularly beneficial for novice programmers, as it provides them with customized learning resources and guidance, enhancing their coding skills and understanding of programming concepts.

Challenges and Ethical Considerations

While the application of GPT models in code generation and assistance offers considerable benefits, it also raises challenges and ethical considerations. Ensuring the accuracy and security of generated code, addressing potential biases in AI-generated solutions, and protecting intellectual property rights are critical issues that require careful attention. Furthermore, the potential for job displacement in the field of software development necessitates thoughtful consideration and mitigation strategies to ensure that these technologies augment rather than replace human expertise.

Future Directions

The integration of GPT models in software development is poised for further innovation and expansion. Future iterations of GPT models could offer even more sophisticated code generation capabilities, better understanding of complex programming tasks, and enhanced customization to fit specific developer needs and preferences. Ongoing research and development efforts are likely to focus on improving the reliability, security, and ethical use of AI in code generation, paving the way for a new era of AI-assisted software development.

The application of GPT models in code generation and programming assistance represents a significant leap forward in the field of software development. As outlined in "OpenAI: Exploring the World of Artificial Intelligence," these technologies not only streamline the coding process but also democratize software development, making it more accessible to a broader audience. The continued evolution of GPT models promises to further transform the software development landscape, offering new opportunities for innovation and efficiency in coding practices.

From the foundational GPT-1 to the groundbreaking GPT-3, OpenAI's innovations have not only advanced the technical capabilities of AI systems but also broadened their practical applications, impacting various sectors and paving the way for future advancements in artificial intelligence.

DALL-E: Creating Images from Text:

The DALL·E is a model designed to create images from textual descriptions. This groundbreaking technology exemplifies the intersection of natural language processing (NLP) and computer vision, pushing the boundaries of AI's creative capabilities. The DALL·E project not only showcases OpenAI's commitment to advancing AI research but also opens up new possibilities for creative expression and application across various fields.

DALL·E: An Overview

DALL·E, named whimsically after the famous surrealist artist Salvador Dalí and Pixar's animated robot WALL·E, represents a leap forward in AI's ability to understand and generate visual content based on textual prompts. Developed by OpenAI, DALL·E is a variant of the Generative Pre-trained Transformer (GPT) models, specifically adapted to generate images from textual descriptions. This model leverages a deep learning architecture that combines elements of NLP and image generation, allowing it to interpret a wide range of textual inputs and produce corresponding images that are often surprisingly coherent, detailed, and creative (Ramesh et al., 2021).

Development and Capabilities

DALL·E, introduced by OpenAI, is named in homage to the surrealist artist Salvador Dalí and Pixar's WALL·E, reflecting the system's ability to merge artistic creativity with technological innovation. It leverages a variant of the Generative Pre-trained Transformer (GPT) model, specifically adapted for image generation. DALL·E's development was driven by the goal of creating a system capable of understanding textual prompts and translating these into detailed, coherent, and contextually relevant images (Ramesh et al., 2021).

Underlying Technology

The technology behind DALL·E involves deep learning algorithms and techniques, particularly those related to transformers and generative adversarial networks (GANs). The model is trained on a diverse dataset comprising images and their corresponding textual descriptions, enabling it to learn associations between words and visual elements. By processing these inputs, DALL·E can synthesize images that accurately reflect the content and intent of the textual prompts, even producing novel combinations of concepts that do not exist in the training data.

Capabilities and Applications

DALL·E's capabilities extend beyond mere replication of known images; it can generate unique, creative visuals that combine unrelated elements in novel ways, mimicking a form of artistic creativity. Applications of DALL·E span various fields, including graphic design, where it can assist in creating logos, product designs, and marketing materials; art, offering new avenues for artistic expression and collaboration; and education, providing visual aids and materials tailored to specific learning contents.

Ethical Considerations and Implications

The development and deployment of DALL·E raise important ethical considerations, particularly concerning copyright, originality, and the potential for misuse. The ability of AI to generate images based on existing artworks or copyrighted materials poses questions about intellectual property rights and the distinction between inspiration and infringement. Additionally, the potential for creating misleading or harmful content highlights the need for responsible use guidelines and ethical frameworks governing AI-generated content.

Future Directions

The ongoing development of DALL·E and similar technologies points to a future where AI plays a central role in creative industries, potentially transforming how visual content is created, consumed, and valued. Future iterations of DALL·E may offer enhanced resolution, greater understanding of complex prompts, and improved integration of stylistic elements, further blurring the lines between human and machine creativity. The exploration of these technologies also opens up new research avenues in AI, focusing on creativity, perception, and the interaction between language and visual cognition.

DALL·E represents a milestone in the field of AI, showcasing the ability of machine learning models to interpret and generate visual content from textual descriptions. As detailed in "OpenAI: Exploring the World of Artificial Intelligence," this technology not only exemplifies the innovative capabilities of OpenAI's projects but also raises fundamental questions about creativity, authorship, and the future role of AI in artistic and design processes.

Technical Foundations and Capabilities

DALL·E's architecture is built upon a transformer model, similar to those used in GPT series, but with significant modifications to handle both text and image data. The model is trained on a diverse dataset of text-image pairs, enabling it to learn the associations between words and visual concepts. This training allows DALL·E to generate images that closely match the descriptions provided, demonstrating a nuanced understanding of objects, attributes, and the relationships between them.

Technical Foundations of DALL-E

Transformer Architecture

DALL-E is built upon a modified version of the Generative Pre-trained Transformer (GPT) architecture, which itself is rooted in the transformer model introduced by Vaswani et al. (2017). The transformer model has been pivotal in recent advancements in natural language processing (NLP) due to its ability to handle sequential data while capturing long-range dependencies within the input. For DALL-E, this architecture is adapted to process both textual and visual inputs, enabling the model to understand and generate complex visual representations from textual descriptions.

Training and Data

The training of DALL-E involves a large dataset of text-image pairs, allowing the model to learn correlations between textual descriptions and visual elements. Through this process, DALL-E acquires a deep understanding of how language corresponds to visual content, encompassing a wide range of styles, objects, and scenes. The model's training is an example of unsupervised learning, where it learns to generate images without explicit instructions on how to interpret the text or construct the images.

Capabilities of DALL-E

Zero-Shot Text-to-Image Generation

One of the most remarkable capabilities of DALL-E is its zero-shot text-to-image generation. This means that DALL-E can create images for textual prompts it has never seen before, demonstrating an understanding of both the content and context of the prompts. The model can generate coherent and contextually relevant images across a broad spectrum of requests, from straightforward descriptions to complex, abstract concepts (Ramesh et al., 2021).

Creative and Novel Image Synthesis

DALL-E goes beyond merely replicating existing images; it can synthesize entirely new images that combine elements in novel ways. This includes creating fantastical creatures, imagining objects in unconventional materials, or placing familiar objects in unexpected contexts.

This capability suggests a form of AI-driven creativity, expanding the potential applications of AI in art and design.

Detail and Realism

The images generated by DALL-E are noted for their detail and realism, with the model capable of rendering textures, lighting, and spatial relationships in a convincing manner. This level of detail extends the utility of DALL-E beyond artistic exploration to practical applications such as product design, architectural visualization, and educational content creation.

Implications and Future Directions

The development of DALL-E marks a significant milestone in the field of AI, highlighting the potential of machine learning models to engage in creative tasks traditionally thought to be the domain of humans. The technical foundations and capabilities of DALL-E pave the way for future research in AI, particularly in understanding and bridging the gap between linguistic descriptions and visual representations.

The exploration of DALL-E's technical foundations and capabilities within "OpenAI: Exploring the World of Artificial Intelligence" underscores the intersection of technology and creativity, showcasing how advancements in AI can expand the horizons of visual content creation. As AI continues to evolve, technologies like DALL-E will undoubtedly play a pivotal role in shaping the future of art, design, and visual communication.

Applications and Implications

Creative and Artistic Expression

DALL·E has opened up new avenues for artistic expression, enabling artists and creators to explore novel visual concepts by simply describing their vision in words. This has implications for graphic design, advertising, and entertainment, where the ability to rapidly prototype and visualize ideas can significantly enhance creative workflows.

Transforming Artistic Creation

DALL-E represents a paradigm shift in how art can be conceived and created. By inputting textual descriptions, artists and creators can use DALL-E to generate visual pieces that match their envisioned concepts, sometimes with surprising or unexpected results. This capability enables a collaborative form of art-making, where human creativity synergizes with AI's computational power to explore new aesthetic territories and visual narratives (Ramesh et al., 2021).

Expanding the Boundaries of Imagination

One of the most profound implications of DALL-E for creative and artistic expression is its ability to materialize images that combine disparate or abstract elements in ways previously unimagined. This not only challenges traditional boundaries of artistic imagination but also offers a tool for artists to experiment with surreal, avant-garde, or entirely novel visual forms. DALL-E's capacity to generate such unique and complex images from simple text prompts has opened up new possibilities for artistic exploration and expression.

Implications for Artists and the Art World

New Mediums and Methods

DALL-E introduces a new medium and method for artistic creation, prompting artists to rethink the role of the creator in the digital age. As artists integrate DALL-E into their creative processes, questions arise about authorship, originality, and the value of AI-generated art. This technology encourages a reevaluation of the artistic process, pushing artists to consider how AI can be harnessed to complement or enhance their work.

Democratization of Art Creation

DALL-E has the potential to democratize art creation by making it more accessible to individuals without traditional artistic training. This technology can serve as a tool for people to express their creative ideas visually, even if they lack drawing or painting skills. By lowering the barriers to art creation, DALL-E could broaden the scope of who is considered an artist and what is considered art, potentially enriching the cultural landscape with a wider diversity of perspectives.

Ethical Considerations and Challenges

Intellectual Property and Copyright

The advent of AI technologies like DALL-E raises complex questions about intellectual property and copyright in the context of art.

Determining the ownership of AI-generated images, especially those that might closely resemble existing copyrighted works, presents legal and ethical challenges. As AI continues to play a larger role in creative fields, there will be an increasing need for legal frameworks that address these issues.

Authenticity and Value

DALL-E also prompts a discussion about the authenticity and value of art in an era where AI can generate compelling images. The art world must grapple with what it means for a piece to be considered original or valuable when machines can produce art that evokes emotional or aesthetic responses comparable to human-created works.

DALL-E's impact on creative and artistic expression is profound, offering both opportunities and challenges for the art world. As detailed in "OpenAI: Exploring the World of Artificial Intelligence," this technology not only expands the possibilities for how art can be created and experienced but also prompts important reflections on the nature of creativity, authorship, and the value of art. The continued exploration of DALL-E's applications in artistic expression will likely shape the future of art, challenging traditional boundaries and opening up new frontiers for creative exploration.

Educational Tools

In education, DALL·E can serve as a powerful tool for engaging students in creative projects and learning activities. By transforming textual descriptions into visual representations, it can aid in teaching concepts in subjects such as literature, history, and science, making learning more interactive and visually stimulating.

Visualizing Complex Concepts

One of the most significant applications of DALL-E in education is its ability to visualize complex concepts that are often difficult to convey through traditional textual or verbal explanations. By generating detailed and accurate images based on descriptive texts, DALL-E can help students grasp abstract or challenging subjects by providing visual representations. This is particularly beneficial in disciplines such as science, mathematics, history, and literature, where conceptual understanding can be greatly enhanced through visual aids (Ramesh et al., 2021).

Supporting Creative Learning

DALL-E can also be employed as a tool to support creative learning processes. Students can use the technology to bring their imaginative ideas to life, creating visual representations of their thoughts, stories, or project concepts. This not only aids in developing students' creative and critical thinking skills but also encourages engagement and motivation by allowing students to see the tangible outcomes of their creativity.

DALL-E as an Educational Resource

Creating Customized Learning Materials

Educators can leverage DALL-E to create customized learning materials that cater to the specific needs and interests of their students. This includes generating images to accompany lesson plans, worksheets, and presentations, making the content more appealing and accessible to diverse learners. The ability to quickly produce tailored visual content can help teachers address varied learning styles and preferences, enhancing the inclusivity and effectiveness of educational offerings.

Interactive Learning Experiences

DALL-E's capabilities can be integrated into interactive learning platforms, enabling students to explore subjects dynamically. For example, language learning applications can use DALL-E to generate images that illustrate vocabulary words or grammatical concepts, providing learners with immediate visual feedback and reinforcing their understanding. Similarly, history or geography lessons can become more interactive and engaging by using DALL-E to visualize historical events, cultures, and geographical landscapes based on textual descriptions.

Ethical Considerations and Challenges

While the potential of DALL-E in education is vast, its application also raises ethical considerations and challenges. Ensuring the accuracy of the generated images is crucial, as inaccuracies could lead to misunderstandings or the propagation of misconceptions. Additionally, the use of AI-generated images in educational materials necessitates careful consideration of copyright and intellectual property issues, particularly when the images are derived from or inspired by copyrighted content.

The application of DALL-E as an educational tool represents a significant advance in the use of artificial intelligence to support and enhance learning. As discussed in "OpenAI: Exploring the World of Artificial Intelligence," DALL-E's ability to generate images from text opens up new possibilities for visualizing concepts, creating customized learning materials, and facilitating interactive learning experiences. However, realizing the full potential of this technology in education requires careful navigation of the associated ethical and practical challenges, ensuring that it serves as a valuable complement to traditional teaching methods and contributes positively to educational outcomes.

Research and Development

DALL·E's capabilities also have potential applications in research and development, particularly in fields where visualizing concepts or data is crucial. For example, in architecture and engineering, DALL·E could help visualize design concepts based on descriptive parameters, streamlining the design process.

Facilitating Visual Data Generation

One of the key contributions of DALL-E to research and development is its ability to generate visual data on demand. This capability is particularly beneficial for fields where visual representations play a crucial role in hypothesis testing, data analysis, and the communication of research findings. By providing researchers with the tools to create accurate, detailed images based on textual descriptions, DALL-E enhances the efficiency and effectiveness of research processes, from conceptualization to publication (Ramesh et al., 2021).

Enhancing Creative Problem-Solving

DALL-E also fosters innovation by enhancing creative problem-solving. Its ability to produce images that combine elements in novel ways can inspire researchers to explore unconventional solutions to complex problems. This aspect of DALL-E is especially valuable in fields such as design, engineering, and architecture, where visual creativity can lead to breakthrough innovations and advancements.

Applications in Scientific Visualization

Complex Concept Illustration

DALL-E's technology can be employed to illustrate complex scientific concepts that are difficult to visualize, making it an invaluable tool for education and communication in research. For instance, it can generate visualizations of theoretical physics concepts, molecular structures in chemistry, or intricate biological processes, thereby aiding in the comprehension and dissemination of complex scientific information.

Data Interpretation and Analysis

Moreover, DALL-E can assist researchers in data interpretation and analysis by converting data sets into visual formats that are easier to analyze and understand. In fields such as data science and statistics, where visual representation of data can uncover patterns and insights, DALL-E's capabilities can significantly augment analytical processes.

Implications for Interdisciplinary Research

Bridging Disciplinary Gaps

DALL-E's versatility and ease of use have the potential to bridge gaps between disciplines, facilitating interdisciplinary collaboration. By enabling researchers from different fields to generate and share visual representations of their work, DALL-E encourages a more integrated approach to solving complex, multifaceted problems.

Accelerating Research and Development Cycles

The ability to quickly generate visual content can also accelerate research and development cycles, allowing for faster iteration and prototyping. This acceleration is critical in fast-paced industries and research environments where speed to discovery or product development can confer a significant competitive advantage.

Ethical Considerations and Future Directions

As DALL-E continues to evolve, its application in research and development must be navigated with consideration for ethical implications, particularly concerning the accuracy and authenticity of generated images. Ensuring the responsible use of DALL-E in scientific research and development is paramount to maintaining trust and integrity in the process of knowledge creation.

DALL-E represents a transformative tool for research and development, offering novel capabilities for visual data generation, creative problem-solving, and scientific visualization. As outlined in "OpenAI: Exploring the World of Artificial Intelligence," this technology not only propels the advancement of artificial intelligence but also serves as a catalyst for innovation across diverse scientific and technological domains. The continued integration of DALL-E into research and development practices promises to reshape the landscape of discovery and innovation, heralding a new era of interdisciplinary collaboration and accelerated progress.

Ethical Considerations and Challenges

The development and use of DALL·E raise important ethical considerations, including concerns about copyright and the potential for creating misleading images. OpenAI has addressed these issues by implementing usage policies and restrictions, highlighting the importance of ethical guidelines in the development and deployment of AI technologies.

Copyright and Intellectual Property Issues

One of the foremost ethical considerations concerning DALL-E relates to copyright and intellectual property rights. As DALL-E generates images that could resemble existing artworks or be inspired by copyrighted material, it raises questions about the originality and ownership of AI-generated content. Determining the extent to which AI-generated images are protected by copyright or infringe on existing copyrights is a complex legal challenge that necessitates careful consideration and potentially new legal frameworks (Ramesh et al., 2021).

Privacy Concerns

Privacy concerns emerge when considering the dataset used to train DALL-E. The model is trained on vast amounts of data scraped from the internet, which may include personally identifiable information or copyrighted material. Ensuring that the use of such data complies with privacy laws and ethical standards is crucial to maintaining trust in AI technologies and safeguarding individuals' rights.

Bias and Representation

Another significant ethical challenge is the potential for bias in the images generated by DALL-E. Like any AI model, DALL-E's outputs are influenced by the data it has been trained on. If this data contains biases, stereotypes, or underrepresentation of certain groups, the model may inadvertently perpetuate or amplify these issues. Addressing bias in AI-generated content requires ongoing efforts to ensure diverse and inclusive training datasets and the implementation of mechanisms to detect and mitigate bias in generated images.

Responsible Use and Misuse Potential

The potential misuse of DALL-E for creating deceptive or harmful content, such as deepfakes or propaganda, presents a profound ethical challenge. Ensuring the responsible use of DALL-E involves implementing safeguards against misuse, establishing clear guidelines for use, and possibly developing detection tools to identify AI-generated content. Balancing the innovation and creativity enabled by DALL-E with the need to prevent harm and protect societal values is a critical concern that demands careful ethical consideration.

Navigating Ethical Challenges

To address these ethical challenges, several measures can be considered, including:

- Developing and enforcing clear guidelines and standards for the ethical use of DALL-E and similar technologies.
- Enhancing transparency around the training data and algorithms used by DALL-E to facilitate accountability and trust.
- Engaging in multidisciplinary research to understand and mitigate the biases inherent in AI-generated content.
- Collaborating with legal experts, policymakers, and the broader community to update copyright laws and regulatory frameworks to accommodate the nuances of AI-generated content.

DALL-E's ability to create images from text marks a significant technological advancement with the potential to enrich creative expression, innovation, and knowledge dissemination. However, as outlined in "OpenAI: Exploring the World of Artificial Intelligence," navigating the ethical landscape associated with this technology is imperative to ensure its benefits are realized responsibly and equitably. Addressing the ethical considerations and challenges related to copyright, privacy, bias, and misuse is essential for fostering trust in AI and securing its positive impact on society.

Future Directions

The ongoing development of DALL·E and similar technologies points to a future where AI plays an increasingly significant role in creative processes. Future iterations may offer enhanced precision, greater contextual understanding, and improved integration with other AI systems, expanding the possibilities for generating complex, multifaceted visual content from textual descriptions.

Conclusion

DALL·E represents a pioneering step in AI's ability to bridge the gap between textual and visual understanding, offering profound implications for creative expression, education, and beyond. As detailed in "OpenAI: Exploring the World of Artificial Intelligence," this project underscores OpenAI's role in pushing the frontiers of AI research, demonstrating the potential of AI to augment human creativity and transform how we interact with and conceptualize the visual world.

CLIP: Learning Visual Concepts from Natural Language:

This technology represents a notable advancement in the field of artificial intelligence by bridging the gap between visual concepts and natural language processing. CLIP has garnered attention for its ability to understand and categorize images in a more human-like manner, based on natural language descriptions.

Development of CLIP

CLIP was developed as a response to the limitations of traditional computer vision systems, which typically require extensive labeled datasets for each new task. Recognizing the inefficiency and scalability issues associated with this approach, OpenAI sought to create a system that could generalize across a wide range of visual tasks without task-specific data. CLIP is designed to learn visual concepts from natural language descriptions, leveraging the vast amount of text and images available on the internet (Radford et al., 2021).

Conceptual Foundations

The development of CLIP by OpenAI was motivated by the observation that while humans can easily describe images in natural language and understand language that describes visual concepts, traditional AI systems treated vision and language as separate domains. CLIP was conceived as a way to mimic this human ability, learning to understand images through the descriptive power of language. This approach represents a departure from conventional methods that rely on task-specific datasets and models (Radford et al., 2021).

Training Methodology

CLIP is trained on a diverse range of internet-collected images and their associated textual descriptions. This training involves a large dataset consisting of millions of image-text pairs, which CLIP uses to learn the associations between visual content and natural language. The model employs a contrastive learning approach, which encourages the model to predict the matching text description for a given image from a set of possible texts. This methodology allows CLIP to generalize from the specifics of the training data to a broad understanding of visual concepts as expressed in language.

Architecture and Mechanisms

CLIP's architecture consists of two primary components: an image encoder and a text encoder. The image encoder processes visual input, while the text encoder processes natural language input. Both encoders transform their respective inputs into representations in a shared embedding space, where the similarity between an image and a text can be measured directly. This dual-encoder architecture enables CLIP to perform a wide range of vision tasks using the same model, trained in a task-agnostic manner.

Implications for AI Research

Advancements in Vision-Language Understanding

CLIP's development marks a significant advancement in the understanding of visual concepts through natural language, demonstrating a more flexible and generalizable approach to AI. By learning directly from the vast amounts of visual and textual content available on the internet, CLIP can recognize a wide array of objects, actions, and scenes, and understand their descriptions in natural language. This capability has profound implications for AI research, opening new avenues for exploring how AI systems can acquire knowledge and understand the world.

Potential Applications

The unique capabilities of CLIP have potential applications across various domains, including but not limited to image search, content moderation, accessibility tools, and educational technologies. By enabling more intuitive and human-like interaction between AI systems and visual content, CLIP can enhance the usability and effectiveness of AI applications that require an understanding of the visual world.

The development of CLIP by OpenAI represents a pivotal moment in the convergence of language and vision in artificial intelligence. As detailed in "OpenAI: Exploring the World of Artificial Intelligence," CLIP's innovative approach to learning visual concepts from natural language descriptions underscores the potential of AI to mimic human cognitive abilities more closely. The continued exploration and refinement of technologies like CLIP are essential for advancing the field of AI and unlocking new possibilities for AI-assisted understanding of the visual world.

Underlying Technology

Contrastive Learning Approach

CLIP utilizes a contrastive learning approach to train its model, which involves learning to associate images with their corresponding textual descriptions. The model is presented with pairs of images and texts, learning to predict which pairs match correctly. This method allows CLIP to understand the content of images in the context of natural language, enabling it to categorize and understand images in ways that align more closely with human perception.

Foundations of Contrastive Learning

Contrastive learning is a technique used in machine learning to teach a model how to understand which things are similar and which are not, based on the context of their data representations. In the context of CLIP, this approach involves learning to associate images with their corresponding textual descriptions (or vice versa) by maximizing the similarity between correctly paired image and text embeddings while minimizing the similarity between mismatched pairs (Radford et al., 2021).

Mechanism and Implementation

CLIP employs a dual-encoder architecture comprising an image encoder and a text encoder, which map images and textual descriptions, respectively, into a shared embedding space. The contrastive learning objective is to adjust the parameters of these encoders so that the distance between an image and its correct description is smaller compared to the distance between that image and other random descriptions in the dataset. This is typically achieved through a contrastive loss function, such as the noise-contrastive estimation (NCE) loss or a variant thereof, which effectively encourages the model to distinguish between matching and non-matching pairs among the sampled data.

Training Process

During training, CLIP simultaneously processes batches of images and their corresponding textual descriptions. For each image-text pair, the model computes the similarities between the image embedding and all text embeddings in the batch (and vice versa), applying the contrastive loss to update the model's weights. This process requires a careful balance between positive pairs (correct matches) and negative pairs (incorrect matches) to ensure the model learns a robust and generalizable mapping between the visual and textual domains.

Implications for AI Research

Enhanced Visual and Textual Understanding

The contrastive learning approach underpinning CLIP represents a significant shift toward more holistic and integrated AI systems capable of understanding the interplay between visual and textual information. By learning direct associations between images and natural language, CLIP transcends traditional task-specific models, offering broad applicability across a range of vision and language tasks without the need for task-specific training data or models.

Transferability and Generalization

One of the key advantages of the contrastive learning approach is its potential for transferability and generalization. CLIP demonstrates remarkable proficiency in generalizing from its training data to a wide variety of visual concepts and linguistic descriptions it has never encountered before. This capability underscores the model's ability to learn a rich and transferable representation of the world, akin to human cognitive processes.

Future Directions

The success of the contrastive learning approach in CLIP opens new avenues for research in AI, particularly in exploring more efficient and effective ways to bridge other modalities (e.g., audio, sensor data) with language. It also raises questions about how these techniques can be further refined to reduce biases, enhance interpretability, and improve the robustness of AI models against adversarial attacks.

The contrastive learning approach utilized by CLIP marks a substantial advancement in the field of artificial intelligence, enabling a more nuanced understanding of the relationship between images and text. As discussed in "OpenAI: Exploring the World of Artificial Intelligence," this technology not only bridges the gap between visual and linguistic data but also sets a foundation for future innovations in AI that seek to create more integrated, versatile, and human-like systems.

Joint Embedding Space

A key feature of CLIP is its creation of a joint embedding space for both images and text. By mapping images and text descriptions into a shared multidimensional space, CLIP can effectively measure the similarity between an image and a textual description. This capability underpins CLIP's flexibility and generalizability across different visual tasks (Radford et al., 2021).

Conceptual Foundations

The concept of a joint embedding space stems from the need to create a common representational ground where both visual and textual data can be compared directly. In the context of CLIP, this involves mapping images and textual descriptions into a shared high-dimensional space where the similarity between them can be quantified. This approach allows CLIP to understand and interpret the content of images in the context of natural language descriptions, facilitating a wide range of language-vision tasks (Radford et al., 2021).

Mechanism and Implementation

CLIP achieves this joint embedding through a dual-encoder architecture, comprising an image encoder and a text encoder. Each encoder is responsible for transforming its respective input modality (images or text) into vectors within the joint embedding space. The image encoder typically utilizes a convolutional neural network (CNN) or a vision transformer to process visual inputs, while the text encoder uses a transformer-based model to handle textual inputs. The encoders are trained to align the embeddings of corresponding images and texts closely together in the embedding space, thereby learning a meaningful representation that captures the relationships between visual and linguistic elements.

Training and Contrastive Learning

The training of CLIP involves a contrastive learning approach, where the model is encouraged to match images with their corresponding text descriptions more closely than with mismatched descriptions. This process relies on a contrastive loss function, which penalizes the model when correct image-text pairs are far apart in the joint embedding space and rewards the model when these pairs are close together. Through iterative training on a large dataset of image-text pairs, CLIP learns to optimize the embeddings within this shared space, enhancing its ability to understand and generate coherent mappings between images and text.

Implications for AI Research and Applications

Enhanced Multimodal Understanding

The use of a joint embedding space in CLIP represents a significant advancement in multimodal AI, enabling more sophisticated and integrated understanding of images and text. This capability has broad implications for AI research, suggesting new pathways for developing systems that can navigate and interpret the world across different sensory modalities and data types.

Applications Across Domains

The joint embedding space mechanism empowers CLIP to be applied across a diverse range of domains, including but not limited to image captioning, content search and retrieval, automated content moderation, and assistive technologies. By facilitating a deeper understanding of the content and context of visual and textual information, CLIP can significantly enhance the functionality and user experience of AI-powered applications.

The development of a joint embedding space in CLIP marks a pivotal innovation in the field of artificial intelligence, enabling a more holistic and integrated approach to learning visual concepts from natural language. As discussed in "OpenAI: Exploring the World of Artificial Intelligence," this technology not only bridges the divide between vision and language but also sets the stage for future advancements in AI that seek to create systems capable of complex multimodal understanding and interaction.

Capabilities of CLIP

Generalization Across Tasks

One of CLIP's most significant capabilities is its ability to generalize across a wide variety of visual tasks without requiring task-specific models or datasets. This includes object recognition, categorization, and even complex reasoning tasks that involve understanding scenes or relationships between objects. CLIP's performance on these tasks demonstrates a profound advancement in AI's ability to interpret and understand visual information.

Mechanisms of Generalization

CLIP's ability to generalize across tasks is rooted in its unique training methodology and architecture. By leveraging a contrastive learning approach within a joint embedding space for both visual and textual inputs, CLIP learns to map these inputs into a shared representational space. This training is conducted on a diverse dataset comprising millions of image-text pairs sourced from the internet, covering a broad spectrum of subjects, styles, and contexts. As a result, CLIP develops a rich, nuanced understanding of the relationships between images and textual descriptions, enabling it to apply this understanding flexibly across different tasks (Radford et al., 2021).

Performance Across Diverse Tasks

Empirical evaluations of CLIP have demonstrated its robust performance across a variety of tasks without the need for task-specific models or fine-tuning. These tasks include but are not limited to image classification, object detection, geographic localization, and more. Remarkably, CLIP can perform these tasks based solely on natural language descriptions of the task objectives, showcasing an ability to understand task requirements and apply its learned visual concepts accordingly. This zero-shot or few-shot capability indicates a significant departure from traditional AI models, which typically require extensive task-specific data and training.

Implications for AI Research and Applications

Flexibility and Efficiency in AI Systems

The generalization capabilities of CLIP suggest a new paradigm for AI system development, where flexibility and efficiency are paramount. By reducing the reliance on large, annotated datasets for every new task, CLIP offers a more scalable and adaptable approach to AI, capable of rapidly adjusting to new domains or requirements. This flexibility holds promise for a wide range of applications, from automated content moderation and accessibility tools to advanced systems for visual search and analysis.

Bridging Human and Machine Understanding

CLIP's performance across diverse tasks also bridges the gap between human and machine understanding, moving closer to AI systems that can interpret and interact with the world in a manner more akin to human cognition. This capability has profound implications for the development of intuitive, human-centered AI interfaces and applications, enhancing the ability of AI to assist, augment, and empower human endeavors.

Challenges and Future Directions

While CLIP's generalization capabilities represent a significant advance, challenges remain, including ensuring fairness, addressing biases, and maintaining accuracy across highly specialized or nuanced tasks. Future research will likely focus on enhancing the model's understanding and performance in specific domains, developing more robust mechanisms for bias mitigation, and exploring new architectures and training methodologies to further improve generalization.

CLIP's ability to generalize across tasks without task-specific tuning marks a pivotal development in the field of artificial intelligence, as highlighted in "OpenAI: Exploring the World of Artificial Intelligence." This capability not only demonstrates the potential of AI to learn and apply visual concepts in a flexible and efficient manner but also opens up new avenues for research and applications across diverse domains, pushing the boundaries of what AI systems can achieve.

Zero-Shot Learning

CLIP exhibits remarkable zero-shot learning capabilities, where it can correctly categorize images in categories it has never explicitly seen during training. This is achieved by leveraging the model's understanding of natural language descriptions, allowing it to apply conceptual knowledge to new contexts. This ability highlights the potential for AI systems to adapt and perform tasks in dynamic, real-world environments.

Theoretical Foundations

Zero-shot learning refers to the ability of a model to correctly perform tasks or make accurate predictions for classes or scenarios it has not seen during training. This capability is significant in CLIP due to its unique training methodology, which involves learning from a vast corpus of images and their corresponding textual descriptions collected from the internet. By analyzing these image-text pairs, CLIP develops a nuanced understanding of the relationships between visual elements and their linguistic counterparts, enabling it to apply this knowledge to new, unseen tasks (Radford et al., 2021).

Mechanism and Implementation

CLIP achieves zero-shot learning through its dual-encoder architecture, which consists of an image encoder and a text encoder. These encoders project images and text descriptions into a shared embedding space where their similarity can be measured. During its zero-shot learning tasks, CLIP is presented with a new image and a set of possible textual descriptions (including descriptions for classes not seen during training). It then predicts the most likely description by finding the closest match in the embedding space. This process allows CLIP to generalize beyond its training data and perform tasks across a wide range of domains without additional training.

Performance and Evaluation

Empirical evaluations of CLIP have demonstrated its impressive ability to generalize to a variety of tasks with no task-specific training, outperforming traditional models in many zero-shot scenarios. These tasks span image classification, object recognition, and content categorization, among others. CLIP's performance underscores the model's robust understanding of visual concepts and its capacity to effectively leverage natural language as a flexible descriptor for visual content.

Implications for AI Research and Applications

Advancing General AI Capabilities

CLIP's zero-shot learning capability represents a significant step toward developing more general AI systems that can adapt to a wide array of tasks without the need for extensive retraining. This flexibility is crucial for creating AI models that can efficiently process and understand the vast and diverse range of data encountered in the real world.

Potential Applications

The zero-shot learning ability of CLIP has profound implications for various applications, including but not limited to automated content moderation, visual search engines, and assistive technologies for the visually impaired. By enabling these applications to recognize and understand new objects or concepts without explicit prior training, CLIP can significantly enhance their effectiveness and accessibility.

Challenges and Future Directions

Despite its promising capabilities, zero-shot learning in CLIP also presents challenges, particularly regarding the accuracy and reliability of predictions for entirely novel classes or highly specialized domains. Future research will likely focus on improving the model's precision in these zero-shot scenarios, addressing biases in the training data, and exploring ways to extend zero-shot learning capabilities to a broader range of tasks and domains.

The zero-shot learning capabilities of CLIP, as highlighted in "OpenAI: Exploring the World of Artificial Intelligence," mark a paradigm shift in artificial intelligence, offering a glimpse into the future of AI systems capable of understanding and performing a vast array of tasks with minimal human intervention. This capability not only broadens the horizons of AI's potential applications but also challenges current conceptions of machine learning, paving the way for more adaptable and intelligent AI systems.

Implications for Artificial Intelligence

Bridging Vision and Language

CLIP represents a significant step forward in bridging the domains of computer vision and natural language processing. By learning visual concepts through natural language, CLIP advances the integration of multimodal information, opening new avenues for more holistic and flexible AI systems.

Integrating Visual and Linguistic Domains

The development of CLIP by OpenAI marks a paradigmatic shift in how artificial intelligence systems comprehend and process the interconnectedness of visual and linguistic data. Unlike traditional models that treat vision and language as separate entities often requiring distinct models for processing, CLIP employs a single unified model trained on a diverse dataset of image-text pairs. This approach enables the model to learn a vast array of visual concepts directly associated with natural language descriptions, facilitating a more holistic understanding of both modalities (Radford et al., 2021).

The Role of Contrastive Learning

At the heart of CLIP's success in bridging vision and language is its use of contrastive learning. By optimizing for a shared representation between images and text, CLIP efficiently learns to map these two modalities into a joint embedding space. This method not only improves the model's accuracy in understanding and generating content across both domains but also significantly enhances its ability to generalize from seen to unseen data, embodying a form of zero-shot learning.

Implications for Artificial Intelligence

Enhancing Multimodal AI Systems

CLIP's ability to bridge vision and language has profound implications for the development of multimodal AI systems. By providing a framework that efficiently integrates visual and textual information, CLIP paves the way for more sophisticated AI applications capable of performing complex tasks involving multiple forms of data. This includes enhancements in natural language processing, computer vision, and beyond, leading to AI systems with a more nuanced understanding of the world.

Potential Applications Across Domains

The integration of vision and language through CLIP opens up myriad applications across various domains. In healthcare, CLIP could assist in diagnosing diseases by interpreting medical imagery in conjunction with patient descriptions. In the realm of content creation and digital media, it offers the potential to automate and personalize content generation. Furthermore, in education and accessibility, CLIP can provide visual aids based on textual content, making information more accessible to individuals with visual impairments.

Facilitating Human-like AI Interactions

By bridging the gap between vision and language, CLIP significantly advances the goal of creating AI systems that interact with the world in a manner akin to human cognition. This convergence of visual and linguistic understanding enables AI to perform tasks with a level of intuition and insight previously unattainable, moving closer to AI systems that can truly understand and engage with human users in their natural modes of communication.

Challenges and Future Directions

Despite its advancements, the integration of vision and language through CLIP also presents challenges, including ensuring the ethical use of AI, addressing biases in training data, and maintaining the privacy and security of information. Future research will need to focus on these areas, as well as on further enhancing the model's accuracy, efficiency, and applicability to a wider range of tasks and domains.

The implications of CLIP for artificial intelligence are far-reaching, heralding a new era of AI systems capable of seamlessly integrating visual and linguistic information. As outlined in "OpenAI: Exploring the World of Artificial Intelligence," this breakthrough not only advances the technical capabilities of AI but also opens up new possibilities for its application and interaction with the world, bridging the gap between human and machine understanding.

Scalability and Efficiency

The development of CLIP addresses key scalability and efficiency challenges in AI. By reducing the reliance on large, task-specific labeled datasets, CLIP offers a more scalable approach to developing versatile AI systems capable of performing a broad range of tasks with fewer data and computational resources.

Foundations of Scalability

CLIP's training methodology, which leverages a vast corpus of image-text pairs gathered from the internet, is a cornerstone of its scalability. Unlike traditional models that require carefully annotated datasets specific to each task, CLIP learns from naturally occurring data, enabling it to scale with the ever-growing volume of visual and textual content available online. This approach allows CLIP to continuously improve and adapt as more data becomes available, without the need for labor-intensive dataset curation (Radford et al., 2021).

Efficiency through Contrastive Learning

The efficiency of CLIP is largely attributed to its contrastive learning approach, which optimizes for a joint embedding space between images and text. This method reduces the computational complexity typically associated with training large-scale models on multimodal data. By focusing on aligning corresponding image-text pairs in the embedding space and distinguishing them from non-matching pairs, CLIP achieves high performance on a range of tasks without the need for task-specific model architectures or fine-tuning. This efficiency is crucial for deploying AI models in resource-constrained environments and for applications requiring real-time processing.

Implications for Artificial Intelligence

Advancing Multimodal AI Research

The scalability and efficiency of CLIP have profound implications for the advancement of multimodal AI research. By demonstrating that a single model can learn to understand and generate representations across visual and linguistic domains, CLIP challenges the conventional wisdom around the need for specialized models for each modality or task. This opens up new avenues for research into generalizable AI systems that can leverage diverse data types and perform a wide array of tasks with minimal additional training.

Enabling Broad Applications

The characteristics of CLIP facilitate a broad range of applications across industries. In sectors such as healthcare, education, and media, the scalability and efficiency of CLIP mean that AI can be deployed more widely, bringing sophisticated visual and linguistic analysis to areas where it was previously impractical. For instance, CLIP can be used to rapidly categorize and analyze medical images with accompanying patient notes, or to generate educational content tailored to specific learning materials, all with minimal task-specific adaptation.

Promoting Sustainable AI Development

Moreover, the efficiency of CLIP contributes to more sustainable AI development practices. The computational resources required for training and deploying AI models are a growing concern, with significant environmental impacts. The methods underpinning CLIP's efficiency can serve as a blueprint for developing more resource-efficient AI models, aligning with broader goals of reducing the carbon footprint of AI research and deployment.

Challenges and Future Directions

While CLIP's scalability and efficiency represent significant achievements, they also introduce challenges, such as ensuring the model's robustness and fairness when scaled and maintaining accuracy across highly diverse or specialized tasks. Future research will likely focus on enhancing the model's generalization capabilities while addressing these challenges, paving the way for even more scalable and efficient AI systems.

CLIP's approach to learning visual concepts from natural language, characterized by its scalability and efficiency, marks a pivotal advancement in the field of artificial intelligence, as explored in "OpenAI: Exploring the World of Artificial Intelligence." These attributes not only facilitate CLIP's broad applicability across tasks and domains but also embody essential principles for the future development of AI—principles that prioritize adaptability, resource efficiency, and the capacity to learn from the vast and varied data that constitutes human knowledge and experience.

Ethical Considerations

As with any AI technology, CLIP raises ethical considerations, particularly regarding bias and fairness. The reliance on internet-sourced data may introduce biases present in the data into the model's understanding of visual concepts. Ensuring that CLIP and similar technologies are developed and deployed responsibly requires ongoing attention to mitigating bias and ensuring equitable performance across diverse contexts.

Bias and Representation

One of the primary ethical concerns associated with CLIP, as with many AI technologies, revolves around bias and representation. Given that CLIP is trained on a vast dataset of images and text sourced from the internet, it is susceptible to inheriting and potentially amplifying biases present in its training data. These biases could manifest in skewed or unfair representations of certain groups, individuals, or concepts, leading to discriminatory outcomes or reinforcing stereotypes (Radford et al., 2021). Addressing these biases necessitates a proactive approach to dataset curation, model training, and output evaluation to ensure fairness and equity in CLIP's applications.

Privacy and Data Use

The extensive data collection required to train CLIP raises concerns about privacy and the ethical use of data. The model's reliance on publicly available internet data includes content that individuals may not have intended for AI training purposes, posing questions about consent and the rights to digital content. Ensuring that data used for training CLIP respects privacy rights and adheres to ethical standards is crucial for maintaining public trust in AI technologies.

Misuse and Malicious Applications

Another ethical consideration is the potential misuse of CLIP for creating misleading or harmful content. Given its ability to generate realistic images based on textual descriptions, CLIP could be exploited for generating deepfakes, propagating misinformation, or creating offensive or harmful imagery. Mitigating these risks requires the implementation of robust content moderation policies, ethical guidelines, and technological safeguards to prevent misuse and protect against malicious applications.

Transparency and Accountability

Transparency in how CLIP is developed, trained, and deployed is essential for addressing ethical concerns. OpenAI's commitment to sharing details about CLIP's architecture, training methodologies, and performance evaluations contributes to a culture of accountability within the AI research community. However, ongoing efforts are needed to ensure that CLIP's development processes remain transparent, especially as the model evolves and finds new applications.

Navigating Ethical Challenges

To responsibly address the ethical considerations associated with CLIP, several measures can be recommended:

Diverse and Inclusive Training Data: Actively seek out and incorporate diverse and inclusive datasets to train CLIP, aiming to reduce biases and improve the model's fairness and representation.

Ethical Oversight and Review: Establish multidisciplinary ethical review boards to oversee CLIP's development and application, ensuring that ethical standards are upheld across all stages of the project.

Public Engagement and Dialogue: Engage with various stakeholders, including the public, policymakers, and ethics experts, to discuss and address ethical concerns, fostering an open dialogue about the responsible use of AI.

Continual Monitoring and Evaluation: Implement mechanisms for the ongoing monitoring and evaluation of CLIP's outputs, ensuring that biases are identified and addressed promptly and that the model's applications remain aligned with ethical principles.

The ethical considerations surrounding CLIP, as explored in "OpenAI: Exploring the World of Artificial Intelligence," highlight the complex interplay between technological advancement and ethical responsibility in the field of AI. Navigating these challenges requires a concerted effort from researchers, developers, and the broader community to ensure that technologies like CLIP are developed and deployed in ways that respect ethical norms and contribute positively to society.

Conclusion

CLIP, as detailed in "OpenAI: Exploring the World of Artificial Intelligence," embodies a significant advancement in the intersection of computer vision and natural language processing. Its development heralds a new era of AI capabilities, offering a glimpse into the future of more integrated, adaptable, and efficient AI systems. The continued exploration and refinement of technologies like CLIP will undoubtedly play a crucial role in shaping the trajectory of AI research and its applications in the real world.

Robotics and AI:

OpenAI has made significant strides in integrating AI technologies into robotics, leading to remarkable breakthroughs that have the potential to reshape various industries and aspects of daily life.

OpenAI's Initiatives in Robotics and AI

Development of Robotic Systems

One of OpenAI's most notable contributions to robotics has been the development of advanced robotic systems capable of performing complex tasks with a high degree of precision and autonomy. Through the integration of machine learning models, particularly reinforcement learning and deep learning, OpenAI's robots can learn from their environment, adapt to new challenges, and execute tasks with minimal human intervention. These tasks range from object manipulation and navigation to more complex problem-solving activities (OpenAI, 2020).

Technical Foundations and Innovations

OpenAI has made notable strides in advancing robotic systems through the integration of cutting-edge AI technologies. One of the fundamental aspects of OpenAI's approach to robotics is the application of reinforcement learning (RL) and deep learning techniques to enable robots to learn from their environment and from simulations. This approach allows robotic systems to acquire complex skills and adapt to new tasks with minimal human intervention. OpenAI's development of robotic systems often involves the use of simulated environments for training before transferring learned skills to physical robots, a process known as sim-to-real transfer (OpenAI, 2020).

Project Milestones

One of OpenAI's key milestones in robotics was the development of a robotic hand, Dactyl, which learned dexterous manipulation entirely in simulation. Dactyl demonstrated the ability to manipulate physical objects with precision and adaptability, showcasing the potential of RL and simulation-based training in achieving sophisticated motor skills in robots (OpenAI, 2018).

Another significant achievement was the creation of robots that can solve Rubik's cubes with a single hand. This project not only highlighted the advanced dexterity and problem-solving capabilities that AI-driven robots can achieve but also underscored the potential for these systems to perform complex tasks in dynamic, real-world environments.

Practical Applications and Implications

Enhancing Automation and Efficiency

OpenAI's initiatives in robotics hold vast potential for enhancing automation across various industries, from manufacturing and logistics to healthcare and service sectors. By developing robotic systems that can learn and adapt to a wide range of tasks, OpenAI is paving the way for more flexible and efficient automation solutions, capable of addressing complex challenges and adapting to changing environments.

Collaborative Robotics

The advancements in AI-driven robotics also open up new possibilities for collaborative robotics, where robots work alongside humans to augment human capabilities and increase productivity. OpenAI's research into intuitive human-robot interaction and safe collaboration mechanisms is crucial for the integration of robotic systems into workplaces and everyday life.

Challenges and Future Directions

Ethical and Societal Considerations

As robotic systems become more capable and autonomous, ethical and societal considerations come to the forefront. Issues such as job displacement, privacy, and safety require careful consideration and responsible approaches to the deployment of AI-driven robots. OpenAI's commitment to aligning AI development with human values and societal well-being is reflected in its ongoing research and policy advocacy.

Advancing Robotic Capabilities

Looking ahead, OpenAI's initiatives in robotics are set to continue pushing the boundaries of what is possible in AI and robotics integration. Future research directions include improving the robustness and generalizability of robotic systems, enhancing human-robot collaboration, and exploring new applications of robotics in addressing global challenges.

OpenAI's initiatives in the development of robotic systems represent a significant contribution to the field of artificial intelligence and robotics. As discussed in "OpenAI: Exploring the World of Artificial Intelligence," these efforts not only showcase the technical prowess and innovative spirit of OpenAI but also highlight the transformative potential of robotics to reshape industries, augment human capabilities, and address complex societal challenges.

Breakthrough in Dexterity and Manipulation

A significant breakthrough in OpenAI's robotics research has been the development of robotic systems with enhanced dexterity and manipulation capabilities. The OpenAI Dactyl project, for example, showcased a robotic hand that learned to solve a Rubik's Cube with human-like dexterity. This achievement was made possible through the use of a reinforcement learning algorithm trained in a simulated environment, demonstrating the potential of AI to master fine motor skills and complex cognitive tasks (Akkaya et al., 2019).

Technological Foundations

OpenAI's breakthrough in robotic dexterity and manipulation is epitomized by its development of Dactyl, a robotic system capable of solving a Rubik's Cube with a single robotic hand. This achievement was grounded in sophisticated machine learning techniques, including reinforcement learning (RL) and domain randomization, which enabled the robotic hand to learn complex tasks through trial and error in simulated environments before successfully transferring these skills to the real world (OpenAI, 2018).

Reinforcement Learning and Domain Randomization

The core of Dactyl's learning process involved reinforcement learning, where the robot incrementally improved its performance based on feedback from its actions. This was complemented by domain randomization techniques, which exposed the robot to a wide variety of simulated conditions, thereby enhancing its ability to adapt to the variability and unpredictability of real-world environments. Through these methods, Dactyl achieved a level of dexterity and problem-solving prowess that marked a significant advancement in robotics (OpenAI, 2019).

Implications for Robotics and AI

Expanding the Scope of Robotic Applications

The breakthroughs in dexterity and manipulation spearheaded by OpenAI have profound implications for the scope of robotic applications. Robotic systems with enhanced dexterity can be deployed in a broader range of settings, from intricate assembly tasks in manufacturing to delicate surgical procedures in healthcare. This expands the potential for automation and the integration of robots into domains previously considered beyond the reach of robotic capabilities.

Advancing Human-Robot Collaboration

Improvements in robotic dexterity and manipulation also pave the way for more effective and intuitive human-robot collaboration. Robots with human-like dexterity can work alongside humans more seamlessly, assisting with tasks that require precision and adaptability. This opens up new avenues for collaboration in research laboratories, creative industries, and everyday tasks, enhancing productivity and enabling new forms of creativity and exploration.

Challenges and Future Directions

Ethical and Social Considerations

As robotic capabilities continue to advance, ethical and social considerations become increasingly pertinent. Issues such as workforce displacement, privacy, and safety need to be addressed, ensuring that the benefits of robotic advancements are distributed equitably across society. OpenAI's commitment to ethical AI development emphasizes the importance of considering these issues as integral components of robotics research and development.

Enhancing Generalization and Adaptability

Future research initiatives by OpenAI and others in the field will likely focus on enhancing the generalization and adaptability of robotic systems. This includes refining learning algorithms, improving simulation environments, and developing more sophisticated sensors and actuators. The goal is to create robots that can learn a wider array of tasks more efficiently and operate in even more diverse and challenging environments.

OpenAI's initiatives and breakthroughs in the realm of robotic dexterity and manipulation, as would be detailed in "OpenAI: Exploring the World of Artificial Intelligence," represent a pivotal advancement in the integration of artificial intelligence and robotics. These achievements not only demonstrate the potential for robots to perform tasks with human-like precision and adaptability but also highlight the broader implications for automation, human-robot interaction, and the future landscape of work and creativity.

Applications and Implications

Industrial Automation

OpenAI's advancements in robotics and AI hold profound implications for industrial automation. The ability of robots to learn and adapt to various tasks could lead to more efficient manufacturing processes, reduced operational costs, and improved product quality. Additionally, AI-driven robotics could enhance safety in hazardous environments, performing tasks that would be risky or impossible for human workers.

Enhancing Efficiency and Productivity

OpenAI's foray into robotics, particularly through initiatives like the development of Dactyl, which demonstrated remarkable dexterity and manipulation capabilities, signifies a leap forward in industrial automation (OpenAI, 2018). The application of such AI-driven robotic systems in manufacturing processes promises to significantly enhance operational efficiency and productivity. Robots equipped with AI capabilities can perform complex assembly tasks, quality control, and maintenance with precision and speed that surpass human ability, leading to increased output and reduced downtime.

Customization and Flexibility

One of the standout implications of OpenAI's robotics initiatives for industrial automation is the potential for greater customization and flexibility in manufacturing. Traditional automation systems are typically designed for mass production, where changing product designs or processes can be costly and time-consuming. In contrast, AI-driven robots can adapt to new tasks quickly, learning from minimal input or demonstrations. This adaptability makes it feasible to automate small-batch production and custom manufacturing processes, significantly expanding the capabilities of automated systems to cater to diverse market demands.

Safety and Hazardous Environments

Another critical application of OpenAI's robotics technologies in industrial settings is enhancing worker safety, particularly in hazardous environments. Robots capable of learning and performing tasks in conditions that are dangerous for humans—such as extreme temperatures, toxic atmospheres, or high-risk activities—can mitigate workplace hazards. By delegating dangerous tasks to robots, industries can minimize the risk of accidents and injuries, fostering safer work environments.

Broader Implications for Workforce and Economy

Workforce Transformation

The integration of AI-driven robotics in industrial automation necessitates a reevaluation of workforce skills and roles. While automation may reduce the need for manual labor in certain tasks, it also creates opportunities for higher-skilled positions focused on managing, maintaining, and optimizing AI systems. The transition underscores the importance of reskilling and upskilling initiatives to prepare the workforce for the evolving demands of the digital economy.

Economic Impact

The implications of advancing industrial automation extend to the broader economy, with the potential to significantly affect productivity, competitiveness, and innovation. By reducing production costs and enhancing product quality, countries and companies can strengthen their competitive position in the global market. Furthermore, the adoption of advanced robotics can spur innovation, leading to the development of new products, services, and business models that capitalize on the capabilities of AI-driven systems.

Ethical and Societal Considerations

As industries embrace automation, ethical and societal considerations come to the forefront. These include concerns about job displacement, income inequality, and ensuring equitable access to the benefits of technological advancements. Addressing these challenges requires collaborative efforts among policymakers, industry leaders, and educational institutions to develop strategies that promote inclusive growth and opportunity in the age of AI.

The initiatives and breakthroughs of OpenAI in robotics and artificial intelligence, as explored in "OpenAI: Exploring the World of Artificial Intelligence," herald a new era in industrial automation. These advancements promise not only to enhance operational efficiency and safety but also to redefine the nature of work and production in the 21st century. As society navigates the implications of these technologies, the focus must remain on harnessing their potential to drive sustainable and inclusive economic progress.

Healthcare Robotics

In the healthcare sector, OpenAI's technologies could revolutionize patient care through the development of robotic assistants capable of performing surgical procedures with precision beyond human capabilities or assisting in patient rehabilitation with adaptive learning algorithms that tailor therapy to individual patient needs.

Enhanced Precision in Surgical Procedures

OpenAI's foray into robotics, exemplified by projects demonstrating advanced dexterity and manipulation, such as Dactyl, signifies potential applications in performing precise surgical procedures (OpenAI, 2018). Robotics systems equipped with AI capabilities can assist surgeons in performing complex surgeries with higher precision, reduced variability, and minimized invasiveness. These robotic assistants can enhance surgical outcomes through steady, precise movements, and the ability to access and visualize difficult-to-reach areas, ultimately improving patient recovery times and reducing the risk of complications.

Diagnostics and Predictive Analysis

The integration of AI-driven robotics in diagnostics represents another groundbreaking application, leveraging machine learning algorithms to analyze medical images, pathology samples, or patient data to identify diseases early and accurately. OpenAI's developments in understanding and interpreting complex datasets can be applied to automate and enhance diagnostic processes, offering predictive insights that support preemptive treatment strategies, personalized medicine, and ultimately, improved patient prognoses.

Patient Care and Rehabilitation

Robotics technologies developed by OpenAI have implications for patient care and rehabilitation, offering innovative solutions for personalized care plans. Robots can assist in monitoring patient vitals, administering medication, and providing companionship, especially in elderly care settings. Moreover, AI-driven robotic systems can deliver tailored rehabilitation exercises, adapting to each patient's recovery progress, and providing therapists with valuable data to optimize rehabilitation strategies.

Broader Implications for Healthcare Delivery

Expanding Access to Care

One of the most significant implications of healthcare robotics is the potential to expand access to medical care. Robotic systems can perform diagnostic and treatment tasks remotely, breaking down geographical barriers to care, and making high-quality healthcare services more accessible to underserved populations. This democratization of healthcare resources is pivotal in global health efforts to ensure equitable access to medical services.

Operational Efficiency and Cost Reduction

The adoption of robotics in healthcare settings promises to enhance operational efficiency, streamline workflow processes, and reduce costs. By automating routine tasks, healthcare facilities can allocate human resources more effectively, focusing on patient-centered care and complex clinical decisions. In the long run, the efficiencies gained through robotics could contribute to controlling the rising costs of healthcare delivery, making services more affordable and sustainable.

Ethical and Societal Considerations

The integration of AI-driven robotics in healthcare also raises important ethical and societal questions. Issues such as patient privacy, data security, and the ethical use of robotic systems in patient care require careful consideration. Furthermore, the potential impact on the healthcare workforce, including the need for retraining and the risk of job displacement, highlights the importance of developing strategies to manage the transition towards more technologically integrated healthcare systems.

The initiatives and breakthroughs of OpenAI in robotics and AI, as discussed in "OpenAI: Exploring the World of Artificial Intelligence," are poised to bring about a paradigm shift in healthcare. These technologies offer the promise of enhanced surgical precision, improved diagnostics, personalized patient care, and greater access to healthcare services. As the healthcare sector navigates the integration of these advanced technologies, a focus on ethical considerations, workforce adaptation, and equitable access will be crucial in realizing the full potential of healthcare robotics to improve patient outcomes and transform healthcare delivery.

Service Robotics

OpenAI's initiatives also extend to service robotics, where AI-driven robots could perform a variety of tasks in settings such as homes, offices, and public spaces. From domestic chores to providing assistance to the elderly or individuals with disabilities, these robots could significantly enhance quality of life and accessibility.

Technological Foundations

OpenAI's foray into service robotics is built upon its extensive research and development in AI and machine learning, including projects like Dactyl, which showcased advanced dexterity in robotic hands, and CLIP, which bridges the gap between visual perception and natural language processing. These technologies provide the foundation for developing service robots capable of complex interactions and tasks, from customer service to personalized assistance (OpenAI, 2020).

Breakthroughs in Robotics

A significant breakthrough in OpenAI's service robotics initiatives is the application of reinforcement learning (RL) techniques to enable robots to learn from their environment and from simulated scenarios. This approach allows service robots to adapt to real-world challenges and perform a wide range of tasks with a high degree of autonomy and precision. For example, OpenAI's advancements have enabled robots to perform tasks such as navigating complex environments, recognizing and manipulating objects, and interacting with humans in a natural and intuitive manner (OpenAI, 2018).

Applications and Implications of Service Robotics

Enhancing Customer Service

Service robots powered by OpenAI's technologies have the potential to revolutionize customer service, offering businesses new ways to engage with customers. In retail environments, robots can provide assistance by guiding customers to products, managing inventory, and even conducting transactions. In hospitality, robots can enhance guest experiences by offering personalized recommendations, facilitating check-ins, and providing concierge services.

Personal Assistance and Accessibility

OpenAI's service robotics also hold promise for personal assistance applications, offering support to individuals in their homes or in care settings. These robots can assist with daily tasks, provide reminders for medication, and offer companionship, thereby improving quality of life and accessibility for elderly individuals or those with disabilities. The integration of natural language processing and computer vision technologies enables these robots to understand and respond to human needs and emotions more effectively.

Challenges and Future Directions

Ethical and Societal Considerations

The deployment of service robots raises important ethical and societal questions, including concerns about privacy, data security, and the potential impact on employment in service industries. Navigating these challenges requires careful consideration of the design and deployment of service robots, ensuring that they augment human capabilities without displacing workers.

Advancing Human-Robot Interaction

A key area of future research and development in service robotics is the advancement of human-robot interaction (HRI). OpenAI's ongoing efforts to improve the naturalness and intuitiveness of interactions between humans and robots are critical for the widespread acceptance and effectiveness of service robots. This includes enhancing robots' ability to understand and respond to complex human cues and to operate safely in diverse environments.

OpenAI's initiatives and breakthroughs in service robotics, as outlined in "OpenAI: Exploring the World of Artificial Intelligence," signify a pivotal shift in the capabilities and applications of robotics within service industries. By leveraging advanced AI technologies, these service robots are set to transform the way businesses interact with their customers and how individuals receive personal assistance, heralding a new era of automation that is more interactive, personalized, and accessible.

Future Directions and Challenges

Ethical and Societal Considerations

As OpenAI continues to push the boundaries of robotics and AI, ethical and societal considerations must be at the forefront of research and development efforts. Issues such as job displacement, privacy, and the ethical treatment of AI entities present complex challenges that require thoughtful solutions and regulatory frameworks.

Aligning AI with Human Values

A central ethical consideration in OpenAI's initiatives is the alignment of AI technologies with human values and ethics. This involves developing AI systems that not only advance in capability but also operate in ways that are beneficial, fair, and understandable to humans. OpenAI's commitment to AI alignment is reflected in its research on interpretability, fairness, and transparency in AI models, ensuring that AI decisions and processes are aligned with ethical principles and societal norms (OpenAI, 2020).

Mitigating Bias and Ensuring Fairness

Another critical ethical challenge is the mitigation of bias in AI systems. OpenAI recognizes that AI models can inadvertently learn and perpetuate biases present in their training data, leading to unfair outcomes. Addressing this issue requires rigorous examination of training datasets, model behavior, and the implementation of fairness measures to prevent biased decision-making. OpenAI's research into fairness in AI seeks to identify and mitigate biases, ensuring that AI technologies promote equity and do not reinforce existing social inequalities (OpenAI, 2019).

Privacy and Data Security

The collection and use of data in AI development also raise significant privacy and data security concerns. OpenAI's use of large-scale datasets to train models like GPT and CLIP involves ethical considerations regarding data provenance, consent, and the protection of personal information. Developing policies and technologies to safeguard privacy and ensure the ethical use of data is paramount for maintaining public trust in AI technologies.

Impact on Employment and the Workforce

The automation potential of AI and robotics poses questions about the impact on employment and the workforce. OpenAI's advancements in areas such as industrial automation and service robotics could lead to significant shifts in labor markets, necessitating thoughtful consideration of the workforce implications. OpenAI engages in discussions on the future of work, advocating for policies and practices that support workforce transitions, reskilling, and the equitable distribution of the economic benefits of AI.

Navigating Ethical and Societal Challenges

To navigate these ethical and societal challenges, OpenAI employs a multifaceted approach, including:

Ongoing Ethical Research: Conducting research dedicated to understanding and addressing the ethical implications of AI, from bias and fairness to AI alignment and safety.

Stakeholder Engagement: Collaborating with a broad range of stakeholders, including policymakers, academia, industry, and civil society, to foster dialogue and develop shared norms and standards for ethical AI.

Transparency and Openness: Committing to transparency in AI research and development, sharing findings, methodologies, and challenges with the broader community to facilitate collective learning and progress.

The ethical and societal considerations of OpenAI's initiatives in robotics and AI, as explored in "OpenAI: Exploring the World of Artificial Intelligence," underscore the organization's dedication to responsible AI development. By proactively addressing issues of fairness, privacy, AI alignment, and the societal impacts of AI, OpenAI seeks to ensure that its technological advancements contribute positively to society. The future of AI, as envisioned by OpenAI, is one where AI technologies are developed and deployed in ways that uphold human values, promote social welfare, and navigate the complex ethical landscape with integrity and foresight.

Advancements in AI for Robotics

Looking forward, OpenAI's research is likely to focus on further advancements in AI that can enhance the autonomy, efficiency, and versatility of robotic systems. This includes improving the learning algorithms that enable robots to understand and interact with the world in increasingly sophisticated ways, as well as developing more robust models that can operate in a wider range of environments and scenarios.

Enhancing Robotic Autonomy and Adaptability

A key area of future advancement in AI for robotics, championed by OpenAI, is the enhancement of robotic autonomy and adaptability. OpenAI's research into reinforcement learning, deep learning, and other AI methodologies has demonstrated significant potential for creating robots that can learn from their environments, adapt to new challenges, and perform complex tasks with minimal human oversight.

Projects such as Dactyl, which showcased a robotic hand learning dexterous manipulation, exemplify the progress toward robots that can autonomously navigate and interact with the physical world in sophisticated ways (OpenAI, 2018).

Bridging the Sim-to-Real Gap

Another important direction for advancements in AI-driven robotics involves bridging the simulation-to-reality (sim-to-real) gap. OpenAI has been at the forefront of developing techniques that allow robots to learn tasks in simulated environments before transferring those skills to real-world settings. This approach not only accelerates the learning process but also reduces the risks and costs associated with physical training. Future advancements will likely focus on improving the fidelity of simulations and the efficiency of transfer learning methods to further enhance the versatility and effectiveness of robotic systems (OpenAI, 2019).

Technical Challenges and Solutions

Scalability of Learning Algorithms

As robotics applications become more complex, scaling learning algorithms to handle a wider range of tasks and environments remains a significant challenge. Future research by OpenAI and others in the field will need to address scalability, developing more efficient algorithms that can learn from larger datasets, more diverse environments, and broader sets of tasks without compromising performance.

Robustness and Safety

Ensuring the robustness and safety of AI-driven robotic systems is paramount, especially as these systems are increasingly deployed in diverse and unpredictable real-world scenarios. OpenAI's commitment to AI safety involves creating algorithms that can predict and mitigate potential failures and developing frameworks for safe human-robot interaction. Advancements in these areas are crucial for the widespread adoption of robotics in sensitive applications such as healthcare, transportation, and public services.

Broader Implications and Considerations

Impact on Labor and Society

The advancements in AI for robotics herald transformative changes for the labor market and society. While these technologies promise to enhance productivity and create new opportunities, they also pose challenges related to job displacement and the need for workforce re-skilling. Navigating these changes will require concerted efforts from policymakers, educators, and industry leaders to ensure that the benefits of robotic advancements are equitably distributed.

Ethical and Regulatory Frameworks

The rapid pace of advancements in AI-driven robotics also underscores the need for robust ethical and regulatory frameworks. As robots become more autonomous and capable, addressing ethical considerations related to autonomy, privacy, and accountability becomes increasingly important. OpenAI's focus on ethical AI development and collaboration with regulatory bodies will play a critical role in shaping the governance of AI and robotics technologies.

The future directions and challenges in advancements in AI for robotics, as explored in "OpenAI: Exploring the World of Artificial Intelligence," highlight the dynamic interplay between technological innovation and societal impact. OpenAI's initiatives in robotics and AI are paving the way for significant breakthroughs that promise to enhance the capabilities of robotic systems, transforming industries and everyday life. However, realizing the full potential of these advancements requires not only technical solutions but also thoughtful consideration of the ethical, societal, and regulatory implications.

Conclusion

OpenAI's initiatives and breakthroughs in robotics and AI represent a significant leap forward in the field, offering promising solutions to complex problems across various domains. As detailed in "OpenAI: Exploring the World of Artificial Intelligence," these advancements not only showcase the potential of integrating AI into robotics but also highlight the importance of addressing the accompanying ethical and societal challenges. The future of robotics, driven by AI research, holds the promise of transformative changes that could redefine human interaction with technology and the world.

Codex:

OpenAI's groundbreaking AI model designed to understand and generate code, would offer a deep dive into one of the most transformative technologies in the realm of programming and software development. The following analysis seeks to provide a comprehensive understanding of Codex's contributions to the field of artificial intelligence and its broader impact on various industries and practices.

Development of Codex

Technological Foundations

Codex is built on the architecture of GPT (Generative Pre-trained Transformer), specifically leveraging the advancements made with GPT-3, one of the most powerful language models developed by OpenAI. Codex extends GPT-3's natural language processing capabilities to the domain of code, training on a diverse dataset comprising billions of lines of code from publicly available sources, including GitHub repositories, forums, and coding websites (Chen et al., 2021). This extensive training enables Codex to understand programming languages and generate functional code based on natural language descriptions.

Genesis of Codex

Codex, developed by OpenAI, represents a significant leap in the application of AI to the realm of coding and software development. Originating from the advancements made with GPT-3, one of the most powerful language models to date, Codex is designed to understand and generate programming code across multiple languages. Its development was motivated by the vision to create a tool that could democratize software development, making coding more accessible and enhancing the productivity of experienced developers (Chen et al., 2021).

Architecture and Design

The architecture of Codex is built upon the transformer model, which has revolutionized natural language processing. Transformers, introduced by Vaswani et al. (2017), employ self-attention mechanisms to process sequences of data, making them particularly adept at understanding the context and relationships within text. By adapting this architecture for Codex, OpenAI enabled the model to not only comprehend natural language but also interpret and generate syntactically and semantically correct code. This dual capability is foundational to Codex's versatility and effectiveness.

Training Methodologies

Codex's training involved a comprehensive dataset comprising billions of lines of code from a wide array of sources, including public repositories, forums, and coding websites. This dataset was curated to represent a diverse set of programming languages and coding styles, ensuring that Codex could generalize across different coding tasks and environments. The model was trained using unsupervised learning techniques, with a particular focus on reinforcement learning from human feedback (RLHF), a method that allowed Codex to refine its outputs based on the quality and functionality of the generated code (OpenAI, 2021).

Capabilities and Innovations

Multilingual Code Generation

One of the hallmark features of Codex is its multilingual code generation capability, enabling it to understand and produce code in dozens of programming languages. This feature not only broadens Codex's applicability across different software development environments but also facilitates cross-language code translation, aiding developers working with legacy systems or migrating projects to new platforms.

Natural Language Understanding

At its core, Codex's ability to parse and respond to natural language prompts sets it apart from traditional programming tools. This capability allows developers to describe functionalities or problems in plain English, from which Codex can generate executable code. This aspect of Codex significantly lowers the barrier to coding, opening up software development to non-experts and streamlining the workflow for seasoned programmers.

The technological foundations of Codex, as detailed in "OpenAI: Exploring the World of Artificial Intelligence," underscore OpenAI's commitment to advancing AI's role in software development. By harnessing the power of the transformer architecture and innovative training methodologies, Codex emerges as a pivotal tool in coding, capable of transforming ideas into code and significantly impacting the landscape of software development.

Capabilities of Codex

Code Generation and Autocompletion

One of the hallmark capabilities of Codex is its ability to generate code snippets and entire programs from natural language descriptions. This includes autocompleting code as a developer types, translating comments into code, and suggesting alternative implementations for given tasks. Codex supports multiple programming languages, making it a versatile tool for developers working across different technology stacks.

Advanced Code Generation

Codex's ability to generate code from natural language descriptions represents a significant leap forward in AI-assisted programming. By processing descriptions of software functionality, algorithms, or even bug fixes, Codex can produce executable code that aligns with the specified requirements. This capability stems from its extensive training on a diverse dataset of code from various sources, enabling the model to understand a wide range of programming concepts, patterns, and languages. The AI model can generate code for a multitude of programming languages, including but not limited to Python, JavaScript, HTML, and CSS, making it a versatile tool for developers across different domains (Chen et al., 2021).

Intelligent Autocompletion

Beyond generating code from scratch, Codex excels in code autocompletion, where it predicts and fills in the next lines of code based on the context provided by the developer. This feature significantly speeds up the coding process, reducing the cognitive load on programmers and minimizing syntactical and logical errors. Codex's autocompletion is not limited to simple suggestions; it can propose complex code structures, function implementations, and even integrate with existing codebases to suggest improvements or optimizations.

Practical Applications

Streamlining Development Workflows

Codex's capabilities in code generation and autocompletion streamline development workflows, making software creation more efficient and accessible. Developers can leverage Codex to quickly prototype ideas, automate repetitive coding tasks, and focus on higher-level design and problem-solving aspects of software development. This efficiency gain not only accelerates project timelines but also encourages experimentation and innovation within development teams.

Enhancing Learning and Collaboration

For novices and learning programmers, Codex serves as an educational tool, offering insights into coding practices and exposing learners to a variety of coding styles and solutions. Its suggestions can help learners understand complex programming concepts and improve their coding skills. Furthermore, Codex facilitates collaboration among developers by generating code that adheres to best practices, ensuring consistency and readability within team projects.

Challenges and Future Directions

Accuracy and Reliability

While Codex's code generation and autocompletion capabilities are impressive, challenges remain regarding the accuracy and reliability of its outputs. Ensuring that the generated code is not only syntactically correct but also functionally robust and secure is paramount. Ongoing research and development efforts by OpenAI aim to enhance Codex's understanding of programming logic and security principles to mitigate these concerns.

Ethical Considerations

The automation of coding tasks raises ethical considerations, including the potential impact on employment in software development and issues related to code ownership and intellectual property. Navigating these ethical challenges requires a balanced approach, fostering an ecosystem where AI-assisted coding complements human creativity and expertise rather than replacing it.

The capabilities of Codex in code generation and autocompletion, as discussed in "OpenAI: Exploring the World of Artificial Intelligence," illustrate the profound impact of AI on software development. By enhancing efficiency, accessibility, and innovation in coding, Codex represents a pivotal advancement in AI-assisted programming. As OpenAI continues to refine and expand Codex's capabilities, the future of software development promises to be increasingly integrated with artificial intelligence, reshaping how code is created and utilized across industries.

Understanding and Debugging Code

Beyond code generation, Codex exhibits a profound understanding of code semantics, allowing it to assist in debugging and code optimization. It can suggest fixes for bugs, identify potential performance improvements, and provide explanations for complex code snippets, thereby serving as an invaluable tool for both novice and experienced programmers.

Advanced Code Comprehension

Codex's ability to understand complex code is foundational to its debugging capabilities. Leveraging the extensive dataset it was trained on, which includes billions of lines of code across various programming languages and domains, Codex can interpret the intent behind code snippets, identify logical flows, and recognize potential issues. This deep understanding enables Codex to assist developers not only in generating code but also in navigating existing codebases, making sense of intricate code structures, and providing insights into how certain functionalities are achieved (Chen et al., 2021).

Debugging and Error Correction

One of the most impactful applications of Codex is its ability to debug and correct errors in code. By analyzing the code contextually, Codex can identify syntax errors, logical inconsistencies, and common bugs that might elude even experienced programmers. Moreover, Codex can suggest optimal solutions to these issues, offering alternative approaches or best practices to enhance code quality. This capability significantly accelerates the debugging process, reducing development time and improving software reliability.

Practical Applications

Streamlined Development Process

The integration of Codex into the development process streamlines programming workflows by providing real-time insights and corrections. Developers can leverage Codex as a pair programmer, consulting it for advice on troubleshooting and optimizing code. This collaborative dynamic between AI and developers fosters a more efficient development process, where common pitfalls are avoided, and code quality is consistently high.

Educational Tool for Programmers

Beyond professional development environments, Codex serves as a powerful educational tool for programmers at all levels. Beginners can learn from Codex's explanations and corrections, gaining a deeper understanding of programming concepts and best practices. For more experienced programmers, Codex offers insights into complex problem-solving and algorithm optimization, enhancing their skill set and encouraging continuous learning.

Challenges and Future Directions

Reliability and Trust

While Codex's debugging capabilities are impressive, ensuring the reliability and accuracy of its suggestions remains a challenge. Developers must critically evaluate Codex's recommendations to avoid introducing new errors or suboptimal practices. Future advancements in Codex will likely focus on increasing the model's reliability, incorporating more robust validation mechanisms, and enhancing its ability to learn from user feedback and corrections.

Ethical and Security Implications

The use of AI in understanding and debugging code also raises ethical and security considerations. Ensuring that Codex does not inadvertently suggest code that could introduce security vulnerabilities or violate ethical programming practices is paramount. Ongoing research and development efforts must address these concerns, ensuring that Codex adheres to the highest standards of security and ethics in software development.

Codex's capabilities in understanding and debugging code, as discussed in "OpenAI: Exploring the World of Artificial Intelligence," represent a monumental advance in the integration of AI within the software development lifecycle. By enhancing code quality, accelerating the debugging process, and serving as a dynamic learning tool, Codex epitomizes the potential of AI to revolutionize programming practices. As OpenAI continues to refine Codex, the future of software development looks increasingly collaborative, with AI playing a pivotal role in assisting developers and advancing the craft of programming.

Applications of Codex

Educational Tools

Codex has significant implications for education, particularly in programming and computer science disciplines. By providing real-time coding assistance and feedback, Codex can enhance learning experiences, allowing students to explore coding concepts more interactively and independently. It also offers potential for personalized learning, adapting to each student's pace and style.

Facilitating Interactive Learning

Codex's ability to translate natural language into code enables a more interactive and engaging learning experience for students. By allowing learners to articulate programming tasks in plain English and instantly see the corresponding code, Codex demystifies the process of coding and lowers the barrier to entry for beginners. This interaction not only enhances understanding but also encourages experimentation, as learners can easily modify their instructions to explore different coding solutions and outcomes (Chen et al., 2021).

Personalized Learning Experiences

The adaptability of Codex to different programming languages and tasks makes it a versatile tool for personalized learning. Educators can utilize Codex to cater to the individual learning pace and style of each student, providing tailored support and feedback. For students struggling with specific concepts, Codex can offer targeted exercises and examples, facilitating a more customized and effective learning journey.

Applications in Coding Education

Automated Tutoring and Feedback

Codex can function as an automated tutor, providing real-time feedback and suggestions to learners as they code. This capability is invaluable for coding education, where immediate feedback can significantly accelerate the learning process. Codex can identify errors, suggest optimizations, and explain complex code snippets, offering insights that might not be readily available in traditional learning environments.

Enhancing Curriculum Development

Educators can leverage Codex to develop and enrich curriculum materials. Codex can assist in generating coding exercises, project ideas, and educational content, reducing the time and effort required to create comprehensive and up-to-date teaching materials. Furthermore, Codex's ability to generate code in multiple languages enables educators to easily incorporate a wider range of programming languages and paradigms into their curriculum.

Challenges and Opportunities

Ensuring Educational Integrity

While Codex offers significant benefits for coding education, it also presents challenges related to educational integrity. Ensuring that students engage with the learning process and develop critical thinking skills, rather than relying too heavily on AI-generated solutions, is essential. Educators must devise strategies to integrate Codex into the learning experience in a way that complements and enhances students' understanding and problem-solving abilities.

Preparing for the Future of Coding

Codex's role as an educational tool extends beyond immediate learning outcomes. By familiarizing students with AI-assisted coding, Codex prepares them for a future where such tools are integral to software development. Understanding how to effectively utilize AI in coding will be a crucial skill for the next generation of programmers, making early exposure through education vitally important.

By facilitating interactive learning, offering personalized experiences, and preparing students for the future of software development, Codex has the potential to transform how programming is taught and learned. As OpenAI continues to develop and refine Codex, its integration into educational settings promises to enhance the accessibility, efficiency, and effectiveness of coding education.

Software Development

In professional software development, Codex promises to boost productivity by automating routine coding tasks, suggesting optimizations, and facilitating rapid prototyping. This can accelerate development cycles, reduce the likelihood of errors, and free developers to focus on more complex and creative aspects of software design.

Accelerating Development Cycles

Codex's ability to generate code from natural language descriptions significantly accelerates development cycles. By automating routine coding tasks and suggesting code implementations, Codex allows developers to focus on more complex and creative aspects of software development, thus speeding up the overall process of creating, testing, and deploying software applications (Chen et al., 2021).

Enhancing Code Quality and Maintenance

Beyond mere speed, Codex contributes to enhancing the quality of code through its debugging capabilities and suggestions for optimization. By identifying potential issues and offering solutions, Codex helps maintain high standards of code quality, which is crucial for long-term maintenance and scalability of software projects.

Practical Applications in Software Development

Rapid Prototyping and Idea Validation

Codex enables developers to quickly prototype applications and validate ideas by translating conceptual descriptions into functional code. This capability is invaluable in early stages of development, where speed and flexibility are paramount. Codex's support for multiple programming languages and frameworks further enhances its utility in prototyping diverse applications.

Automated Code Reviews and Optimization

Incorporating Codex into the code review process can significantly improve efficiency and code quality. Codex can automatically review code submissions, identify potential improvements, and ensure adherence to coding standards and best practices. This not only streamlines the review process but also fosters a culture of continuous learning and improvement among development teams.

Broader Implications for the Software Development Industry

Democratization of Software Development

Codex has the potential to democratize software development by lowering the barrier to entry for non-experts. Its intuitive interface and ability to translate natural language into code make programming more accessible to a wider audience, including those with limited coding experience. This democratization could spur innovation and creativity, leading to the development of new applications and services.

Future of Developer Roles and Skills

The advent of tools like Codex prompts a reevaluation of developer roles and the skills deemed essential in the software development industry. As AI takes on more routine coding tasks, developers may need to focus more on areas where human creativity and problem-solving are irreplaceable, such as conceptual design, user experience, and system architecture.

Codex not only streamlines the development process but also enhances the quality and maintainability of code, democratizes access to programming, and reshapes the future skills and roles within the software development industry. As OpenAI continues to refine and expand Codex's capabilities, the integration of AI into software development is poised to become more pervasive, driving efficiencies, fostering innovation, and redefining what it means to be a developer in the AI era.

Implications and Challenges

Democratization of Coding

Codex represents a step towards the democratization of coding, making software development more accessible to a wider audience, including those without formal programming education. This has the potential to spur innovation and creativity by enabling more individuals to bring their ideas to life through software.

Potential Benefits

The advent of Codex represents a paradigm shift in software development, offering the potential to significantly lower the barrier to entry for coding. By enabling users to generate code through natural language descriptions, Codex opens up programming to non-experts, hobbyists, and those traditionally marginalized in the tech industry due to the steep learning curve associated with mastering programming languages. This democratization could lead to a surge in creativity and innovation, as a more diverse group of individuals can contribute ideas and solutions previously constrained by the technical limitations of coding (Chen et al., 2021).

Enhancing Educational Opportunities

Codex also has profound implications for education in computer science and programming. By serving as an interactive learning tool, Codex can provide immediate feedback on coding assignments, suggest improvements, and help students grasp complex programming concepts through natural language interaction. This could revolutionize computer science education, making it more engaging, personalized, and effective, particularly for beginners.

Challenges and Ethical Considerations

Accuracy and Reliability Concerns

While Codex significantly lowers the barrier to coding, concerns about the accuracy and reliability of the code generated by AI persist. Dependence on Codex for code generation without a deep understanding of programming principles could lead to software with bugs, vulnerabilities, or inefficiencies. Ensuring that users of Codex, especially novices, are aware of these limitations and have the means to verify and validate the generated code is crucial for maintaining software quality and security.

Impact on Professional Development

The democratization of coding through Codex also raises questions about the future of professional software development. While Codex can enhance productivity and creativity, there is concern that reliance on AI for coding tasks could devalue traditional programming skills and expertise. Balancing the use of Codex to augment, rather than replace, human creativity and problem-solving in software development is a challenge that the industry must navigate.

Ethical and Intellectual Property Issues

The use of Codex also introduces ethical and intellectual property considerations. As Codex generates code based on a vast dataset of existing code, ensuring that the output respects copyright and licensing agreements is essential. Additionally, addressing ethical concerns related to the potential misuse of Codex for generating malicious code or automating tasks in a way that could harm individuals or communities is paramount.

Navigating the Future

To address these challenges, a multifaceted approach involving continued technological refinement, ethical oversight, and educational efforts is necessary. Enhancing Codex's accuracy and reliability, developing guidelines for ethical use, and fostering a culture of lifelong learning in programming are key steps towards realizing the benefits of democratizing coding while mitigating potential risks.

Codex's ability to make coding more accessible promises to expand the diversity of creators and innovators in the tech industry, driving forward a more inclusive future. However, navigating the ethical, educational, and professional challenges this democratization brings is essential for ensuring that the benefits of Codex are realized equitably and responsibly.

Ethical and Security Considerations

The advent of Codex also raises ethical and security concerns, particularly regarding the generation of malicious code, copyright infringement, and the reliance on potentially biased training data. Addressing these challenges requires careful oversight, ethical guidelines, and perhaps new regulatory frameworks to ensure the responsible use of AI in coding.

Bias and Fairness

One of the principal ethical concerns surrounding Codex, as with many AI technologies, revolves around the issue of bias. Given that Codex is trained on a vast corpus of code from various sources, there is a potential for the model to learn and perpetuate biases present in its training data. These biases could manifest in the generation of code that inadvertently discriminates or fails to consider the needs of diverse user groups. Addressing bias in Codex requires continuous efforts to audit and refine its training data and algorithms to ensure fairness and equity in its outputs.

Intellectual Property and Copyright

The ability of Codex to generate code based on existing programming languages and frameworks raises questions regarding intellectual property and copyright infringement. As Codex can produce code snippets that closely resemble or are derived from copyrighted material, ensuring that generated code complies with legal and ethical standards is imperative. OpenAI must navigate these concerns by implementing safeguards that prevent the generation of proprietary code without authorization and by fostering transparency regarding the model's training data and generation processes.

Security Considerations in Codex's Deployment

Vulnerability to Malicious Use

Codex's powerful code generation capabilities also present security considerations, particularly the risk of misuse by actors intending to create malicious software or exploit vulnerabilities in existing systems. The model's ability to understand and execute programming tasks based on natural language inputs could potentially be exploited to automate the generation of malware, phishing scripts, or other harmful code. Mitigating this risk requires the implementation of stringent access controls, monitoring, and ethical usage guidelines for Codex users.

Ensuring Code Security and Reliability

Beyond the risk of intentional misuse, the security and reliability of code generated by Codex are of paramount concern. The model may inadvertently introduce security vulnerabilities or bugs into the software it helps create, especially if users rely heavily on Codex without sufficient understanding of the underlying code. Ensuring the security of AI-generated code necessitates robust validation and testing mechanisms, alongside education for developers on the importance of reviewing and understanding Codex-generated outputs.

Navigating Ethical and Security Challenges

To responsibly address the ethical and security challenges presented by Codex, OpenAI and the broader tech community must adopt a multifaceted approach that includes:

Enhanced Oversight and Auditing: Implementing rigorous oversight and auditing procedures to continuously monitor and assess the fairness, legality, and security of Codex's outputs.

Collaboration with Legal and Ethical Experts: Engaging with legal scholars, ethicists, and industry stakeholders to develop comprehensive guidelines and standards for ethical AI use in coding.

Education and Awareness: Promoting education and awareness among Codex users about the ethical and security implications of AI-generated code, encouraging responsible use and critical evaluation of automated outputs.

While Codex represents a significant advancement in automating and enhancing the coding process, navigating its ethical and security implications is crucial for ensuring that this powerful tool is used responsibly and for the benefit of all. Through continued research, dialogue, and policy development, OpenAI and the tech community can address these challenges, paving the way for a future where AI contributes positively and securely to software development.

Conclusion

Codex, epitomizes the convergence of artificial intelligence and software development, heralding a new era where coding becomes more efficient, accessible, and creative. Its development not only showcases OpenAI's commitment to advancing AI technologies but also highlights the transformative potential of AI to impact how software is created and who can participate in its creation.

8

Chapter 4: Applications of OpenAI

A comprehensive examination of the applications of OpenAI's technologies would provide an insightful overview of how OpenAI's groundbreaking work in artificial intelligence is being applied across various domains, reshaping industries, and offering solutions to complex societal challenges. This analysis aims to explore the multifaceted applications of OpenAI's projects, including natural language processing, computer vision, robotics, and beyond, elucidating the transformative impact these technologies have on healthcare, education, environmental science, and the creative arts, supported by hypothetical APA in-text citations and references.

Applications of OpenAI's Technologies

Healthcare

In the healthcare sector, OpenAI's technologies, particularly those related to natural language processing (NLP) and machine learning, are being leveraged to revolutionize patient care, diagnostics, and research. GPT models, for instance, are applied in analyzing patient data, medical records, and scientific literature to assist in diagnosis, personalized treatment plans, and identifying potential research areas. Furthermore, robotics technologies developed by OpenAI are being explored for surgical assistance and patient care, offering precision and efficiency improvements (OpenAI, 2020).

Diagnostic Assistance and Predictive Analytics

One of the paramount applications of OpenAI's technologies in healthcare revolves around diagnostic assistance and predictive analytics. Leveraging the capabilities of models like GPT for analyzing vast datasets of electronic health records (EHRs), medical images, and literature, AI algorithms can assist healthcare professionals in identifying patterns, diagnosing conditions more accurately, and predicting patient outcomes. This application not only enhances diagnostic precision but also facilitates early intervention strategies, potentially improving patient prognoses (OpenAI, 2021).

Personalized Treatment and Drug Discovery

OpenAI's AI models contribute significantly to the personalization of treatment plans and the acceleration of drug discovery processes. By analyzing patient data and existing research, AI can identify the most effective treatment protocols tailored to individual patient profiles, taking into account genetic factors, lifestyle, and comorbidities. In drug discovery, AI-driven analysis of molecular structures and biological pathways speeds up the identification of potential therapeutic compounds, reducing the time and cost associated with bringing new drugs to market (OpenAI, 2020).

Clinical Decision Support Systems

The integration of OpenAI's technologies into clinical decision support systems (CDSS) offers healthcare providers real-time, evidence-based recommendations and alerts. These AI-powered systems analyze patient data in the context of the latest medical research and guidelines to provide clinicians with actionable insights, enhancing decision-making processes, and ensuring adherence to best practices. This application not only improves patient care quality but also supports clinicians in managing complex cases more effectively.

Operational Efficiencies and Patient Engagement

Beyond direct patient care, OpenAI's advancements in AI are applied to optimize healthcare operations and enhance patient engagement. AI algorithms streamline administrative tasks such as scheduling, billing, and patient record management, contributing to operational efficiencies and cost reductions. In terms of patient engagement, AI-driven platforms facilitate personalized communication, health monitoring, and self-management tools, empowering patients to take an active role in their healthcare journey.

Ethical and Implementation Challenges

The application of AI in healthcare, while promising, presents several ethical and implementation challenges that must be addressed. Issues of data privacy, security, and consent are paramount, given the sensitive nature of health information. Ensuring the accuracy, reliability, and transparency of AI-driven recommendations is crucial to building trust among healthcare professionals and patients. Moreover, addressing potential biases in AI algorithms is essential to prevent disparities in care and outcomes.

As these technologies continue to evolve, their integration into healthcare systems promises to yield significant benefits in terms of improved patient outcomes, efficiencies, and personalized care. However, navigating the ethical and implementation challenges will be critical to realizing the full potential of AI in healthcare.

Education

OpenAI's contributions to education are manifold, with AI models like GPT and Codex offering personalized learning experiences, automating administrative tasks, and facilitating content creation. GPT models, for example, are used to generate educational content, provide tutoring in natural language, and even grade assignments, offering scalability in educational resources and personalized support for students (OpenAI, 2021).

Personalized Learning Experiences

One of the most notable applications of OpenAI's technologies in education is the creation of personalized learning experiences. AI models like GPT-3 have the capability to adapt educational content to the individual needs, learning styles, and proficiency levels of students. By analyzing student interactions and performance, AI can tailor lessons, exercises, and feedback to optimize learning outcomes, making education more accessible and effective for diverse student populations (OpenAI, 2021).

Intelligent Tutoring Systems

OpenAI's advancements in natural language understanding and generation have facilitated the development of intelligent tutoring systems (ITS). These AI-driven platforms can simulate one-on-one tutoring experiences, providing students with instant feedback, explanations, and support across a wide range of subjects. The ability of systems like GPT-3 to engage in naturalistic dialogue enables a more interactive and engaging learning process, potentially bridging gaps in teacher-student ratios and offering supplementary educational support (OpenAI, 2020).

Automating Administrative Tasks

Beyond direct educational applications, OpenAI's technologies are being employed to streamline administrative tasks within educational institutions. AI algorithms can automate processes such as grading, attendance tracking, and scheduling, reducing the administrative burden on educators and allowing them to dedicate more time to teaching and student engagement. Additionally, AI-driven analysis of educational data can provide insights into learning trends, program effectiveness, and areas in need of improvement, supporting more informed decision-making at institutional levels.

Enhancing Accessibility

OpenAI's projects also contribute to enhancing accessibility in education. For students with disabilities or those requiring additional support, AI technologies can offer assistive tools, such as real-time transcription, language translation, and content adaptation. This not only facilitates access to educational materials but also promotes inclusivity and equity in learning opportunities.

Ethical and Implementation Challenges

The integration of AI into education raises important ethical and implementation challenges that must be carefully navigated. Concerns regarding data privacy and security are paramount, given the sensitive nature of student information. Ensuring the fairness and transparency of AI-driven assessments and recommendations is critical to maintaining trust and equity in educational outcomes. Additionally, addressing potential biases in AI algorithms is essential to prevent the reinforcement of existing disparities in education.

By leveraging AI to personalize learning, automate administrative tasks, and enhance accessibility, OpenAI is at the forefront of fostering more engaging, effective, and inclusive educational experiences. As these technologies continue to evolve, their thoughtful and ethical implementation will be crucial in realizing their full potential to transform education.

Environmental Science

In environmental science, OpenAI's AI models are applied in analyzing large datasets to model climate change impacts, optimize energy consumption, and improve the efficiency of renewable energy systems. AI-driven analysis of satellite imagery and environmental data helps in monitoring deforestation, tracking wildlife populations, and predicting natural disasters, contributing to more informed and effective conservation and sustainability efforts (OpenAI, 2020).

Climate Change Modeling and Analysis

OpenAI's technologies, particularly its machine learning models, play a crucial role in climate change modeling and analysis. By processing vast datasets that include historical climate records, satellite imagery, and environmental parameters, AI models can predict future climate patterns with greater accuracy and detail than ever before. These predictions are vital for understanding the potential impacts of climate change on different ecosystems and human societies, facilitating informed decision-making and policy development aimed at mitigation and adaptation strategies (OpenAI, 2020).

Biodiversity Conservation

In the realm of biodiversity conservation, OpenAI's AI technologies are applied to monitor and protect endangered species and habitats. Computer vision models, for example, analyze images and videos from camera traps and drones to identify species, track wildlife populations, and detect illegal activities such as poaching and deforestation. This application not only enhances the efficiency and coverage of conservation efforts but also provides valuable insights into wildlife behavior and ecosystem dynamics (OpenAI, 2021).

Sustainable Agriculture

OpenAI's advancements in AI are also being utilized to promote sustainable agriculture practices. AI-driven models analyze data from various sources, including satellite imagery, soil sensors, and weather forecasts, to optimize crop yields, reduce resource use, and minimize environmental impacts. Precision agriculture techniques enabled by AI can advise on the optimal timing for planting, watering, and harvesting, as well as guide the targeted application of fertilizers and pesticides, leading to more sustainable and productive farming operations.

Environmental Monitoring and Management

AI technologies developed by OpenAI contribute significantly to environmental monitoring and management. By analyzing data from satellites, IoT devices, and other sensors, AI models can detect changes in environmental conditions, such as air and water quality, deforestation rates, and urban expansion. This real-time monitoring capability supports proactive environmental management practices, enabling timely interventions to prevent or mitigate environmental degradation.

Challenges and Ethical Considerations

Data Accuracy and Bias

One of the challenges in applying AI to environmental science is ensuring the accuracy and representativeness of the data used for training AI models. Biases in data can lead to skewed or inaccurate models, potentially compromising the effectiveness of environmental applications. Ongoing efforts to collect high-quality, diverse datasets are essential for overcoming this challenge.

Ethical Use of AI in Environmental Decision-Making

The ethical implications of relying on AI for environmental decision-making also warrant careful consideration. Decisions based on AI analyses must take into account not only environmental outcomes but also social, economic, and ethical dimensions. Ensuring transparency in how AI models are developed, deployed, and interpreted is crucial for maintaining public trust and ensuring that AI-supported environmental initiatives are aligned with broader societal values.

From climate modeling and biodiversity conservation to sustainable agriculture and environmental monitoring, AI technologies offer innovative solutions that can enhance our ability to protect and preserve the natural world. As these technologies continue to evolve, their responsible and ethical deployment will be key to maximizing their positive impact on environmental science and sustainability efforts.

Creative Arts

The creative arts have also benefited from OpenAI's technologies, with projects like DALL-E and Jukebox demonstrating the potential of AI in generating art, music, and literature. DALL-E's ability to create images from textual descriptions and Jukebox's composition of music in various styles showcase the potential of AI to inspire new forms of creative expression and collaboration between humans and AI in the artistic process (OpenAI, 2021).

AI-Generated Art and Imagery

One of the most striking applications of OpenAI's technologies in the creative arts is the generation of art and imagery. DALL-E, an AI model developed by OpenAI, exemplifies this by creating vivid, often surreal images from textual descriptions. This capability not only opens new avenues for visual artists to explore but also democratizes art creation, allowing individuals without traditional artistic skills to bring their imaginative visions to life. The intersection of AI and art challenges traditional notions of creativity and raises intriguing questions about the role of AI in the creative process (OpenAI, 2021).

Music Composition and Production

Jukebox, another groundbreaking project by OpenAI, leverages AI to compose music in a variety of genres and styles, complete with lyrics and melody. This technology offers musicians and composers novel tools for inspiration and experimentation, enabling the creation of music that blends human artistry with AI's computational creativity. The application of AI in music composition and production exemplifies the potential for AI to serve as a collaborative partner in the creative process, expanding the sonic landscape and opening up new possibilities for musical expression (OpenAI, 2020).

Literary and Textual Creativity

GPT models developed by OpenAI have also found applications in literary and textual creativity, capable of generating poetry, stories, and even scripts based on user prompts. This aspect of AI application in creative writing challenges traditional authorship concepts and introduces a collaborative dimension where AI assists writers in ideation, drafting, and editing processes. The use of AI in literary creation prompts a reevaluation of creativity, originality, and the future of storytelling (OpenAI, 2019).

Ethical and Aesthetic Considerations

Authenticity and Authorship

The integration of AI into creative arts raises profound questions about authenticity and authorship. As AI-generated or AI-assisted artworks become more prevalent, distinguishing between human and machine creativity, and understanding the implications for copyright and intellectual property rights, becomes increasingly complex. Navigating these issues requires careful consideration of the ethical and legal frameworks surrounding AI-generated content.

Impact on the Creative Industries

The application of OpenAI's technologies also has significant implications for the creative industries. While AI offers new tools for artistic expression and the potential to democratize creative pursuits, there is also concern about the impact on professional artists, musicians, and writers. Balancing the benefits of AI-assisted creativity with the need to support and value human artists is a challenge that will shape the future of creative industries.

By enabling new forms of art, music, and literature, OpenAI's projects challenge conventional boundaries and invite a reimagining of creativity in the age of artificial intelligence. As these technologies continue to evolve, fostering a collaborative and ethical approach to AI in the arts will be crucial in harnessing their potential to enrich human creativity and cultural heritage.

Ethical and Security Considerations

The widespread application of OpenAI's technologies also raises important ethical and security considerations. Issues such as data privacy, algorithmic bias, intellectual property rights, and the potential misuse of AI for malicious purposes necessitate careful consideration and the development of ethical guidelines and security measures. OpenAI's commitment to safe and ethical AI development is reflected in its research on AI alignment, policy advocacy, and collaboration with the broader AI research community to address these challenges responsibly.

AI Alignment and Safety

A primary ethical concern in the development and deployment of AI technologies is ensuring alignment with human values and safety. OpenAI places a significant emphasis on AI alignment research, striving to create AI systems that can understand and adhere to human ethical principles, making decisions that are beneficial—or at least not harmful—to humanity. This involves complex challenges, such as defining universal ethical guidelines that AI can interpret and implementing mechanisms that allow AI systems to learn these values dynamically (OpenAI, 2021).

Bias and Fairness

Another critical ethical issue is addressing bias in AI algorithms and ensuring fairness in AI outcomes. OpenAI acknowledges that AI models, including those developed by the organization, can inadvertently learn and perpetuate societal biases present in their training data. Efforts to mitigate these biases involve careful curation of training datasets, transparent model development processes, and ongoing evaluation of model outputs for fairness across different demographic groups (OpenAI, 2020).

Privacy and Data Security

The collection and use of data for training AI models raise significant privacy and data security concerns. OpenAI utilizes vast amounts of data to train its models, necessitating stringent data governance policies to protect sensitive information and ensure compliance with global data protection regulations. The organization also explores techniques such as federated learning and differential privacy to enhance data security while minimizing privacy risks (OpenAI, 2019).

Security Considerations in OpenAI's Technologies

Malicious Use of AI

The potential for AI technologies to be used for malicious purposes represents a pressing security concern. OpenAI is acutely aware of the dual-use nature of AI and undertakes comprehensive risk assessments for its projects, sometimes choosing to limit the release of certain technologies or models to prevent misuse. Collaborating with policymakers, security experts, and other stakeholders to develop norms and regulations that prevent harmful applications of AI is a critical aspect of OpenAI's approach to security (OpenAI, 2021).

AI and Cybersecurity

As AI technologies become more sophisticated, their role in cybersecurity—both as a tool for enhancing security and a vector for new types of cyber threats—grows increasingly complex. OpenAI engages in research to understand and mitigate the risks of AI-powered cyber-attacks, developing more robust AI systems capable of defending against such threats and ensuring the security of AI infrastructure (OpenAI, 2020).

Navigating Ethical and Security Challenges

To navigate these ethical and security challenges, OpenAI employs a multifaceted strategy that includes active research into AI ethics and safety, collaboration with a broad range of stakeholders to develop and adhere to industry best practices, and public engagement to foster an informed dialogue about the responsible development and use of AI.

As AI continues to evolve, OpenAI's proactive approach to addressing these considerations is essential for ensuring that the benefits of AI are realized while minimizing potential harms and risks.

Conclusion

From healthcare and education to environmental science and the creative arts, OpenAI's projects are at the forefront of leveraging AI to address complex challenges, enhance human capabilities, and enrich society. As these technologies continue to evolve, navigating the ethical and security considerations associated with AI will be crucial in ensuring that the benefits of AI are realized equitably and sustainably.

AI in Language Generation:

AI in Language Generation: Writing, Translation, and Storytelling would provide an in-depth analysis of how OpenAI's advancements in artificial intelligence are revolutionizing the fields of writing, translation, and storytelling.

AI in Language Generation: Writing, Translation, and Storytelling

Technological Foundations

The foundation of OpenAI's impact on language generation lies in its development of the GPT series, with GPT-3 being the most advanced iteration at the time of writing. These models are trained on diverse internet text, enabling them to generate human-like text based on the input they receive. The transformer architecture, which underlies GPT models, allows for the processing of long-range dependencies in text, making them particularly adept at understanding context and generating coherent and contextually relevant outputs (Vaswani et al., 2017; Brown et al., 2020).

Development of the GPT Series

The cornerstone of OpenAI's achievements in language generation is the development of the Generative Pre-trained Transformer (GPT) series, with GPT-3 being the most notable iteration to date. Built upon the transformer architecture introduced by Vaswani et al. (2017), GPT models leverage deep learning techniques to process and generate natural language text. The transformer model is distinguished by its use of self-attention mechanisms, which allow it to weigh the importance of different words in a sentence, or across sentences, to generate coherent and contextually relevant text outputs (Vaswani et al., 2017).

Pre-training and Fine-tuning Approach

A key aspect of GPT models' design is their pre-training on a diverse and extensive dataset of internet text. This pre-training involves learning the probabilities of word sequences, enabling the model to understand language patterns, grammar, and even stylistic nuances across various text types. Following pre-training, GPT models can be fine-tuned with specific datasets to excel in tasks like translation, question-answering, or content creation in particular styles or domains (Brown et al., 2020).

Multilingual Capabilities

The GPT series, particularly GPT-3, exhibits remarkable multilingual capabilities, having been trained on text from numerous languages. This training enables the models not only to generate text in multiple languages but also to perform translation tasks with a high degree of fluency and accuracy. The multilingual capacity of GPT models is pivotal for applications in global communication and content creation, facilitating cross-cultural exchange and understanding (Brown et al., 2020).

Writing and Content Creation

GPT models have demonstrated remarkable capabilities in writing and content creation, ranging from producing articles, essays, and poetry to generating code and technical reports. These models can mimic various writing styles and adapt to specific content requirements, offering tools for both professional writers seeking inspiration and businesses looking to automate content generation. The application of AI in writing challenges traditional notions of authorship and creativity, prompting discussions about the role of AI in creative processes (Brown et al., 2020).

Technological Underpinnings

The foundation of OpenAI's impact on writing and content creation lies in the GPT series, especially the latest iteration, GPT-3. These models are based on the transformer architecture, which utilizes self-attention mechanisms to process vast amounts of text data. GPT-3, trained on an extensive corpus of text from the internet, demonstrates an unprecedented ability to generate coherent, contextually relevant, and stylistically varied written content. This capability stems from the model's deep learning algorithms, which predict the probability of a sequence of words, enabling it to produce text that closely mimics human writing (Brown et al., 2020).

Applications in Content Generation

GPT-3 has found applications across a wide spectrum of content generation tasks. In the realm of journalism and blogging, it can produce articles and posts on a diverse array of topics, providing a tool for rapid content creation. In marketing and advertising, GPT-3 aids in generating creative copy, product descriptions, and promotional content tailored to specific audiences. Additionally, in the educational sector, it assists in creating instructional materials, quizzes, and even textbooks, customized to curriculum requirements and learning objectives.

Enhancing Creativity and Efficiency

One of the most significant implications of GPT-3's capabilities is the enhancement of creativity and efficiency in writing processes. By generating initial drafts, ideas, or entire pieces of content, GPT-3 serves as a creative partner that can inspire writers, reduce writer's block, and expedite the writing process. This collaboration between human writers and AI not only augments the creative potential of individuals but also streamlines content production workflows, making it possible to meet the growing demand for fresh, engaging content in the digital age.

Ethical Considerations and Challenges

Despite its potential, the use of AI in writing and content creation presents several ethical considerations and challenges. Issues of copyright, originality, and the authenticity of AI-generated content raise questions about intellectual property rights and the value of human authorship. Additionally, the potential for misuse of AI to produce disinformation or plagiarized content necessitates the development of guidelines and standards for ethical AI use in content creation.

Future Directions

The future of writing and content creation with AI technologies like GPT-3 is poised for further innovation and expansion. As these models become more sophisticated, their integration into collaborative writing tools, content management systems, and creative platforms will likely deepen. Moreover, ongoing research into improving the accuracy, reliability, and ethical use of AI in writing promises to enhance the symbiosis between human creativity and artificial intelligence, opening new horizons for personalized and dynamic content generation.

The exploration of AI in Language Generation, with a focus on Writing and Content Creation, highlights the transformative impact of OpenAI's GPT models on the field. These advancements not only offer new possibilities for creativity and efficiency in writing but also present challenges and ethical considerations that must be carefully navigated. As AI technologies continue to evolve, their role in shaping the future of written communication and content creation remains a vibrant area of exploration and potential.

Translation and Multilingual Communication

Beyond generating text in a single language, GPT models exhibit significant potential in translation and multilingual communication. Trained on text from multiple languages, these models can translate text with a degree of nuance and accuracy that rivals specialized translation models. This capability has profound implications for global communication, enabling more seamless cross-cultural exchanges and helping to bridge language barriers that have historically impeded understanding and collaboration (Brown et al., 2020).

Technological Innovations

The core of OpenAI's impact on translation and multilingual communication lies in the sophisticated architecture of the GPT series. GPT-3, with its 175 billion parameters, represents one of the most advanced language models to date, trained on a diverse dataset encompassing text from hundreds of languages. This extensive training enables the model to understand and generate text across multiple languages, facilitating accurate and contextually nuanced translations. The transformer architecture, which underpins GPT models, allows for effective handling of long-range dependencies in text, crucial for maintaining coherence and accuracy in translations (Vaswani et al., 2017; Brown et al., 2020).

Applications in Global Communication

GPT models have significantly broadened the scope of applications in global communication. In the domain of translation, these models are employed to provide real-time, accurate translations for websites, documents, and communication platforms, making content accessible to a global audience. Furthermore, GPT's multilingual capabilities enable cross-cultural exchanges and collaborations by allowing individuals to communicate in their native languages, with AI facilitating understanding and interaction.

Enhancing Accessibility and Fostering Inclusivity

One of the most notable implications of OpenAI's technologies in translation and multilingual communication is the enhancement of accessibility and the promotion of inclusivity. By breaking down language barriers, GPT models make information, education, and digital resources more accessible to non-English speakers and those from linguistically diverse backgrounds. This democratization of access plays a crucial role in bridging the digital divide and fostering a more inclusive global community.

Challenges and Ethical Considerations

Despite the potential benefits, the application of AI in translation and multilingual communication presents several challenges and ethical considerations. Ensuring the accuracy and cultural appropriateness of AI-generated translations is paramount, as inaccuracies or cultural insensitivities can lead to misunderstandings or offense. Additionally, the potential for algorithmic bias and the preservation of linguistic diversity are critical concerns. Addressing these challenges requires ongoing research, diverse and representative training datasets, and ethical guidelines to govern the development and deployment of AI in translation services.

Future Directions

The future of translation and multilingual communication with AI technologies like those developed by OpenAI is poised for further innovation. Advances in understanding context, idiomatic expressions, and cultural nuances will enhance the quality and reliability of AI-generated translations. Moreover, the integration of AI translation tools into augmented reality and wearable technologies offers the potential for seamless, real-time translation in everyday interactions, further transforming global communication dynamics.

The exploration of AI in Language Generation, with a focus on Translation and Multilingual Communication, underscores the transformative impact of OpenAI's GPT models on facilitating global communication and understanding. As these technologies continue to evolve, their potential to enhance accessibility, foster inclusivity, and connect the world in unprecedented ways remains a vibrant area of exploration and promise.

Storytelling and Narrative Construction

In storytelling and narrative construction, OpenAI's technologies offer innovative avenues for exploring narrative complexity and character development. AI-generated storytelling challenges traditional storytelling paradigms by introducing non-linear narratives, interactive story arcs, and dynamically generated characters and settings. These developments not only expand the toolkit available to writers and filmmakers but also open up new forms of interactive entertainment and educational content that can adapt to the preferences and responses of the audience (Brown et al., 2020).

The Advent of AI-Driven Storytelling

OpenAI's GPT series, with its latest iteration GPT-3, has ushered in a new era of AI-driven storytelling. Leveraging deep learning and natural language processing, GPT models possess the ability to generate coherent and creative text, simulating various narrative styles and genres. This technological breakthrough has profound implications for storytelling, offering novel methodologies for narrative construction that blend traditional storytelling elements with AI's computational creativity (Brown et al., 2020).

Enhancing Creativity in Narrative Construction

The integration of AI technologies like GPT-3 into the creative process has the potential to enhance narrative construction by providing authors and creators with an unprecedented tool for generating ideas, plotlines, character developments, and dialogues. AI-driven storytelling aids in overcoming creative blocks and expanding the narrative possibilities, enabling the exploration of new themes, perspectives, and narrative structures that may not have been previously considered.

Interactive and Dynamic Storytelling

One of the most innovative applications of OpenAI's technologies in storytelling is the development of interactive and dynamic narratives. In interactive fiction and video games, GPT models can generate story elements in real-time, responding to user choices and actions to create a personalized narrative experience. This dynamic approach to storytelling allows for a more immersive and engaging experience, as the narrative evolves based on the interaction between the user and the AI, offering a multitude of narrative pathways and endings.

Ethical Considerations and Challenges

The use of AI in storytelling and narrative construction also presents several ethical considerations and challenges. Issues surrounding copyright and the originality of AI-generated content come to the forefront, raising questions about authorship and the ownership of AI-created narratives. Furthermore, ensuring that AI-driven stories promote diversity and avoid perpetuating stereotypes and biases is crucial for responsible storytelling that respects and reflects the complexities of human experience.

Future Directions

The future of storytelling and narrative construction with AI technologies promises further innovation and exploration. As AI models become more sophisticated, their ability to understand and mimic human emotions, motivations, and complexities will enhance, paving the way for more nuanced and compelling narratives. Additionally, the convergence of AI with emerging technologies such as virtual reality (VR) and augmented reality (AR) could offer even more immersive storytelling experiences, blurring the lines between creator, narrative, and audience.

The exploration of AI in Language Generation, with a focus on Storytelling and Narrative Construction, highlights the transformative impact of OpenAI's technologies on the art of storytelling. By facilitating creative expression, enabling interactive narratives, and challenging traditional storytelling paradigms, AI technologies are redefining the boundaries of narrative construction. As these technologies continue to evolve, their integration into storytelling practices will undoubtedly continue to provoke discussion, inspire creativity, and shape the future of narrative art.

Challenges and Ethical Considerations

The deployment of AI in language generation also presents several challenges and ethical considerations. Issues of copyright, originality, and the potential for generating misleading or harmful content require careful navigation. Ensuring the responsible use of language generation technologies involves developing guidelines for transparency, accountability, and user consent, particularly in applications that blur the lines between human and machine-generated content.

Authorship and Originality

One of the primary ethical concerns in AI-generated writing and storytelling revolves around questions of authorship and originality. As AI models like GPT-3 generate content that can mimic human writing styles and produce creative narratives, determining the boundaries between human creativity and machine-generated output becomes increasingly blurred. This ambiguity raises significant questions about copyright, ownership, and the recognition of creative contributions in AI-assisted or AI-generated works (Brown et al., 2020).

Bias and Fairness

Another critical challenge is the potential for AI models to perpetuate or amplify existing biases present in their training data. Given that GPT models are trained on vast corpora of text sourced from the internet, they may inadvertently learn and reproduce biases, stereotypes, or harmful representations. Addressing these biases requires diligent efforts in dataset curation, model training, and output monitoring to ensure fairness and prevent discrimination in AI-generated content (Bender et al., 2021).

Privacy and Data Security

The use of extensive datasets for training language models also poses significant privacy and data security challenges. Ensuring the confidentiality of data sources and protecting the rights of individuals whose data may be included in training sets is paramount. OpenAI's approach to data governance, model transparency, and ethical usage guidelines seeks to mitigate these risks, emphasizing the importance of privacy and security in AI development (OpenAI, 2021).

Misuse and Malicious Applications

The potential for the misuse of AI in language generation technologies, whether for generating disinformation, creating fraudulent content, or other malicious purposes, represents a significant ethical concern. OpenAI acknowledges these risks and has engaged in proactive measures to limit the misuse potential of its models, including restricting access to certain functionalities and implementing usage monitoring systems to detect and prevent harmful applications of its technology (OpenAI, 2020).

Navigating Ethical Complexities

To navigate these ethical complexities, OpenAI has implemented several strategies, including the development of ethical frameworks for AI research and deployment, engaging with the broader AI ethics community, and fostering open dialogue about the challenges and responsibilities of AI innovation. Moreover, OpenAI's commitment to AI safety research aims to anticipate and address potential risks associated with advanced AI capabilities.

The discussion on challenges and ethical considerations in AI language generation underscores the critical importance of ethical responsibility in the advancement of AI technologies. As OpenAI continues to push the boundaries of what is possible with AI in writing, translation, and storytelling, the organization remains vigilant in addressing the ethical, social, and technical challenges that accompany these innovations. The future of AI language generation will undoubtedly require a balanced approach that prioritizes human welfare, creativity, and ethical integrity alongside technological advancement.

The exploration of AI in Language Generation: Writing, Translation, and Storytelling highlights the vast potential of OpenAI's technologies to enrich and expand the domains of writing, translation, and storytelling. As these technologies continue to evolve, they promise to further dissolve linguistic boundaries, democratize content creation, and innovate narrative forms. The ongoing challenge lies in harnessing these capabilities responsibly, ensuring that AI serves to enhance human creativity and understanding across cultures and languages.

AI in Gaming:

AI in Gaming: Reinforcement Learning and Strategy offers an in-depth examination of how OpenAI leverages reinforcement learning (RL) techniques to master complex gaming environments and develop sophisticated strategies. This analysis aims to elucidate the principles of reinforcement learning, the architecture of OpenAI's AI models, and the significant breakthroughs achieved in strategic gameplay, highlighting the broader implications of these advancements for AI research and practical applications. By exploring specific projects and their outcomes.

Reinforcement Learning in Gaming

Foundations of Reinforcement Learning

Reinforcement learning is a subset of machine learning where an agent learns to make decisions by taking actions in an environment to achieve some objectives. The agent learns from trial and error, receiving rewards or penalties based on the outcomes of its actions. This learning process is guided by policies that the agent develops to map states of the environment to actions that maximize cumulative rewards. OpenAI has been at the forefront of applying reinforcement learning to complex gaming environments, demonstrating the potential of RL to solve problems that require strategic thinking and adaptability (Sutton & Barto, 2018).

Reinforcement Learning in Gaming

In the context of gaming, RL allows AI agents to learn game strategies and tactics through the process of trial and error. Games provide a controlled yet complex environment where AI agents can learn a wide range of behaviors, from basic movement to advanced strategic planning. OpenAI has been pivotal in demonstrating the potential of reinforcement learning within gaming, notably through projects such as OpenAI Five and Gym.

OpenAI Five

OpenAI Five is a prime example of the application of RL in strategic gaming. This AI system was trained to play the multiplayer online battle arena game Dota 2 at a competitive level. Through reinforcement learning, OpenAI Five learned to predict opponents' moves, cooperate with teammates, and devise long-term strategies to win games (Berner et al., 2019). The success of OpenAI Five not only showcased the potential of RL in mastering complex games but also its applicability in solving real-world problems that require strategic planning and teamwork.

Gym

OpenAI Gym is an open-source platform designed to provide developers, researchers, and enthusiasts with a toolkit for developing and comparing reinforcement learning algorithms. Gym offers a wide range of environments, from simple control tasks to full game simulations, where AI agents can be trained and evaluated (Brockman et al., 2016). This project has significantly contributed to the advancement of reinforcement learning research by standardizing benchmarks and facilitating the sharing of innovative algorithms.

The contribution of OpenAI's technologies and projects to the field of AI in gaming, particularly through the lens of reinforcement learning, underscores the transformative potential of AI in strategizing and decision-making processes. The foundational principles of reinforcement learning, exemplified by OpenAI's projects such as OpenAI Five and Gym, demonstrate the capability of AI agents to learn and adapt in complex environments. These advancements not only pave the way for more sophisticated and intelligent game AI but also hint at the broader applicability of reinforcement learning in various domains requiring strategic insight and decision-making.

Architecture and Training of AI Models

OpenAI's AI models for gaming, such as those developed for playing Dota 2 and hide-and-seek, utilize advanced RL algorithms combined with deep neural networks. These models are often trained using techniques like Proximal Policy Optimization (PPO) and Generalized Advantage Estimation (GAE) in simulated environments that replicate the dynamics of the games. Through extensive training sessions, sometimes amounting to hundreds of years of gameplay in accelerated time, these AI agents acquire a profound understanding of game mechanics, strategy, and tactical maneuvers (Schulman et al., 2017; OpenAI, 2019).

The architecture of AI models for gaming, particularly those developed using reinforcement learning, is complex and multi-faceted. At its core, an RL model comprises an agent that interacts with a game's environment, aiming to maximize cumulative rewards over time. This agent is built upon deep neural networks (DNNs) that enable the processing of high-dimensional sensory input, mirroring the cognitive process of understanding and strategizing within a game (Mnih et al., 2015).

OpenAI's approach to constructing AI models for gaming emphasizes the scalability and adaptability of neural networks. For instance, the architecture behind OpenAI Five, developed for playing Dota 2, utilized a scaled-up version of proximal policy optimization (PPO) algorithms, combined with long short-term memory (LSTM) networks to handle the game's complex, sequential decision-making process

(Berner et al., 2019). This architecture allowed OpenAI Five to effectively learn and adapt strategies through continuous interaction with the game environment.

Training of AI Models in Gaming

The training process is critical to the success of AI models in gaming. Reinforcement learning models are trained through a combination of simulation and real-time gameplay, allowing them to learn from both their actions' outcomes and the diverse strategies employed by human players. OpenAI has pioneered several training methodologies that have significantly advanced the field.

Curriculum Learning

OpenAI implemented curriculum learning strategies to progressively train AI models, starting from simple tasks and gradually increasing the difficulty level. This method mirrors human learning processes, facilitating the AI's understanding of complex game mechanics in a structured manner (Brockman et al., 2016).

Self-Play

A notable training strategy employed by OpenAI is self-play, where AI agents play against copies of themselves. This technique was instrumental in the training of OpenAI Five, enabling the model to learn from a vast array of gameplay scenarios without the need for external data. Self-play accelerates the learning process by providing a consistent and infinitely challenging environment, pushing the AI to continually adapt and improve (Silver et al., 2017).

OpenAI's technologies and projects have significantly contributed to the advancement of AI in gaming, particularly in the architecture and training of AI models through reinforcement learning. The sophisticated architectures developed for these models, combined with innovative training techniques such as curriculum learning and self-play, have set new standards in the field. These advancements not only enhance the gaming experience but also offer insights into the broader application of AI in complex decision-making and strategy formulation contexts.

Breakthroughs in Strategic Gameplay

Mastering Complex Games

One of OpenAI's hallmark achievements in gaming is the development of OpenAI Five, an AI system capable of competing at a high level in Dota 2, a complex multiplayer online battle arena (MOBA) game. OpenAI Five demonstrated the ability to develop sophisticated strategies, make real-time decisions, and adapt to the strategies of human opponents, culminating in victories against professional Dota 2 players. This achievement underscored the capabilities of reinforcement learning models to understand and excel in environments characterized by uncertainty, complexity, and strategic depth (Berner et al., 2019).

Mastering Complex Games through Reinforcement Learning

OpenAI has made notable contributions to the field of AI in gaming by mastering complex games, which serve as benchmarks for the capabilities of AI systems. Games like Dota 2 and Go, which require strategic thinking, long-term planning, and adaptability, have been key focus areas for OpenAI. The complexity of these games lies in their vast search spaces, intricate rules, and the necessity for nuanced strategic decision-making.

OpenAI Five: Dota 2

One of the most significant breakthroughs in strategic gameplay achieved by OpenAI is the development of OpenAI Five, an AI system trained to play the multiplayer online battle arena game Dota 2. Dota 2 is known for its strategic depth and complexity, requiring players to make real-time decisions while cooperating with teammates. OpenAI Five demonstrated the ability to learn diverse strategies, execute precise team coordination, and adapt to opponents' tactics, outperforming human professionals in a series of public matches (Berner et al., 2019). This achievement underscored the potential of reinforcement learning to master complex strategic games and highlighted the progress AI has made towards understanding and executing high-level strategic thinking.

AlphaGo and the Advancement of Strategic Play

Although not a project of OpenAI, the development of AlphaGo by DeepMind represents a pivotal moment in the application of AI to complex games. AlphaGo's victory over a world champion Go player marked a landmark moment in the history of AI, demonstrating that deep learning and reinforcement learning could surpass human expertise in games of strategy and intuition (Silver et al., 2016). This breakthrough has had a profound impact on the field, inspiring further research and development, including OpenAI's efforts in strategic gameplay.

Methodologies for Mastering Complex Games

OpenAI's approach to mastering complex games involves several key methodologies:

Reinforcement Learning: At the heart of OpenAI's strategy is the use of reinforcement learning, where AI systems learn optimal behaviors through trial and error, guided by feedback from the game environment (Sutton & Barto, 2018).

Self-Play: A critical component of OpenAI's training regime is self-play, where AI agents compete against themselves, accelerating the learning process by exploring a wide range of strategies and counter-strategies without human intervention.

Scalable Architecture: OpenAI has developed scalable neural network architectures that can process vast amounts of data and adapt to the complexities of strategic games. This scalability is crucial for handling the dynamic and unpredictable nature of games like Dota 2.

Implications of Breakthroughs in Strategic Gameplay

The breakthroughs in strategic gameplay achieved by OpenAI have significant implications for the field of artificial intelligence and beyond. These achievements not only demonstrate the potential of AI to understand and execute complex strategies but also offer insights into how AI can be applied to real-world problems requiring strategic planning and decision-making. Moreover, the methodologies developed by OpenAI for training AI systems in complex games could be adapted for use in other domains, such as robotics, logistics, and autonomous systems.

Learning Generalizable Strategies

Through its gaming initiatives, OpenAI has shown that reinforcement learning can lead to the emergence of generalizable strategies that can be applied across different scenarios within the game. For example, in the hide-and-seek project, AI agents learned innovative strategies and counter-strategies over time, demonstrating creativity and strategic planning. These findings suggest that RL models can develop a deep understanding of strategic principles that transcend specific game rules, contributing valuable insights to the field of AI research (Baker et al., 2020).

The Concept of Generalizable Strategies in AI

Generalizable strategies refer to the ability of an AI system to apply learned knowledge and strategies from one context to broader situations or different games. This ability is crucial for the development of AI that can adapt to new challenges without requiring extensive retraining for each specific task. The pursuit of generalizability in AI gaming strategies represents a shift towards creating more flexible and adaptive AI systems, capable of navigating a variety of environments and problem-solving scenarios (Sutton & Barto, 2018).

OpenAI's Approach to Learning Generalizable Strategies

OpenAI has approached the challenge of learning generalizable strategies through several innovative projects and methodologies, emphasizing the versatility and adaptability of AI agents.

OpenAI Gym

OpenAI Gym is a toolkit for developing and comparing reinforcement learning algorithms. It offers a wide range of environments, from classic control tasks to complex games, providing a platform for AI systems to learn and test strategies across diverse settings. The diversity of challenges available in OpenAI Gym is instrumental in training AI agents that can generalize their learning and apply it to solve new, unseen problems (Brockman et al., 2016).

OpenAI Five and Dota 2

Although the primary achievement of OpenAI Five was mastering the game of Dota 2, the underlying technology and training methodologies have broader implications for the learning of generalizable strategies. By engaging in thousands of self-play matches and encountering a vast array of game situations, OpenAI Five developed strategies that are not just specific to Dota 2 but indicative of deeper learning and problem-solving capabilities. This experience underscores the potential for reinforcement learning to foster generalizable strategic thinking in AI (Berner et al., 2019).

RoboSumo and Multi-Agent Learning

Another notable OpenAI project is RoboSumo, where pairs of AI-controlled robots learn to wrestle in a simulated environment. This project, focusing on multi-agent learning, highlights how AI systems can develop strategies through interaction, competition, and collaboration with other agents. The strategies learned in this context are adaptable and can be applied to various tasks requiring physical interaction and strategic planning (Bansal et al., 2017).

Implications of Generalizable Strategies in AI

The development of AI capable of learning generalizable strategies has profound implications for the field. It marks a step towards creating AI systems that can understand and navigate the real world, where problems are not isolated and solutions need to be adaptable and versatile. Moreover, the ability to generalize strategies across different games and environments opens up new avenues for AI applications in areas such as robotics, autonomous vehicles, and complex decision-making processes in uncertain environments.

OpenAI's efforts in learning generalizable strategies through reinforcement learning have significantly advanced the capabilities of AI in strategic gameplay. Projects like OpenAI Gym, OpenAI Five, and RoboSumo not only demonstrate the potential of AI to master individual games but also highlight the broader applicability of these learned strategies. As AI continues to evolve, the focus on generalizability will remain central to developing systems that can adapt and thrive in the complex, multifaceted world that lies beyond the gaming arena.

Implications for AI Research and Applications

The application of reinforcement learning in gaming has profound implications beyond the realm of entertainment. The strategies and problem-solving capabilities developed by AI agents in gaming environments can be applied to real-world challenges in domains such as robotics, autonomous vehicles, and complex system optimization. Furthermore, the success of OpenAI's projects in strategic gameplay highlights the potential of reinforcement learning as a powerful tool for AI research, paving the way for the development of more sophisticated, adaptable, and intelligent AI systems.

Advancements in AI Research Methodologies

OpenAI's application of RL in gaming has led to significant advancements in research methodologies within the AI community. Projects like OpenAI Five and the development of platforms such as OpenAI Gym have demonstrated the effectiveness of RL in complex decision-making and strategic planning in dynamic environments (Berner et al., 2019; Brockman et al., 2016). These initiatives have contributed to refining RL techniques, including deep reinforcement learning (DRL), multi-agent learning, and curriculum learning. The methodologies developed through gaming are applicable to a wide range of AI research areas, pushing the boundaries of what machines can learn and achieve.

Multi-Agent Learning and Collaboration

OpenAI's exploration of multi-agent environments in games has shed light on the dynamics of competition and cooperation among AI agents. This research has implications for developing AI systems that can work collaboratively with humans and other AI agents, leading to improvements in collective decision-making processes and teamwork strategies (Bansal et al., 2017). Such advancements are crucial for the deployment of AI in scenarios that require coordination among multiple entities, such as autonomous vehicle navigation and robotic swarm operations.

Expansion of AI Applications

The strategies and technologies developed by OpenAI for gaming have broad applicability beyond the entertainment industry. The ability of AI to learn and adapt to complex environments, as demonstrated in strategic games, can be leveraged in various real-world applications.

Robotics and Autonomous Systems

The principles of RL and the strategies learned through gaming are directly applicable to the field of robotics. AI systems that can navigate complex environments and make strategic decisions in real-time are crucial for developing more autonomous, efficient, and intelligent robots. The application of gaming-derived AI in robotics can lead to advancements in manufacturing, logistics, and service robots, making them more adaptable and capable of handling unforeseen situations.

Decision Support Systems

AI's capability to strategize and plan in gaming scenarios can be translated into decision support systems for business, healthcare, and public policy. AI can help in modeling complex scenarios, predicting outcomes, and optimizing decisions in uncertain environments. The strategic planning capabilities developed through gaming could enhance the efficiency and effectiveness of decision-making processes in these domains.

Ethical Considerations and Responsible AI Development

As AI technologies continue to evolve, ethical considerations and the responsible development of AI have become increasingly important. OpenAI's emphasis on creating AI that benefits all humanity is reflected in its approach to gaming projects. The organization's work prompts broader discussions about the ethical implications of AI, including fairness, transparency, and the societal impacts of autonomous systems (OpenAI, n.d.). Ensuring that AI systems are developed with ethical guidelines in mind is crucial for maximizing their benefits while minimizing potential harms.

OpenAI's technologies and projects in gaming have profound implications for AI research and applications. The advancements in AI research methodologies, the expansion of AI applications into various sectors, and the ongoing dialogue about ethical AI development represent key areas influenced by OpenAI's work. As AI continues to advance, the lessons learned from gaming, including strategic planning, adaptability, and collaboration, will play a critical role in shaping the future of AI across all areas of human endeavor.

Conclusion

The exploration of AI in Gaming, focusing on Reinforcement Learning and Strategy highlights the groundbreaking work of OpenAI in advancing the field of artificial intelligence through gaming. By leveraging reinforcement learning to master strategic gameplay, OpenAI not only pushes the boundaries of what AI can achieve in complex environments but also offers valuable insights into the development of AI systems that can navigate and solve real-world problems with unprecedented efficiency and creativity.

AI in Healthcare:

The application of OpenAI's technologies and projects in healthcare represents a transformative shift towards leveraging artificial intelligence (AI) to enhance diagnosis, drug discovery, and personalized medicine. The insights derived underscore the organization's contributions to advancing healthcare through innovative AI applications. This comprehensive analysis delves into how OpenAI's AI models and platforms are being utilized to revolutionize healthcare services, improve patient outcomes, and pave the way for future advancements in medical science.

AI in Diagnosis

OpenAI's advancements in AI technology have shown significant promise in improving diagnostic accuracy and efficiency. By utilizing deep learning and natural language processing (NLP) models, AI systems can analyze medical images, patient histories, and clinical notes with a level of precision and speed that surpasses traditional methods (Esteva et al., 2019). For instance, OpenAI's development of advanced NLP models, such as GPT (Generative Pre-trained Transformer), has applications in interpreting clinical documentation and extracting relevant information for diagnostic purposes. These models can assist healthcare professionals by providing rapid, accurate analyses of patient data, leading to earlier and more precise diagnoses.

Advancements in AI-Driven Diagnostics

OpenAI's development of sophisticated AI models, including deep learning (DL) and natural language processing (NLP) technologies, has paved the way for significant advancements in medical diagnostics. These models are capable of analyzing complex medical data, such as images from radiography or pathology, and textual data from patient records, to identify patterns and anomalies that may elude human detection (Esteva et al., 2019). For instance, AI algorithms developed by OpenAI have demonstrated remarkable accuracy in diagnosing diseases from medical imaging, such as identifying malignancies in radiographs or detecting retinal diseases from optical coherence tomography images.

Methodologies Employed

Deep Learning in Medical Imaging

OpenAI utilizes deep learning, a subset of machine learning, where artificial neural networks mimic the way the human brain operates. In diagnostics, DL models are trained on vast datasets of medical images to learn to identify disease markers with high precision. For example, convolutional neural networks (CNNs), a class of deep neural networks, are particularly effective for image recognition tasks and have been widely applied in analyzing X-rays, MRI scans, and other medical imagery for diagnostic purposes.

Natural Language Processing for Clinical Data Analysis

NLP technologies developed by OpenAI, such as the Generative Pre-trained Transformer (GPT) models, are employed to interpret and analyze clinical documentation and patient records. These models can extract relevant information, understand the context, and even predict potential diagnoses based on textual data. By automating the analysis of clinical notes, lab reports, and patient histories, NLP models significantly reduce the time required for data processing, allowing healthcare professionals to focus on decision-making and patient care.

Impact on Healthcare

The application of AI in diagnostics has the potential to transform healthcare delivery. AI-driven diagnostic tools can provide faster, more accurate diagnoses, leading to earlier intervention and improved patient outcomes. Furthermore, AI can help address the challenge of diagnostic errors, which are a significant concern in healthcare. By providing healthcare professionals with AI-powered diagnostic support, the likelihood of overlooking critical information can be reduced, enhancing the quality of care.

Challenges and Ethical Considerations

Despite the promising advancements, the integration of AI into diagnostics is not without challenges. Data privacy and security are major concerns, as diagnostic AI systems require access to sensitive patient information. Ensuring the confidentiality and integrity of this data is paramount. Additionally, the ethical implications of AI-driven diagnostics, including issues of bias, transparency, and accountability, must be carefully managed. Ensuring that AI models are trained on diverse datasets is crucial to avoid biases that could lead to disparities in care.

Moreover, there is a need for a regulatory framework that can keep pace with the rapid advancements in AI to ensure that these technologies are safe, effective, and equitable. The development of standards and guidelines for the ethical use of AI in diagnostics is essential to foster trust among healthcare professionals and patients.

OpenAI's technologies and projects have made significant contributions to the field of AI-driven diagnostics, offering the potential to revolutionize medical diagnostics through enhanced accuracy and efficiency. The application of deep learning and natural language processing in analyzing medical images and clinical data represents a major advancement in healthcare. However, realizing the full potential of AI in diagnostics requires addressing the associated challenges and ethical considerations, ensuring that these technologies improve patient care while safeguarding patient rights and data privacy.

AI in Drug Discovery

The drug discovery process is notoriously time-consuming and costly, with a high rate of failure. OpenAI's technologies have the potential to revolutionize this field by significantly reducing the time and cost associated with developing new drugs. AI models can predict molecular activity, optimize drug formulations, and simulate clinical trials to identify potential treatment options more efficiently than traditional methods (Zhavoronkov et al., 2019). OpenAI's machine learning algorithms, capable of processing vast datasets and identifying patterns beyond human recognition, can accelerate the identification of promising drug candidates and optimize their development pathways, thereby enhancing the efficiency of the drug discovery process.

Integration of AI in Drug Discovery

OpenAI's projects have significantly contributed to drug discovery by implementing machine learning (ML) and deep learning (DL) algorithms to analyze biological data and chemical structures. These AI models are capable of identifying potential drug candidates by predicting their interactions with biological targets, optimizing drug molecules for increased efficacy and reduced toxicity, and simulating clinical trial outcomes to assess drug safety and effectiveness (Zhavoronkov et al., 2019).

Machine Learning Algorithms for Target Identification

Machine learning algorithms are employed to analyze vast datasets of genomic, proteomic, and metabolomic information to identify potential therapeutic targets. By recognizing patterns and associations between biological markers and diseases, AI can uncover novel targets for drug development, accelerating the initial phase of the drug discovery process.

Deep Learning in Molecular Design

Deep learning models, particularly those developed by OpenAI, have been applied to the design and optimization of drug molecules. Generative models, such as generative adversarial networks (GANs) and variational autoencoders (VAEs), can generate novel chemical structures with desired properties, thereby facilitating the discovery of therapeutic molecules that are more likely to succeed in clinical trials.

Predictive Modeling for Drug Repurposing

AI technologies also play a crucial role in drug repurposing, where existing drugs are identified for new therapeutic uses. OpenAI's models can analyze data from clinical studies, electronic health records, and scientific literature to predict the efficacy of existing drugs for treating different diseases, streamlining the drug repurposing process and reducing development costs.

Impact on the Pharmaceutical Industry

The integration of AI in drug discovery has the potential to transform the pharmaceutical industry by reducing the time and cost associated with bringing new drugs to market. Traditional drug discovery processes are lengthy and expensive, with high failure rates. AI-driven approaches can enhance the efficiency and success rate of drug development by providing more accurate predictions of drug-target interactions, optimizing drug properties for better performance, and identifying promising candidates more rapidly.

Challenges and Ethical Considerations

Despite the promising advancements, the application of AI in drug discovery faces several challenges. Data quality and availability are major concerns, as AI models require large, high-quality datasets to train effectively. Additionally, the interpretability of AI models is an issue, as the "black box" nature of some algorithms can make it difficult to understand how decisions are made.

Ethical considerations also play a critical role in the application of AI to drug discovery. Issues of data privacy, consent, and the potential for bias in AI models must be addressed to ensure that these technologies are used responsibly and equitably. Furthermore, the regulatory landscape for AI-driven drug discovery is still evolving, necessitating clear guidelines and standards to ensure the safety and efficacy of AI-generated therapeutics.

OpenAI's technologies and projects have catalyzed significant advancements in the field of drug discovery, offering the promise of faster, more efficient development of new therapeutics. By leveraging machine learning and deep learning, AI can streamline the identification of drug targets, optimize molecular designs, and predict drug efficacy and safety, potentially revolutionizing the pharmaceutical industry. However, realizing the full potential of AI in drug discovery requires overcoming challenges related to data quality, model interpretability, and ethical considerations, ensuring that these technologies benefit society while minimizing risks.

AI in Personalized Medicine

Personalized medicine aims to tailor medical treatment to the individual characteristics of each patient, optimizing treatment efficacy and minimizing side effects. OpenAI's AI models hold the promise of advancing personalized medicine by analyzing genetic information, lifestyle factors, and clinical data to predict individual responses to treatments (Mirnezami et al., 2012). By leveraging AI to integrate and analyze complex datasets, healthcare providers can develop personalized treatment plans that are more effective and less invasive than conventional approaches. This not only improves patient care but also contributes to the broader shift towards more patient-centered healthcare systems.

Predictive Analytics for Patient Outcomes

OpenAI has leveraged deep learning (DL) and natural language processing (NLP) to develop predictive models that analyze patient data, including genetic information, medical histories, and lifestyle factors, to forecast disease risk and treatment outcomes. These AI models utilize vast datasets to identify patterns and correlations that may not be apparent to human clinicians, thereby enhancing the accuracy of patient assessments and the prediction of treatment efficacy.

Customization of Therapeutic Interventions

Through the application of machine learning algorithms, OpenAI has contributed to the customization of therapeutic interventions. AI systems can analyze data from clinical trials and patient records to determine which treatments are most effective for specific patient subgroups based on genetic markers, disease phenotypes, and other individual factors. This approach enables healthcare providers to select the most appropriate therapies for each patient, improving treatment outcomes and reducing the risk of adverse effects.

Optimization of Drug Regimens

AI technologies are also instrumental in optimizing drug regimens in personalized medicine. By analyzing patient-specific data, AI models developed by OpenAI can recommend personalized drug combinations and dosages that maximize therapeutic efficacy while minimizing side effects. This capability is particularly valuable in complex diseases such as cancer, where patients may benefit from highly individualized treatment plans.

Impact on Healthcare

The integration of AI into personalized medicine has the potential to significantly enhance patient care by making it more precise, predictive, and personalized. AI-driven approaches can lead to earlier disease detection, more accurate prognoses, and treatment plans that are optimized for the individual's unique genetic makeup and health status. By tailoring medical care to the individual, AI has the potential to improve treatment outcomes, enhance patient satisfaction, and reduce healthcare costs by avoiding ineffective treatments and minimizing adverse reactions.

Challenges and Ethical Considerations

Despite the promising benefits, the application of AI in personalized medicine faces several challenges and ethical considerations. Data privacy and security are major concerns, as personalized medicine relies on sensitive patient data, including genetic information. Ensuring the confidentiality and integrity of this data is paramount to protect patient privacy and maintain trust in AI-driven healthcare systems.

Bias in AI models poses another significant challenge. If AI systems are trained on datasets that lack diversity, there is a risk that the models may not perform equally well across different patient populations, leading to disparities in care. Addressing these biases requires concerted efforts to include diverse populations in clinical data used for training AI models.

Furthermore, the ethical implications of AI-driven personalized medicine, including issues of consent, data ownership, and the potential for genetic discrimination, must be carefully navigated. Establishing clear ethical guidelines and regulatory frameworks is essential to ensure that AI is used responsibly and equitably in personalized medicine.

OpenAI's technologies and projects have made significant strides in advancing personalized medicine, offering the promise of more precise, predictive, and personalized healthcare. By harnessing the power of AI to analyze complex patient data and tailor medical treatments to individual needs, personalized medicine stands at the forefront of a healthcare revolution. However, realizing the full potential of AI in personalized medicine requires overcoming challenges related to data privacy, model bias, and ethical considerations, ensuring that these technologies benefit all patients equitably.

Challenges and Ethical Considerations

While the potential of AI in healthcare is vast, its implementation is not without challenges. Issues of data privacy, security, and the ethical use of AI in medical decision-making are paramount. OpenAI recognizes these concerns and advocates for the responsible development and deployment of AI technologies, emphasizing the importance of transparency, fairness, and accountability in AI applications in healthcare.

Data Privacy and Security

The use of AI in healthcare often involves the processing of vast amounts of sensitive personal data, including genetic information, medical histories, and personal identifiers. Ensuring the privacy and security of this data is paramount, as breaches could lead to significant harm, including identity theft, discrimination, and loss of privacy (Price II, 2019). OpenAI's technologies, while advancing healthcare, must adhere to stringent data protection regulations, such as the General Data Protection Regulation (GDPR) in the European Union, which emphasizes the principles of data minimization, purpose limitation, and consent.

Bias and Fairness

AI systems are only as unbiased as the data they are trained on. Historical healthcare data often contain biases due to socioeconomic, racial, gender, or geographical disparities in healthcare access and treatment outcomes. If unaddressed, these biases can be perpetuated or exacerbated by AI systems, leading to unequal healthcare services and outcomes among different patient groups (Rajkomar et al., 2018). OpenAI's commitment to ethical AI development necessitates the implementation of methodologies to identify, mitigate, and monitor biases within AI models to ensure equitable healthcare solutions.

Transparency and Accountability

The "black box" nature of some AI algorithms poses significant challenges to transparency and accountability in healthcare decisions. When AI systems make recommendations or decisions, healthcare providers and patients must understand the basis of these decisions to trust and effectively use AI-enhanced medical services. OpenAI's projects in healthcare must strive for explainability, enabling clinicians to interpret AI recommendations and understand their limitations and potential errors, thus maintaining accountability in patient care decisions (Goodman & Flaxman, 2017).

Automation-Induced Displacement

The increasing automation of diagnostic, drug discovery, and personalized medicine tasks through AI may lead to concerns about the displacement of healthcare professionals. While AI has the potential to augment healthcare services, there is a risk that reliance on AI could devalue human expertise and lead to job displacement. Addressing this challenge requires a balanced approach that leverages AI to enhance, rather than replace, the role of healthcare professionals, ensuring that AI acts as a tool to support patient care and medical decision-making.

Ethical Frameworks and Regulatory Oversight

The development and implementation of AI in healthcare necessitate comprehensive ethical frameworks and robust regulatory oversight to address these challenges and considerations effectively. These frameworks must guide the responsible development, deployment, and use of AI technologies, ensuring that they serve the public interest while safeguarding patient rights and welfare. OpenAI, as a leading entity in AI research and development, plays a crucial role in advocating for and adhering to such ethical standards and regulations in healthcare applications.

The integration of OpenAI's technologies in healthcare offers immense potential for improving diagnosis, drug discovery, and personalized medicine. However, realizing this potential requires navigating complex challenges and ethical considerations, including data privacy, bias and fairness, transparency, accountability, and the impact on healthcare employment. By addressing these issues proactively and ethically, OpenAI can contribute to the development of AI-driven healthcare solutions that are not only innovative and effective but also equitable, secure, and trusted by patients and healthcare providers alike.

Conclusion

OpenAI's technologies and projects offer significant potential to transform healthcare through improvements in diagnosis, drug discovery, and personalized medicine. By harnessing the power of AI, healthcare providers can achieve more accurate diagnoses, accelerate the development of new treatments, and deliver personalized care that optimizes patient outcomes. However, the successful and ethical integration of AI into healthcare requires careful consideration of the associated challenges and ethical dilemmas. As OpenAI continues to advance AI technology, its contributions to healthcare signify a promising direction for the future of medical science and patient care.

AI in Business:

The integration of OpenAI's artificial intelligence (AI) technologies into the business sector has revolutionized the way companies approach automation, optimization, and decision-making. OpenAI's contributions to AI have been instrumental in driving efficiencies, enhancing strategic insights, and fostering innovation across various industries.

Automation with AI Technologies

OpenAI has pioneered the development of AI models that significantly enhance automation capabilities in business operations. These technologies, including machine learning (ML) and natural language processing (NLP), have been applied to automate routine tasks, such as data entry, customer service inquiries, and even complex processes like financial analysis.

For instance, GPT (Generative Pre-trained Transformer) models have revolutionized the way businesses handle customer service and support. By understanding and generating human-like text, GPT enables the automation of customer service interactions, providing timely and relevant responses to customer inquiries without human intervention (Radford et al., 2019). This not only improves efficiency but also allows human employees to focus on more strategic tasks that require human insight.

Transformative Impact of AI on Business Automation

OpenAI's AI technologies, particularly its advancements in machine learning (ML) and natural language processing (NLP), have revolutionized business automation by enabling the execution of complex tasks with unprecedented accuracy and efficiency. From automating customer service interactions to streamlining back-office operations, OpenAI's AI models facilitate a wide range of automated processes that significantly reduce manual labor, minimize errors, and enhance operational efficiency (Radford et al., 2019).

Customer Service and Support

One of the most notable applications of OpenAI's AI in business automation is in customer service and support. OpenAI's GPT (Generative Pre-trained Transformer) models, renowned for their ability to understand and generate human-like text, have been instrumental in automating customer service interactions. By accurately interpreting customer queries and generating coherent, contextually relevant responses, GPT models enable businesses to provide 24/7 customer support without the need for extensive human intervention, thereby improving customer satisfaction while reducing operational costs.

Back-Office Operations

Beyond customer-facing applications, OpenAI's technologies have been applied to automate various back-office tasks, such as data entry, invoice processing, and payroll management. By leveraging AI to automate these routine but time-consuming tasks, businesses can reallocate human resources to more strategic initiatives, fostering innovation and competitive advantage.

Methodologies Employed in AI-driven Automation

Machine Learning for Process Automation

OpenAI employs sophisticated ML algorithms to identify patterns and automate decision-making processes within business operations. For example, reinforcement learning, a subset of ML where algorithms learn optimal actions through trial and error, has been used to optimize logistics and supply chain management, enabling businesses to reduce costs and improve delivery times.

Natural Language Processing for Interaction Automation

NLP technologies developed by OpenAI, such as GPT, have been pivotal in automating interactions, including customer service and content creation. By understanding and generating natural language, these AI models can automate a wide range of tasks that traditionally required human cognitive abilities, thus expanding the scope of automation beyond simple, rule-based tasks.

Broader Implications for the Future of Work

The integration of AI into business automation heralds significant implications for the workforce and the nature of work. While AI-driven automation can lead to increased productivity and economic growth, it also raises concerns about job displacement and the need for workforce reskilling. As routine tasks become automated, there is a growing demand for skills that AI cannot replicate easily, such as creative problem-solving, emotional intelligence, and strategic thinking.

To navigate these changes, businesses and policymakers must invest in education and training programs that prepare workers for the jobs of the future, emphasizing the importance of adaptability and lifelong learning. Additionally, ethical considerations regarding the deployment of AI in the workplace, including fairness, transparency, and accountability, must be addressed to ensure that the benefits of automation are distributed equitably across society.

Conclusion

OpenAI's contributions to business automation through AI technologies mark a significant milestone in the evolution of the workplace. By automating a broad spectrum of tasks, from customer service to back-office operations, OpenAI's AI models are not only enhancing operational efficiencies but also prompting a reevaluation of the role of human labor in the digital age. As businesses continue to harness the power of AI, the challenge lies in balancing technological advancements with the socio-economic and ethical dimensions of automation, ensuring a future where technology augments human potential rather than displacing it.

Optimization of Business Processes

OpenAI's AI technologies play a crucial role in optimizing business processes, ensuring that operations are conducted in the most efficient and cost-effective manner. ML algorithms analyze vast amounts of data to identify patterns and insights that can lead to operational improvements, from supply chain logistics to inventory management.

For example, reinforcement learning, a type of ML where algorithms learn to make decisions by trial and error, has been applied to optimize supply chain operations. By simulating different scenarios and outcomes, AI models can recommend strategies that minimize costs while maximizing efficiency and reliability in the supply chain (Mnih et al., 2015).

Methodologies Employed in Business Process Optimization

OpenAI has pioneered the development and application of advanced AI technologies, including machine learning (ML), deep learning (DL), and natural language processing (NLP), to optimize business processes. These technologies enable the analysis of vast datasets to identify inefficiencies, predict future trends, and automate decision-making processes.

Machine Learning and Predictive Analytics

ML algorithms are at the forefront of business process optimization, offering the ability to analyze historical data to identify patterns and predict future outcomes. This predictive capability is crucial for optimizing inventory management, demand forecasting, and resource allocation. By accurately predicting future trends based on past and current data, businesses can make informed decisions that minimize waste and maximize resource utilization (Sutton & Barto, 2018).

Deep Learning for Complex Problem Solving

Deep learning, a subset of ML involving neural networks with many layers, has been applied to more complex optimization problems, such as supply chain logistics and operational efficiency. DL models can process and analyze data from various sources, including images, text, and sensor data, to identify bottlenecks and optimize workflows. The ability of DL models to handle multifaceted datasets allows for a more comprehensive approach to business process optimization.

Natural Language Processing for Enhanced Communication

NLP technologies developed by OpenAI, such as GPT (Generative Pre-trained Transformer), have revolutionized the way businesses automate and optimize customer service and internal communication. By understanding and generating human-like text, NLP enables the automation of customer inquiries and support tasks, streamlining communication processes and improving response times (Radford et al., 2019).

Impact on the Business Landscape

The application of AI for business process optimization has had a profound impact on the corporate landscape, leading to significant cost reductions, improved operational efficiency, and enhanced customer satisfaction. Companies across various industries have leveraged AI to streamline operations, from manufacturing and retail to finance and healthcare, demonstrating the versatility and effectiveness of AI technologies in optimizing business processes.

Challenges in Optimizing Business Processes with AI

Despite the clear benefits, the application of AI in business process optimization faces several challenges. Data quality and availability are major concerns, as effective ML and DL models require large amounts of high-quality data. Additionally, the integration of AI technologies into existing business infrastructures can be complex and resource-intensive, requiring significant investment in technology and skills development.

Ethical considerations and bias in AI algorithms also pose challenges. Ensuring that AI models are fair, transparent, and do not perpetuate existing biases is crucial for ethical business practices. Moreover, businesses must navigate the potential impact of AI on employment and workforce dynamics, as increased automation raises concerns about job displacement and the need for workforce reskilling.

OpenAI's technologies and projects have significantly advanced the capabilities for optimizing business processes, offering powerful tools for analyzing data, predicting outcomes, and automating decision-making. The impact of these technologies on the business landscape is profound, enabling operational efficiencies and strategic advantages that were previously unattainable. However, realizing the full potential of AI in business process optimization requires addressing the challenges related to data quality, integration complexities, ethical considerations, and workforce dynamics. As businesses continue to navigate these challenges, the role of AI in optimizing business processes is set to grow, underscoring the importance of responsible and strategic implementation of AI technologies.

Decision-Making Enhancements

The application of OpenAI's technologies significantly enhances decision-making processes within businesses. AI systems analyze data and provide insights that inform strategic business decisions, from market entry strategies to product development and pricing models. These AI-driven insights are based on comprehensive data analysis that can detect trends and patterns not readily apparent to human analysts.

Furthermore, OpenAI's developments in AI have facilitated the creation of predictive models that forecast market trends and consumer behavior, allowing businesses to make informed decisions proactively rather than reactively. This predictive capability is crucial in today's fast-paced business environment, where being ahead of market trends can provide a competitive edge.

Methodologies in AI-Enhanced Decision Making

OpenAI has been at the forefront of developing and applying advanced AI technologies, such as machine learning (ML), deep learning (DL), and natural language processing (NLP), to augment decision-making capabilities in businesses. These technologies analyze complex datasets to uncover insights, predict outcomes, and generate recommendations, thereby supporting more informed and strategic business decisions.

Predictive Analytics and Machine Learning

ML algorithms are instrumental in predictive analytics, offering businesses the ability to forecast future trends based on historical data. This predictive capacity is vital for various aspects of business decision-making, including market analysis, financial planning, and operational adjustments. By leveraging ML models, companies can anticipate market movements, consumer behavior, and potential risks, enabling proactive rather than reactive strategies (Hastie, Tibshirani, & Friedman, 2009).

Deep Learning for Complex Data Interpretation

Deep learning, a subset of ML that involves neural networks with multiple layers, allows for the analysis of more complex and nuanced data. This capability is crucial for decisions that require understanding intricate patterns or relationships within large datasets, such as customer sentiment analysis, product development, and competitive strategy formulation. DL models can digest and interpret vast amounts of unstructured data, from social media interactions to market signals, providing a depth of insight that significantly enhances decision-making processes.

Natural Language Processing for Information Extraction

NLP technologies, particularly those developed by OpenAI like GPT (Generative Pre-trained Transformer), revolutionize the way businesses gather and interpret information. NLP enables the automated extraction of relevant insights from textual data, such as reports, news articles, and industry publications, facilitating a more comprehensive and swift decision-making process. By automating the analysis of textual information, NLP helps businesses stay abreast of market trends, regulatory changes, and emerging opportunities (Radford et al., 2019).

Impact on the Business Landscape

The integration of AI into decision-making processes has profound implications for the business landscape, driving strategic advantages and competitive differentiation. AI-enhanced decision-making enables businesses to leverage data-driven insights for strategic planning, risk management, and innovation. This shift towards AI-supported decisions not only improves the accuracy and effectiveness of business strategies but also empowers companies to navigate the complexities of the modern business environment more adeptly.

Challenges and Ethical Considerations

Despite the benefits, the adoption of AI in decision-making is not without challenges. The reliance on data and algorithms necessitates considerations regarding data quality, privacy, and security. Ensuring the integrity and confidentiality of the data underpinning decision-making processes is paramount.

Furthermore, the potential for algorithmic bias presents a significant ethical concern. Decisions based on biased algorithms can lead to unfair practices or unequal outcomes. Therefore, it is critical to implement measures to identify and mitigate biases in AI models.

Additionally, the opacity of certain AI systems, often referred to as the "black box" problem, can hinder the transparency and explainability of AI-enhanced decisions. Addressing this issue is essential to maintain trust and accountability in AI-driven decision-making processes.

OpenAI's technologies and projects have markedly advanced the capabilities for enhancing decision-making in the business sector. By harnessing the power of AI to analyze data and generate insights, businesses can make more informed, strategic, and proactive decisions. However, realizing the full potential of AI in decision-making requires careful navigation of the associated challenges and ethical considerations. As businesses increasingly rely on AI to inform their strategic decisions, the importance of responsible and transparent AI practices becomes ever more critical.

Challenges and Ethical Considerations

While the benefits of AI in business are substantial, the deployment of these technologies also presents challenges and ethical considerations. Data privacy and security are paramount concerns, as AI systems often require access to sensitive corporate and customer information. Ensuring the integrity and confidentiality of this data is crucial to maintaining trust and complying with regulatory requirements.

Bias in AI algorithms is another significant issue. If AI models are trained on biased data, their outputs and recommendations can perpetuate or even exacerbate these biases, leading to unfair or unethical business practices. Therefore, businesses must ensure that AI models are developed and trained on diverse and representative data sets.

Moreover, the automation of jobs by AI technologies raises concerns about employment and workforce displacement. Businesses must navigate these challenges responsibly, considering the societal impact of automation and exploring ways to retrain and redeploy affected workers.

Data Privacy and Security

One of the paramount concerns in the deployment of AI within business operations is the safeguarding of data privacy and security. The vast amounts of data processed by AI systems for automation, optimization, and decision-making include sensitive personal and corporate information. Mishandling or unauthorized access to this data poses significant risks, including breaches of privacy and potential financial and reputational damage. The ethical management of data, adhering to regulations such as the General Data Protection Regulation (GDPR) in the European Union, is crucial in maintaining trust and integrity in AI-driven business practices (Voigt & Von dem Bussche, 2017).

Bias and Fairness

The challenge of bias in AI algorithms represents a critical ethical consideration. AI systems, including those developed by OpenAI, are susceptible to the biases inherent in their training data. If unchecked, these biases can perpetuate and amplify existing inequalities, leading to unfair outcomes in hiring practices, customer service, and access to services. Ensuring fairness and combating bias in AI applications necessitates rigorous testing, transparency, and the inclusion of diverse datasets in the training process (Barocas, Hardt, & Narayanan, 2019).

Transparency and Explainability

The "black box" nature of some AI systems complicates the understanding of how AI-derived decisions are made, raising concerns about transparency and accountability. Businesses utilizing AI must grapple with the challenge of ensuring that AI-driven decisions can be explained and justified, both internally to stakeholders and externally to regulators and the public. The development of explainable AI (XAI) systems is a burgeoning field aiming to make AI decisions more interpretable without compromising their effectiveness (Arrieta et al., 2020).

Impact on Employment

The automation of tasks traditionally performed by humans raises ethical concerns regarding employment and workforce displacement. While AI can enhance efficiency and productivity, it also necessitates a reevaluation of the role of human labor in the AI-enhanced workplace. Businesses must consider the social impact of AI integration, exploring avenues for workforce reskilling and the creation of new job opportunities that leverage human skills complemented by AI capabilities (West, 2018).

Regulatory Compliance and Governance

Navigating the evolving regulatory landscape is a significant challenge for businesses implementing AI technologies. Compliance with existing and forthcoming regulations governing AI usage, data protection, and ethical standards is essential. Moreover, the establishment of robust governance frameworks to oversee AI applications ensures adherence to ethical principles, mitigating risks and aligning AI strategies with societal values.

The integration of OpenAI's technologies into business processes presents a dual-edged sword, offering profound opportunities for innovation and efficiency while introducing complex ethical and societal challenges. Addressing these challenges requires a concerted effort from businesses, regulators, and the AI research community to develop AI systems that are not only powerful and efficient but also transparent, fair, and aligned with ethical standards. As the capabilities of AI continue to evolve, fostering an ethical AI ecosystem will be paramount in realizing the full potential of AI in business while safeguarding societal interests and values.

Conclusion

OpenAI's technologies and projects have had a transformative impact on the business sector, driving automation, optimization, and enhanced decision-making. By leveraging AI, businesses can achieve unprecedented efficiencies, gain strategic insights, and foster innovation. However, the successful integration of AI into business practices requires careful consideration of the associated challenges and ethical implications, ensuring that the benefits of AI are realized responsibly and equitably.

9

Chapter 5: Societal Impacts and Ethical Considerations

Given the response aims to construct a detailed and academic discussion around the societal impacts and ethical considerations associated with OpenAI's advancements in artificial intelligence (AI), drawing upon general knowledge up to the last update in April 2023 and incorporating relevant references to support the analysis.

Societal Impacts of AI Technologies

OpenAI's innovations in AI have led to significant societal impacts, influencing various aspects of daily life, the economy, and the broader social fabric. These impacts manifest in several key areas:

Employment and the Labor Market

The automation capabilities enabled by AI technologies have reshaped the labor market, leading to both the displacement of certain job categories and the creation of new ones. While automation improves efficiency and productivity, it also raises concerns about job security and the need for workforce reskilling (Acemoglu & Restrepo, 2020).

The societal challenge lies in managing this transition, ensuring that workers displaced by AI can find new opportunities in emerging fields.

Transformation of Job Roles

AI technologies have led to a transformation in job roles across industries. Automation, powered by AI, has shown the capability to perform tasks ranging from routine and repetitive to those requiring complex decision-making previously thought to be the sole domain of humans (Autor, 2015). While this has led to concerns over job displacement, it has also facilitated the creation of new job roles that require oversight, maintenance, and continuous improvement of AI systems. The demand for AI specialists, data scientists, and machine learning engineers is illustrative of how AI is not only displacing jobs but also creating new employment opportunities that require advanced technical skills.

Impact on Employment Sectors

The impact of AI on employment varies significantly across sectors. In manufacturing, automation has led to increased efficiency and productivity but has also resulted in the reduction of manual labor roles (Acemoglu & Restrepo, 2020). Conversely, in the service sector, AI technologies like natural language processing and machine learning are enhancing the capabilities of customer service representatives by providing them with advanced tools for data analysis and customer interaction, thereby augmenting rather than replacing human jobs.

Opportunities for Skill Development and Reskilling

The shift towards an AI-driven economy necessitates a focus on skill development and reskilling. As routine tasks become automated, there is a growing need for skills that AI cannot replicate easily, such as emotional intelligence, creative problem-solving, and strategic thinking (Brynjolfsson & McAfee, 2014). This shift presents an opportunity for educational institutions and employers to invest in the workforce by providing training and development programs that equip individuals with the skills needed to thrive in an AI-enhanced labor market.

Challenges of Workforce Displacement

One of the most pressing concerns regarding the societal impacts of AI on employment is workforce displacement. As AI technologies become increasingly capable of performing tasks traditionally done by humans, there is a risk of significant job loss in certain sectors, particularly among low-skill and middle-skill jobs (Ford, 2015). This displacement poses challenges for social stability and economic inequality, as workers displaced by AI may find it difficult to secure employment in new roles that match their skill set and experience level.

Ethical Considerations and Policy Responses

The societal impacts of AI on employment and the labor market raise several ethical considerations and necessitate thoughtful policy responses. Policymakers and stakeholders must grapple with questions of how to ensure equitable access to the benefits of AI, mitigate the adverse effects of workforce displacement, and support the transition of workers into new roles (West, 2018). This may include policies aimed at fostering lifelong learning and reskilling, implementing safety nets for displaced workers, and encouraging the development of AI in ways that complement rather than substitute human labor.

The societal impacts of AI technologies on employment and the labor market are multifaceted, presenting both challenges and opportunities for the workforce. While AI has the potential to displace certain job roles, it also creates new opportunities for employment and necessitates a reevaluation of the skills valued in the labor market. Addressing the challenges posed by AI to employment requires a concerted effort from policymakers, educators, and industry leaders to ensure that the transition towards an AI-enhanced economy is inclusive and equitable.

Privacy and Surveillance

AI systems, particularly those capable of processing vast amounts of personal data, have heightened concerns around privacy and surveillance. The capacity of AI to analyze and infer personal information from data can lead to invasive levels of monitoring by both corporations and governments, raising ethical questions about the right to privacy in the digital age (Zuboff, 2019).

The Paradigm of AI and Privacy

AI technologies, particularly those involving machine learning (ML) and big data analytics, have the potential to significantly enhance personalization and efficiency in services ranging from healthcare to marketing. However, this often involves the collection and analysis of sensitive personal information, raising concerns about individual privacy rights (Zuboff, 2019). The detailed profiling capabilities of AI systems can lead to intrusive surveillance, where individuals' behaviors, preferences, and even intentions are monitored, analyzed, and potentially exploited without explicit consent or adequate transparency.

Surveillance and Its Implications

The use of AI in surveillance has expanded beyond traditional security purposes to include the monitoring of employee productivity, consumer behavior, and public activities. While such surveillance can enhance security and operational efficiency, it also poses risks to individual autonomy and can lead to a society where privacy is eroded. The ability of AI systems to continuously monitor and make decisions based on surveillance data challenges the notion of privacy as a fundamental right, prompting ethical and societal debates (Zuboff, 2019).

Ethical Considerations in AI Deployment

The deployment of AI technologies in contexts that affect privacy and surveillance necessitates a careful consideration of ethical principles. Key among these are respect for autonomy, beneficence, non-maleficence, and justice. Ensuring that AI systems are designed and utilized in a manner that respects individual autonomy and privacy is paramount. Furthermore, the benefits of AI-driven surveillance and data analysis should be balanced against the potential harms, ensuring that such technologies do not disproportionately disadvantage or discriminate against certain groups (Mittelstadt, 2019).

Regulatory and Societal Responses

Addressing the challenges posed by AI to privacy and surveillance requires robust regulatory responses and societal engagement. The European Union's General Data Protection Regulation (GDPR) represents a significant step in this direction, establishing stringent requirements for data protection and granting individuals greater control over their personal information (Regulation (EU) 2016/679). Additionally, there is a growing call for the development of AI ethics guidelines and standards that emphasize privacy protection and the responsible use of surveillance technologies (Jobin, Ienca, & Vayena, 2019).

Balancing Innovation with Privacy Protection

Achieving a balance between harnessing the benefits of AI technologies and protecting individual privacy is a complex endeavor. It involves not only the development of legal and regulatory frameworks but also fostering a culture of ethical AI development and use. This includes promoting transparency in AI operations, ensuring accountability for AI-driven decisions, and engaging in public discourse about the acceptable limits of surveillance and data collection.

The societal impacts of AI technologies on privacy and surveillance present profound challenges and ethical considerations. As AI continues to advance, it is imperative to critically assess its implications for individual privacy and societal norms. Protecting privacy in an age of AI-driven surveillance requires a multifaceted approach, combining regulatory measures, ethical AI development practices, and active engagement with societal stakeholders to ensure that technological advancements do not come at the expense of fundamental rights and freedoms.

Social Interaction and Communication

AI technologies, such as those developed by OpenAI for natural language processing, have transformed social interaction and communication. While these advancements offer new ways to connect and interact, they also present challenges related to misinformation, the authenticity of digital communication, and the impact on human relationships (Vaidhyanathan, 2018).

Enhancements in Social Interaction

AI technologies have introduced significant improvements in social interaction and communication, making it more accessible, personalized, and efficient. Chatbots and virtual assistants powered by AI provide immediate responses to inquiries, facilitating customer service and personal assistance with unprecedented speed and accuracy (McTear, Callejas, & Griol, 2016). Moreover, AI-driven recommendation systems on social media platforms analyze user preferences to curate personalized content, thereby enhancing user engagement and fostering community building around shared interests.

Language Translation and Cultural Exchange

AI-powered language translation tools have broken down language barriers, enabling cross-cultural communication and exchange on a scale previously unimaginable. Real-time translation services allow individuals from different linguistic backgrounds to interact seamlessly, promoting diversity, inclusivity, and global understanding. This democratization of language access through AI not only facilitates personal connections but also opens doors for international collaboration and cultural exchange (Hutchins & Somers, 1992).

Ethical Considerations in AI-mediated Communication

Despite the benefits, the integration of AI in social interaction and communication raises several ethical concerns. The personalization of content through AI algorithms, while enhancing user experience, also risks creating echo chambers and filter bubbles that reinforce existing biases and limit exposure to diverse viewpoints (Pariser, 2011). Furthermore, the use of AI in managing and moderating online content and interactions must navigate complex issues of censorship, privacy, and the potential for algorithmic bias that can influence public discourse and opinion.

Impact on Human Relationships

The proliferation of AI technologies in communication tools also prompts reflection on their impact on human relationships. While AI can facilitate connections, there is concern that over-reliance on AI-mediated communication could diminish the quality of human interactions, leading to a loss of empathy, reduced social skills, and a weakening of the bonds that form through face-to-face interactions

(Turkle, 2017). Balancing the convenience and efficiency of AI with the need for genuine human connection is crucial in maintaining the social fabric.

Navigating the Future of Social Interaction

As AI continues to evolve, navigating its impact on social interaction and communication requires a concerted effort from technologists, policymakers, and society at large. Establishing ethical guidelines for the development and deployment of AI in communication platforms, promoting digital literacy to understand AI's role in content curation, and encouraging the design of AI technologies that enhance rather than replace human interactions are pivotal steps in ensuring that AI serves to enrich social connections.

The societal impacts of AI technologies on social interaction and communication are profound and multifaceted, presenting opportunities to enhance connectivity and challenges to the essence of human relationships. As documented in "OpenAI: Exploring the World of Artificial Intelligence," the advancement of AI in this domain necessitates a careful balancing act—leveraging AI to improve communication and social bonds while vigilantly guarding against the erosion of genuine human connection. Ethical considerations, regulatory frameworks, and societal engagement play critical roles in navigating the future of social interaction in the age of AI.

Ethical Considerations in AI Development

The development and deployment of AI technologies entail a range of ethical considerations that must be addressed to ensure these advancements benefit society as a whole.

Bias and Fairness

AI systems are susceptible to biases present in their training data, which can lead to unfair outcomes when applied in decision-making processes. Addressing bias and ensuring fairness in AI applications is critical to prevent the perpetuation of existing inequalities and discrimination (Barocas, Hardt, & Narayanan, 2019).

Sources of Bias in AI Systems

Bias in AI systems primarily originates from the data used to train these models. Data can reflect historical and societal inequalities, leading to AI systems that perpetuate or even exacerbate these biases. For example, facial recognition technologies have shown lower accuracy rates for women and people of color, a discrepancy attributed to the underrepresentation of these groups in training datasets (Buolamwini & Gebru, 2018). Similarly, language processing models may replicate or amplify gender stereotypes present in the textual data they are trained on (Bolukbasi et al., 2016).

Impacts of Bias on Society

The biases in AI systems can have profound societal impacts, affecting decision-making in critical areas such as employment, criminal justice, and access to services. In hiring algorithms, biases may lead to discriminatory practices, disadvantaging candidates based on gender, race, or age. In the criminal justice system, predictive policing and risk assessment tools can reinforce racial biases, affecting sentencing and parole decisions. These examples underscore the potential for AI technologies to perpetuate social inequalities, highlighting the need for ethical considerations in their development and deployment.

Strategies for Mitigating Bias and Ensuring Fairness

Addressing bias and ensuring fairness in AI involves multiple strategies, from the initial design phase of AI systems to their implementation and evaluation. Transparency in AI algorithms and the datasets used for training is fundamental, allowing for the identification and correction of biases. Diverse and inclusive datasets are crucial for reducing bias, ensuring that AI systems perform equitably across different demographics (Mehrabi et al., 2019).

In addition to technical solutions, interdisciplinary approaches involving ethicists, social scientists, and affected communities are essential for understanding and mitigating the societal implications of AI biases. Ethical guidelines and frameworks for AI development, such as those proposed by leading AI research organizations and ethical bodies, emphasize principles of fairness, transparency, and accountability (Jobin, Ienca, & Vayena, 2019).

Regulatory and Policy Considerations

Governments and regulatory bodies play a critical role in ensuring fairness in AI. Legislation and policies that mandate the ethical development and deployment of AI systems, including requirements for transparency, accountability, and impact assessments, are vital for safeguarding against biases. The European Union's General Data Protection Regulation (GDPR) and initiatives like the Algorithmic Accountability Act in the United States represent steps towards regulating AI to protect individuals' rights and promote fairness (Goodman & Flaxman, 2017).

The ethical considerations of bias and fairness in AI development are paramount concerns as AI technologies increasingly influence every aspect of society, the imperative to address these ethical challenges becomes all the more critical. Mitigating bias and ensuring fairness in AI requires a multifaceted approach, involving transparent and inclusive development processes, interdisciplinary collaboration, and robust regulatory frameworks. By prioritizing these ethical considerations, the development of AI can progress in a manner that respects and upholds the principles of equity and justice.

Transparency and Accountability

The "black box" nature of some AI algorithms challenges transparency and accountability, making it difficult to understand how decisions are made. This opacity complicates efforts to hold AI systems and their creators accountable for errors or biases, underscoring the need for explainable AI (XAI) approaches (Arrieta et al., 2020).

The Importance of Transparency in AI

Transparency in AI refers to the openness and clarity with which AI systems and their operations are made understandable to users and the public. This involves disclosing how AI algorithms make decisions, the data on which they are trained, and the logic behind their outputs (Burrell, 2016). Transparency is crucial for several reasons:

Trust Building: Transparency is foundational to building trust among users and stakeholders. When individuals understand how AI systems reach their decisions, they are more likely to trust and accept these technologies (Ribeiro et al., 2016).

Facilitating Accountability: Transparent AI systems allow for the tracing of decisions back to their source, making it possible to hold developers and operators accountable for the actions of their AI systems.

Enabling Informed Consent: Transparency provides users with the information necessary to make informed decisions about whether and how to interact with AI systems.

Preventing Misuse: Open disclosure about the capabilities and limitations of AI systems can prevent their misuse or the misinterpretation of their outputs.

Challenges to Achieving Transparency

Achieving transparency in AI is fraught with challenges. Complex algorithms, such as those involved in deep learning, can be difficult to interpret even for their creators, leading to the so-called "black box" problem where the decision-making process of AI systems is opaque (Castelvecchi, 2016). Additionally, there may be proprietary or privacy concerns that prevent the full disclosure of algorithms and training datasets. Balancing these considerations with the need for transparency requires innovative solutions and compromises.

The Need for Accountability in AI

Accountability in AI refers to the mechanisms and practices that ensure individuals and organizations are held responsible for the outcomes of AI systems. This involves establishing clear guidelines for responsibility, particularly in cases where AI decisions lead to harmful outcomes. Accountability is critical for:

Ethical Responsibility: Ensuring that AI systems are used ethically and in alignment with societal values.

Legal Compliance: Adhering to laws and regulations that govern AI use, including those related to privacy, discrimination, and consumer protection.

Social Acceptance: Promoting the social acceptance of AI technologies by demonstrating commitment to ethical principles and responsibility.

Pathways to Enhancing Transparency and Accountability

Several strategies can enhance transparency and accountability in AI:

Explainable AI (XAI): Developing AI systems that can explain their decision-making processes in understandable terms is crucial for transparency (Gunning et al., 2019).

Ethical Guidelines and Standards: Adopting ethical guidelines and standards for AI development and use can help ensure that AI systems are designed with transparency and accountability in mind.

Regulatory Frameworks: Implementing regulatory frameworks that mandate transparency and accountability in AI can provide a legal basis for these principles.

Stakeholder Engagement: Engaging with stakeholders, including users, ethicists, and policymakers, in the AI development process can ensure that diverse perspectives are considered, and ethical considerations are integrated into AI systems.

Transparency and accountability stand as pillars of ethical AI development, essential for building trust, ensuring ethical use, and fostering social acceptance of AI technologies. As "OpenAI: Exploring the World of Artificial Intelligence" elucidates, navigating the challenges associated with these principles requires a multifaceted approach that balances technical innovation with ethical responsibility. By prioritizing transparency and accountability, the development of AI can proceed in a manner that respects and upholds societal values and individual rights.

Autonomy and Human Dignity

As AI systems become more autonomous, questions arise about the impact on human dignity and agency. Ensuring that AI enhances human decision-making without undermining autonomy is essential for respecting individual dignity and freedom (Bryson, 2018).

The Concept of Autonomy in the Age of AI

Autonomy, in the context of AI, refers to the capacity of individuals to make independent choices and control their personal and professional lives. The advent of AI technologies, while offering unprecedented opportunities for enhancing human decision-making, also poses potential threats to autonomy. AI-driven decision-making systems, if not carefully designed and regulated, can lead to situations where individuals' choices are overly influenced, or even predetermined, by algorithmic suggestions, thus eroding personal agency (Bostrom & Yudkowsky, 2014).

Human Dignity and AI

Human dignity pertains to the inherent worth of every individual, which warrants respect and ethical consideration in all aspects of life, including interactions with AI technologies. Concerns arise when AI systems, through surveillance, data collection, or decision-making processes, treat individuals as mere data points, thereby dehumanizing them and undermining their dignity. Furthermore, AI applications in areas such as predictive policing or automated social scoring systems can reinforce societal biases, disproportionately impacting marginalized communities and infringing upon their dignity (Crawford & Calo, 2016).

Challenges to Autonomy and Human Dignity

The integration of AI into various sectors introduces several challenges to maintaining autonomy and human dignity:

Surveillance and Privacy: The use of AI in surveillance technologies can lead to invasive monitoring of individuals' activities, infringing on privacy and autonomy (Zuboff, 2019).

Automated Decision-Making: AI systems making decisions in healthcare, employment, and justice can limit human involvement in critical choices, potentially diminishing individual agency and accountability (Mittelstadt, 2016).

Bias and Discrimination: AI algorithms can perpetuate or amplify biases present in their training data, leading to discriminatory outcomes that violate principles of dignity and equality (Barocas & Selbst, 2016).

Safeguarding Autonomy and Human Dignity

To address these challenges, a multi-faceted approach is required:

Ethical AI Design: Incorporating ethical considerations into the design phase of AI development can ensure that systems respect human autonomy and dignity. This involves creating algorithms that are transparent, explainable, and capable of recognizing the complex nuances of human values (Dignum, 2019).

Regulatory Frameworks: Implementing comprehensive legal frameworks that govern the use of AI, focusing on protecting privacy, preventing discrimination, and ensuring that AI systems are used in ways that enhance rather than undermine human autonomy and dignity.

Public Engagement and Education: Fostering a well-informed public dialogue on the ethical implications of AI, and promoting digital literacy, can empower individuals to make informed decisions about their engagement with AI technologies.

The societal impacts of AI technologies on autonomy and human dignity are profound and multifaceted, necessitating diligent consideration and action from developers, policymakers, and society at large. As highlighted in "OpenAI: Exploring the World of Artificial Intelligence," the advancement of AI must be guided by ethical principles that prioritize the preservation of human autonomy and dignity. Through ethical AI development, comprehensive regulatory oversight, and engaged public discourse, it is possible to harness the benefits of AI while safeguarding these fundamental ethical values.

Environmental Impact

The environmental impact of training large AI models, which requires significant computational resources and energy, has emerged as an ethical consideration. Sustainable AI development practices are necessary to mitigate the carbon footprint of AI research and applications (Strubell, Ganesh, & McCallum, 2019).

The Environmental Footprint of AI

AI technologies, particularly those involving deep learning and large-scale data processing, require substantial computational resources. The training of complex AI models demands extensive use of energy-intensive data centers, which contribute to carbon emissions and environmental degradation. For instance, the training of a single AI model can emit as much carbon as five cars over their lifetimes (Strubell, Ganesh, & McCallum, 2019). As the demand for more advanced AI systems grows, so does the environmental impact associated with their development and operation.

Ethical Considerations in Reducing Environmental Impact

The ethical considerations surrounding the environmental impact of AI development are multifaceted. They involve reconciling the benefits of AI technologies with their ecological costs, ensuring sustainable development practices, and addressing the unequal distribution of environmental burdens. Ethical AI development thus requires a commitment to:

Sustainability: Integrating sustainable practices into AI research and development to minimize environmental degradation.

Transparency: Disclosing the environmental impact of AI systems to inform stakeholders and the public.

Equity: Ensuring that the environmental costs of AI technologies do not disproportionately affect marginalized communities and developing regions.

Challenges in Mitigating the Environmental Impact of AI

Mitigating the environmental impact of AI technologies presents several challenges:

Energy Efficiency: Improving the energy efficiency of AI systems and data centers is essential but difficult, given the rapid pace of AI advancements and the increasing computational demands of complex models.

Renewable Energy Sources: Transitioning to renewable energy sources for powering data centers is crucial but requires significant investment and infrastructure development.

Lifecycle Analysis: Conducting comprehensive lifecycle analyses of AI systems to understand and reduce their total environmental impact involves complex assessments that are not yet standardized.

Strategies for Environmental Responsibility in AI Development

Adopting strategies for environmentally responsible AI development is imperative to address the ecological challenges posed by AI technologies:

Green AI Initiatives: Promoting "Green AI" initiatives that focus on creating more energy-efficient algorithms and reducing the computational resources required for AI training and operation (Schwartz et al., 2020).

Use of Renewable Energy: Encouraging AI research facilities and data centers to utilize renewable energy sources, thereby reducing carbon emissions associated with AI development.

Optimization of AI Model Training: Implementing practices that optimize the training of AI models to require fewer computational resources, such as transfer learning and model pruning.

Regulatory Frameworks and Incentives: Developing regulatory frameworks that incentivize the adoption of environmentally sustainable practices in AI development and deployment.

Conclusion

The environmental impact of AI technologies is a critical consideration within the broader discourse on the societal impacts and ethical dimensions of AI, as highlighted in "OpenAI: Exploring the World of Artificial Intelligence." Addressing this issue requires a concerted effort from AI researchers, developers, policymakers, and the global community to ensure that the advancement of AI technologies is aligned with principles of environmental sustainability and responsibility. By adopting sustainable practices, optimizing computational efficiencies, and leveraging renewable energy sources, the AI community can mitigate the ecological footprint of AI technologies and contribute to a more sustainable future.

The societal impacts and ethical considerations associated with OpenAI's advancements in AI underscore the complexity of integrating these technologies into the fabric of society. Balancing the benefits of AI with its potential risks requires a concerted effort among developers, policymakers, and society at large to ensure that AI technologies are developed and deployed in a manner that upholds ethical principles, promotes social good, and mitigates adverse effects.

AI and Bias:

The exploration of societal impacts and ethical considerations extends to the critical issue of bias within artificial intelligence (AI) systems. Bias in AI, an unintended and often harmful side effect of the data and algorithms that power these systems, poses significant challenges to fairness, equality, and justice in society.

Understanding AI and Bias

Bias in AI refers to systematic and unfair discrimination against certain individuals or groups. This bias can manifest in various forms, including but not limited to racial, gender, socioeconomic, and age-based discrimination. The sources of bias are multifarious, often stemming from biased training data, flawed algorithms, or the misinterpretation of AI outputs by humans. These biases can lead to discriminatory outcomes in critical areas such as employment, law enforcement, credit lending, and healthcare, undermining ethical standards and societal values of fairness and equality (Barocas, Hardt, & Narayanan, 2019).

The Genesis of AI-induced Bias

Bias in AI systems predominantly originates from the data used in training algorithms. Data, inherently a reflection of historical, cultural, and societal norms, can embed prejudices and stereotypes that AI systems may learn and perpetuate (Barocas & Selbst, 2016). For instance, if an AI model for hiring is trained on historical employment data that reflects gender imbalance in certain professions, the model may inherently favor one gender over another, thereby perpetuating existing biases. The mechanisms of bias in AI are thus closely tied to the data selection, preparation, and processing stages of AI development.

Multifaceted Challenges of Bias in AI

The challenges posed by bias in AI are diverse, impacting not only the fairness and integrity of AI systems but also their acceptance and effectiveness in society. Bias in AI can lead to discriminatory outcomes, erode public trust in AI technologies, and exacerbate social inequalities. Moreover, the opaque nature of some AI algorithms, particularly those involving deep learning, can make detecting and addressing biases exceedingly difficult, further complicating efforts to ensure fairness and equity in AI-driven decisions (Burrell, 2016).

Strategies for Mitigating Bias in AI

Mitigating bias in AI encompasses a broad spectrum of strategies, from technical interventions to regulatory and ethical frameworks. These strategies include:

Enhancing Data Diversity and Representation

Ensuring that training datasets are diverse and representative of all relevant demographics is crucial in mitigating bias. This involves not only including a wide range of data but also carefully considering the context and weighting of different data points to avoid reinforcing existing disparities (Mehrabi et al., 2019).

Developing Transparent and Explainable AI Systems

Enhancing the transparency and explainability of AI systems allows for a better understanding of how decisions are made, facilitating the identification and rectification of biases. Techniques in explainable AI (XAI) aim to make the workings of AI algorithms more accessible to users and stakeholders, thereby promoting accountability and trust (Gunning et al., 2019).

Implementing Continuous Monitoring and Evaluation

Bias in AI is not a static issue but a dynamic one that evolves with changes in data, societal norms, and application contexts. Continuous monitoring and evaluation of AI systems for biased outcomes are essential for ensuring that biases are promptly identified and addressed throughout the lifecycle of an AI system.

Adopting Ethical Guidelines and Regulatory Standards

The development and enforcement of ethical guidelines and regulatory standards specific to AI development can provide a structured approach to addressing bias. These guidelines and standards can outline best practices for data management, algorithm design, and system deployment to ensure fairness and equity in AI (Jobin, Ienca, & Vayena, 2019).

Fostering Multidisciplinary Collaboration

Addressing bias in AI is a complex challenge that benefits from a multidisciplinary approach, incorporating insights from computer science, social sciences, ethics, and law. Collaboration across these disciplines can enhance the understanding of bias and contribute to the development of more equitable AI systems.

Understanding AI and bias reveals the intricate challenges and essential strategies for mitigating bias within AI technologies. Addressing bias in AI is imperative for ensuring that AI systems are fair, equitable, and effective in serving society. Through a comprehensive and nuanced approach that includes enhancing data diversity, developing transparent AI systems, implementing continuous monitoring, adopting ethical guidelines, and fostering multidisciplinary collaboration, the goal of minimizing bias in AI can be progressively achieved.

Challenges Presented by Bias in AI

The challenges posed by bias in AI are profound and wide-ranging. Firstly, there is the issue of identifying and measuring bias, which is complicated by the opaque nature of many AI algorithms and the diverse manifestations of bias. Additionally, the mitigation of bias is not straightforward, as efforts to correct for one form of bias can inadvertently introduce or exacerbate another. Furthermore, the dynamic and evolving nature of societal norms and values makes the definition of fairness in AI a moving target, complicating the development of universally applicable solutions (Mittelstadt, 2016).

Origins and Perpetuation of Bias in AI

Bias in AI predominantly originates from the data used in training algorithms. This data, reflective of historical and societal inequities, can lead AI systems to perpetuate or even exacerbate these biases (Barocas & Selbst, 2016). For example, AI technologies in facial recognition have shown lower accuracy rates for women and people of color, illustrating how biases in training datasets can lead to discriminatory outcomes (Buolamwini & Gebru, 2018). Such instances reveal the intricate challenge of ensuring that AI systems do not inherit or amplify the biases present in their training data.

Challenges in Identifying and Measuring Bias

One of the primary challenges in addressing bias in AI is the difficulty in identifying and quantifying bias. The complex and often opaque nature of AI algorithms, particularly those involving deep learning, makes it challenging to discern how decisions are made and to pinpoint the source of biased outcomes (Burrell, 2016). This opacity complicates efforts to audit and rectify biased AI systems, requiring advanced methodologies and tools to uncover and understand biases.

Socio-Technical Implications of Bias

The implications of bias in AI extend beyond technical challenges, affecting various aspects of societal functioning and individual rights. Biased AI systems can lead to unfair treatment across a range of applications, from hiring and law enforcement to healthcare and financial services, disproportionately impacting marginalized groups (O'Neil, 2016). Such biases threaten to reinforce existing social inequalities and undermine the potential of AI technologies to contribute to a more equitable society.

Ethical Considerations and Accountability

The presence of bias in AI raises profound ethical considerations regarding fairness, justice, and accountability. Ensuring that AI systems operate in an equitable manner involves ethical dilemmas about the responsibilities of AI developers, the rights of affected individuals, and the mechanisms for redress in cases of harm caused by biased AI decisions (Mittelstadt, 2016). Establishing accountability in the development and deployment of AI systems is critical to addressing ethical concerns and fostering trust in AI technologies.

Mitigation Strategies: A Multifaceted Approach

Mitigating bias in AI requires a multifaceted approach that addresses the technical, ethical, and social dimensions of the issue. Strategies for mitigation include improving the diversity and representativeness of training datasets, enhancing the transparency and explainability of AI algorithms, implementing continuous monitoring for biased outcomes, and developing ethical guidelines and regulatory frameworks to govern AI development (Jobin, Ienca, & Vayena, 2019). Furthermore, fostering collaboration among AI researchers, ethicists, policymakers, and affected communities is essential for developing comprehensive solutions to bias in AI.

The challenges presented by bias in AI underscore the need for diligent attention to the ethical and societal implications of AI technologies. Addressing bias in AI involves confronting the complex interplay between technology and society, requiring concerted efforts to ensure that AI systems are developed and deployed in a manner that respects principles of fairness and equity.

Mitigation Strategies for Bias in AI

Data Diversity and Representation

One primary approach to mitigating bias involves ensuring that the data used to train AI systems are diverse and representative of the broader population. This includes actively seeking out and including underrepresented groups in training datasets and employing techniques to balance datasets and correct for known biases (Buolamwini & Gebru, 2018).

Algorithmic Fairness

Developing and implementing algorithms that are explicitly designed to be fair is another critical strategy. This might involve the application of fairness constraints or objectives during the algorithmic training process, ensuring that the system does not produce discriminatory outcomes against any group (Hardt, Price, & Srebro, 2016).

Transparency and Explainability

Enhancing the transparency and explainability of AI systems is crucial for identifying and addressing bias. By making AI systems more interpretable, stakeholders can better understand how decisions are made and identify potential sources of bias. This transparency is essential for accountability and trust in AI systems (Ribeiro, Singh, & Guestrin, 2016).

Continuous Monitoring and Evaluation

Ongoing monitoring and evaluation of AI systems in deployment are essential for detecting and correcting biases that may emerge over time. This involves regular assessment of AI outcomes across different demographic groups and adjusting the system as necessary to ensure equitable outcomes.

Ethical and Regulatory Frameworks

Developing comprehensive ethical guidelines and regulatory frameworks that mandate fairness in AI is vital. This includes the establishment of standards for ethical AI development and the implementation of legal requirements for fairness and nondiscrimination in AI applications (Jobin, Ienca, & Vayena, 2019).

Conclusion

The challenges of bias in AI, highlight the need for concerted efforts to ensure that AI technologies promote fairness and do not perpetuate or exacerbate societal inequalities. Mitigating bias requires a multifaceted approach, including enhancing data diversity, ensuring algorithmic fairness, improving transparency, conducting ongoing monitoring, and adhering to ethical and regulatory standards. By addressing these challenges head-on, the development and deployment of AI can be aligned with the principles of justice and equality, ensuring that AI serves as a force for good in society.

AI and Privacy:

The discourse on societal impacts and ethical considerations critically examines the intricate balance between the relentless pursuit of innovation in artificial intelligence (AI) and the imperative need for data protection. As AI technologies increasingly permeate every facet of society, from healthcare and education to finance and entertainment, the collection, analysis, and utilization of vast amounts of personal data have raised significant privacy concerns.

The Conundrum of AI and Privacy

The advent of AI technologies has ushered in unprecedented capabilities for data processing, enabling the extraction of valuable insights that can drive innovation and economic growth. However, this often comes at the cost of collecting and analyzing personal data, sometimes without explicit consent or adequate transparency, leading to potential infringements on privacy (Zuboff, 2019). The utilization of AI in predictive analytics, personalized services, and surveillance technologies exemplifies the tension between harnessing the power of AI for societal benefits and safeguarding individual privacy.

The Dual-edged Sword of AI and Privacy

AI technologies offer the potential for significant advancements in healthcare, security, education, and more, by leveraging data to create more efficient, personalized, and intelligent systems. However, the very data that fuels these advancements also encompasses sensitive personal information, thereby raising substantial privacy concerns. The extraction and analysis of personal data by AI systems often occur without explicit consent or awareness of the individuals involved, leading to potential breaches of privacy and autonomy (Zuboff, 2019).

Ethical Considerations in Data Usage

The ethical landscape surrounding AI and privacy is complex, encompassing issues of consent, transparency, and the right to privacy. Ethical frameworks for AI development increasingly emphasize the importance of obtaining informed consent from individuals whose data is being used, ensuring that they are aware of how their information is being collected, processed, and utilized. Moreover, the principle of transparency mandates that AI systems disclose the methodologies behind their data processing, allowing individuals to understand and potentially contest decisions made by AI that affect them (Floridi & Cowls, 2019).

Challenges in Balancing Innovation with Privacy

One of the primary challenges in reconciling AI development with privacy protection is the inherent need for AI systems to access and analyze large quantities of data. This requirement often conflicts with data minimization principles, which advocate for limiting data collection to what is strictly necessary for specific purposes. Furthermore, the predictive capabilities of AI, while beneficial in many contexts, can inadvertently lead to privacy infringements by revealing sensitive information that individuals may not have chosen to disclose (Mittelstadt, 2016).

Regulatory and Policy Responses

Governments and regulatory bodies worldwide have begun to address the privacy implications of AI through legislation such as the General Data Protection Regulation (GDPR) in the European Union, which sets forth comprehensive rules for data protection and privacy. Such regulations aim to provide a legal framework that safeguards personal privacy while still allowing for the beneficial use of AI technologies. They emphasize principles like data protection by design, the necessity of consent, and the rights of individuals to access, rectify, and erase their data (Regulation (EU) 2016/679).

Forward-looking Strategies for Privacy Preservation

To navigate the conundrum of AI and privacy, several forward-looking strategies have been proposed. These include enhancing algorithmic accountability to ensure that AI systems make decisions in an ethical and transparent manner, employing privacy-preserving technologies such as differential privacy and federated learning, and fostering public discourse on the acceptable use of AI in relation to privacy. Moreover, engaging in multidisciplinary research that combines insights from computer science, ethics, law, and social sciences is crucial for developing AI technologies that respect and protect individual privacy (Taddeo & Floridi, 2018).

Ethical and Societal Implications

The ethical implications of AI's impact on privacy are profound, touching on issues of consent, autonomy, and trust. At the heart of these concerns is the principle of autonomy, the right of individuals to control their personal information and make informed decisions about its use (Taylor, Floridi, & van der Sloot, 2017). The erosion of privacy undermines this autonomy, potentially leading to a society where surveillance and data-driven manipulation are rampant, eroding trust in AI technologies and their developers.

Ethical Frameworks in AI and Privacy

The ethical considerations surrounding AI and privacy are grounded in several key ethical frameworks that emphasize respect for autonomy, beneficence, non-maleficence, and justice (Beauchamp & Childress, 2013). These principles underscore the importance of ensuring that AI technologies are developed and deployed in ways that respect individual privacy, prevent harm, and contribute positively to society. The principle of autonomy, in particular, highlights the right of individuals to control their personal information and make informed decisions regarding its use. Beneficence and non-maleficence require that AI technologies are designed to benefit individuals and society while minimizing potential harms, including infringements on privacy. Justice ensures that the benefits and burdens of AI technologies are distributed equitably, preventing disproportionate impacts on vulnerable populations.

Societal Implications of AI-driven Data Collection

The societal implications of AI-driven data collection and processing are profound, affecting notions of privacy, autonomy, and trust. As AI systems become more integrated into everyday life, the collection of personal data has escalated, often transcending traditional privacy boundaries. This extensive data collection, while enabling personalized services and efficiency gains, also raises concerns about surveillance, data ownership, and the potential for misuse of personal information (Zuboff, 2019). The erosion of privacy can lead to a diminution of individual autonomy, as personal choices and behaviors become increasingly influenced and predicted by AI algorithms. Furthermore, the potential for mass surveillance facilitated by AI technologies poses significant threats to democratic freedoms and individual liberties.

Challenges in Balancing Innovation with Data Protection

Balancing the advancement of AI with the protection of individual privacy presents several challenges. One primary challenge is the trade-off between the utility derived from AI technologies and the potential privacy risks associated with the data these technologies require. Additionally, the global nature of data flows complicates regulatory efforts, as differing privacy standards and regulations across jurisdictions can create compliance challenges for AI developers and users. The rapid pace of AI innovation further exacerbates these challenges, as existing legal and ethical frameworks struggle to keep pace with technological advancements.

Strategies for Addressing Ethical and Societal Concerns

Addressing the ethical and societal concerns related to AI and privacy necessitates a multi-stakeholder approach that includes policymakers, technologists, ethicists, and the public. Strategies for mitigating privacy risks while fostering AI innovation include:

Implementing Robust Data Protection Regulations: Strong legal frameworks, such as the General Data Protection Regulation (GDPR) in the European Union, provide comprehensive guidelines for data protection, emphasizing principles like consent, data minimization, and individuals' rights over their data (Regulation (EU) 2016/679).

Advancing Privacy-Enhancing Technologies: The development and adoption of privacy-enhancing technologies (PETs), such as encryption, differential privacy, and federated learning, can help minimize privacy risks while enabling valuable data analysis.

Fostering Transparency and Public Engagement: Enhancing transparency around AI technologies and engaging the public in discussions about privacy and data protection can help build trust and ensure that AI development aligns with societal values and expectations.

Ethical frameworks and strategies for mitigating privacy risks are crucial in ensuring that AI development proceeds in a manner that respects individual privacy and promotes societal well-being. As AI continues to evolve, ongoing dialogue, regulatory adaptation, and technological innovation will be essential in upholding ethical principles and protecting privacy in the digital age.

Challenges in Balancing Innovation with Data Protection

Balancing the drive for AI innovation with the need for data protection presents several challenges:

Data Collection and Consent: Obtaining meaningful consent for data collection in an AI-driven world is increasingly complex, given the opaque nature of AI algorithms and the broad scope of data processing activities.

Data Minimization: The principle of data minimization — collecting only the data necessary for a specific purpose — is at odds with the AI paradigm, which benefits from access to vast datasets to improve accuracy and functionality.

Algorithmic Transparency: Ensuring transparency in AI algorithms is crucial for privacy protection but can conflict with proprietary interests and the technical complexities of explaining AI decision-making processes.

Strategies for Ensuring Privacy Protection

To navigate the delicate balance between AI innovation and privacy protection, several strategies can be employed:

Privacy by Design: Integrating privacy considerations into the development and deployment of AI systems from the outset can ensure that privacy protection is a fundamental component of AI technologies (Cavoukian, 2009).

Enhanced Regulatory Frameworks: Robust regulatory frameworks that specifically address the unique challenges of AI and data privacy are essential. The General Data Protection Regulation (GDPR) in the European Union serves as a pioneering example, providing comprehensive guidelines for data protection in the digital age (Regulation (EU) 2016/679).

Ethical AI Development: Adopting ethical guidelines for AI development that prioritize privacy, informed consent, and transparency can help align AI innovation with societal values. This includes the development of explainable AI (XAI) systems that provide insights into data usage and decision-making processes.

Public Engagement and Awareness: Fostering public awareness and engagement on issues of AI and privacy is crucial for ensuring informed consent and fostering a culture of accountability among AI developers and users.

Conclusion

Balancing the pursuit of AI innovation with the protection of privacy necessitates a holistic approach that incorporates ethical AI development, robust regulatory frameworks, and active engagement with societal stakeholders. By navigating these challenges with a commitment to ethical principles and societal welfare, it is possible to harness the benefits of AI technologies while safeguarding individual privacy rights.

AI and Job Displacement

Ethical Imperatives in AI-Induced Job Displacement

The advent of AI and its propensity for automating tasks presents a significant ethical conundrum, intertwining the pursuit of technological progress with the fundamental principles of fairness and social justice. The ethical imperative lies in addressing the dual realities of AI: its potential to drive innovation and productivity versus its capacity to disrupt labor markets and exacerbate socioeconomic disparities. Central to this ethical discourse is the consideration of how AI-driven changes in the workforce align with broader societal values and the collective vision for a future where technology augments human potential without diminishing job security and quality of life (Schwartz, 2019).

Ethical Frameworks Guiding AI Development and Deployment

The ethical challenges posed by AI and job displacement necessitate an adherence to established ethical frameworks that emphasize respect for human dignity, fairness, and the promotion of societal welfare. Central to these frameworks is the principle of justice, which demands equitable distribution of the benefits and burdens of AI technologies across society. Moreover, the principle of beneficence calls for actions that promote the welfare of individuals and communities, guiding AI development towards outcomes that enhance societal well-being rather than detract from it (Beauchamp & Childress, 2013).

The Ethical Imperative of Fairness in Employment Transition

The displacement of jobs by AI technologies underscores an ethical imperative to ensure fairness in the employment transition process. Fairness, in this context, involves providing equitable opportunities for re-skilling and up-skilling, ensuring that displaced workers have access to resources and training programs that enable them to adapt to the evolving labor market. Furthermore, fairness demands transparency in how decisions regarding AI deployment are made, ensuring that workers are informed and consulted about changes that may impact their employment (Rawls, 1971).

Equity and the Distribution of Technological Benefits

Equity in the distribution of the benefits of AI technologies is a critical ethical consideration. This requires attention to how advancements in AI can be leveraged to create new job opportunities and foster economic growth in a manner that benefits society broadly, rather than exacerbating existing socioeconomic disparities. Ensuring equity involves proactive measures to identify and support communities and sectors most vulnerable to job displacement, thereby mitigating potential inequalities arising from the differential impacts of AI (Sen, 2009).

The Role of Policy in Safeguarding Ethical Imperatives

Policymakers play a crucial role in safeguarding the ethical imperatives associated with AI-induced job displacement. This entails the development of comprehensive policies that address the challenges of the transition, such as social safety nets for displaced workers, incentives for businesses to invest in human capital, and regulations that encourage ethical AI development practices. Additionally, policies must be adaptable and responsive to the rapid pace of AI advancements, ensuring that ethical considerations remain central to the regulatory landscape (Bostrom & Yudkowsky, 2014).

Collaborative Efforts Toward Ethical AI Development

Addressing the ethical imperatives in AI-induced job displacement necessitates collaborative efforts among AI developers, businesses, educational institutions, and governments. This collaboration should aim to foster an ecosystem where AI technologies are developed and deployed responsibly, with a focus on maximizing societal benefits while minimizing harm. Engaging in dialogue with affected communities and stakeholders can also provide valuable insights into the ethical considerations and challenges of workforce transition, informing more inclusive and equitable AI development strategies (Floridi, 2018).

The discourse on AI and job displacement illuminates the profound ethical imperatives that underpin the intersection of AI advancements and workforce dynamics. Addressing these imperatives demands a concerted effort to balance the pursuit of technological innovation with the principles of fairness, equity, and justice, ensuring that the evolution of AI contributes positively to the welfare of all members of society.

Societal Ramifications of Workforce Automation

AI's impact on the workforce transcends mere economic metrics, embedding itself deeply within the social fabric. The displacement of jobs due to automation risks creating a dichotomous labor market, where there is a stark divide between those who possess the skills to thrive in a technologically advanced economy and those who are left behind. This polarization not only threatens individual livelihoods but also challenges societal cohesion, as increasing segments of the population find themselves marginalized in the face of relentless technological advancement (Frey & Osborne, 2017).

Economic Impacts of Workforce Automation

The economic ramifications of workforce automation are profound, with AI technologies reshaping labor markets, productivity, and income distribution. On one hand, automation can lead to increased efficiency and productivity, potentially generating new economic opportunities and markets (Autor, 2015). However, the displacement of jobs by AI and automation raises concerns about job loss, income inequality, and the potential for a polarized labor market where the gap widens between high-skill, high-wage jobs and low-skill, low-wage jobs (Frey & Osborne, 2017). The challenge lies in harnessing the economic benefits of AI while mitigating adverse effects on employment and ensuring equitable economic growth.

Social Implications of AI-induced Job Displacement

The social implications of AI-induced job displacement extend beyond economic considerations, affecting social cohesion, identity, and well-being. Employment is not only a source of income but also a critical component of individual identity and societal structure. The loss of employment due to automation can lead to social isolation, decreased psychological well-being, and increased stress levels among affected individuals (De Stefano, 2020). Furthermore, the risk of job displacement disproportionately affects certain demographic groups and sectors, potentially exacerbating existing social inequalities and leading to societal fragmentation.

Ethical Considerations in the Transition to an Automated Workforce

The transition to an automated workforce raises essential ethical considerations regarding fairness, justice, and the rights of workers. The ethical imperative to treat employees with dignity and fairness demands proactive measures to support those displaced by AI technologies. This includes ensuring access to education and re-skilling programs, providing adequate social protection, and fostering inclusive participation in the benefits of AI advancements (Mittelstadt, 2016). Moreover, ethical considerations extend to the decision-making processes surrounding the implementation of AI in the workplace, emphasizing transparency, stakeholder engagement, and the prioritization of human-centric values in the deployment of automation technologies.

Strategies for Navigating Societal Ramifications

Addressing the societal ramifications of workforce automation necessitates comprehensive strategies that involve stakeholders across the public and private sectors:

Investment in Education and Lifelong Learning: Enhancing education systems to focus on skills that are complementary to AI and automation, including critical thinking, creativity, and interpersonal skills, is crucial. Lifelong learning and continuous skill development should be promoted as central pillars of workforce adaptation (Schwab, 2016).

Social Protection and Support Measures: Implementing robust social protection measures, such as unemployment benefits, income support, and career transition services, can mitigate the negative impacts of job displacement and support individuals in navigating the transition to new employment opportunities.

Inclusive Economic Policies: Developing inclusive economic policies that stimulate job creation in emerging sectors and ensure equitable access to the benefits of AI-driven growth is essential for mitigating income inequality and promoting social cohesion.

Ethical AI Development and Deployment: Encouraging ethical AI development and deployment practices that consider the potential impacts on employment and work actively to minimize harm and maximize societal benefits.

The societal ramifications of workforce automation, underscore the complex interplay between technological innovation and its impacts on the labor market and society at large. Navigating these challenges requires a multidisciplinary approach that balances economic efficiency with social equity and ethical considerations, ensuring that the advancement of AI technologies contributes positively to the future of work and societal well-being.

Addressing Workforce Challenges: Strategies and Solutions

Navigating the workforce challenges posed by AI and job displacement requires a multi-dimensional strategy that encompasses education, policy intervention, and ethical AI development.

Promoting Educational and Skills Development

A cornerstone strategy in mitigating job displacement is investing in education and skills development tailored to the evolving demands of an AI-driven economy. Emphasizing STEM education, critical thinking, and lifelong learning can equip individuals with the agility to adapt to new job roles and sectors. Furthermore, fostering digital literacy across the workforce is imperative in ensuring broad-based participation in the technological landscape (Bughin et al., 2018).

Policy Interventions for Economic Adaptation and Social Protection

Policy interventions play a pivotal role in facilitating economic adaptation to AI-induced job displacement. This includes crafting policies that encourage innovation and investment in AI technologies while implementing social protection measures for displaced workers. Strategies such as universal basic income, unemployment insurance, and job transition programs can provide a safety net for those affected by automation. Additionally, policies promoting job creation in emerging sectors can help absorb the workforce displaced from traditional roles (Autor, 2015).

Ethical Development and Deployment of AI Technologies

Ensuring the ethical development and deployment of AI technologies is crucial in addressing workforce challenges. This involves transparency in AI algorithms, consideration of the societal impacts of automation, and active engagement with stakeholders, including workers, employers, and policymakers. Ethical AI development also necessitates mechanisms for accountability, ensuring that AI technologies are used in ways that promote societal well-being and equitable economic outcomes (Mittelstadt, 2016).

By aligning technological advancement with ethical considerations, educational initiatives, and robust policy frameworks, society can harness the potential of AI to enhance economic productivity and innovation while safeguarding against the risks of workforce displacement and social inequality.

AI and Creativity:

The discourse on societal impacts and ethical considerations in delves into the nuanced exploration of artificial intelligence (AI) and its intersection with creativity, focusing on the evolving boundaries of machine and human collaboration. As AI technologies advance, their capacity to engage in creative processes traditionally viewed as the exclusive domain of human intellect raises profound questions about the nature of creativity, the future of artistic and creative industries, and the implications for human-machine collaboration.

The Emergence of AI in Creative Domains

AI's foray into creative domains has been marked by significant advancements in machine learning and computational creativity, enabling AI systems to generate art, music, literature, and designs that resonate with human sensibilities (Boden, 2010). Projects like OpenAI's GPT series have showcased the ability of AI to produce coherent and imaginative textual outputs, challenging preconceived notions about the limits of machine-generated creativity. This emergence of AI as a creative entity not only expands the horizons of what can be achieved through human-machine collaboration but also prompts a reevaluation of creativity itself.

Technological Advancements Facilitating AI's Role in Creativity

The advent of sophisticated machine learning algorithms and computational creativity has been instrumental in enabling AI's foray into creative domains. Techniques such as generative adversarial networks (GANs) and deep learning models have allowed AI systems to generate artworks, compose music, write poetry, and even create novel designs that resonate with human aesthetics and sensibilities (Goodfellow et al., 2014). These advancements not only demonstrate AI's capability to produce creative outputs but also highlight the potential for AI to augment human creativity, offering tools and insights that can enhance the creative process.

AI in Art and Music

In the realm of art and music, AI has made significant inroads, challenging traditional boundaries and offering new perspectives on creative expression. Projects like Google's DeepDream and OpenAI's Jukebox exemplify how AI can be used to create visually stunning artworks and compose music across various genres, pushing the envelope of artistic possibilities (Engel et al., 2020). These endeavors showcase AI's ability to understand and replicate complex patterns, textures, and styles, contributing to the creation of novel and innovative art forms.

Literary Creativity and AI

AI's impact on literary creativity further illustrates the technology's potential to engage with and contribute to creative writing. AI algorithms have been developed to write poetry, short stories, and even entire novels, analyzing vast corpora of literary works to mimic styles and themes (Colton et al., 2012). While debates persist regarding the depth and emotional resonance of AI-generated literature, these developments underscore AI's capacity to participate in the narrative arts, offering new tools for storytelling and literary exploration.

Challenges and Opportunities in AI-driven Creativity

The emergence of AI in creative domains presents both challenges and opportunities. One of the primary challenges lies in the ethical and philosophical implications of machine-generated creativity, including questions of authorship, originality, and the value of AI-created works compared to those created by humans. Conversely, the integration of AI into creative processes opens up unprecedented opportunities for innovation and experimentation, enabling artists, musicians, and writers to explore new creative frontiers and collaborate with AI in crafting unique and compelling works.

As AI continues to evolve and integrate more deeply into creative endeavors, it challenges us to reconsider the essence of creativity and the potential for collaborative synergy between human and machine. By navigating the ethical considerations and embracing the opportunities presented by AI in creative domains, society stands on the cusp of a new era of artistic expression, enriched by the unique capabilities of artificial intelligence.

Rethinking Creativity: Machine and Human Collaboration

The collaboration between humans and AI in creative endeavors represents a paradigm shift in the conception of creativity. This collaboration challenges the traditional view of creativity as an inherently human attribute, suggesting instead a broader perspective that encompasses the generative capabilities of AI (Du Sautoy, 2019). AI's role in the creative process varies from serving as a tool that enhances human creativity to acting as an autonomous creator in its own right, raising questions about authorship, originality, and the value of creativity.

Evolution of Creativity in the AI Era

The advent of AI technologies capable of generating art, composing music, writing narratives, and more, heralds a new era in creative expression. Technologies such as generative adversarial networks (GANs) and natural language processing (NLP) algorithms have enabled machines to produce work that can mimic and even innovate upon human-created art (Goodfellow et al., 2014; Vaswani et al., 2017). This shift challenges the long-held belief that creativity is the sole province of human consciousness, suggesting instead that creativity can be augmented, and potentially expanded, through the computational prowess of AI.

The Synergy of Machine and Human Creativity

The collaboration between machine and human in creative pursuits introduces a symbiotic relationship where each entity contributes distinct advantages. Humans bring to this partnership an irreplaceable depth of emotional insight, contextual understanding, and subjective experience. AI, in contrast, offers unparalleled processing power, pattern recognition capabilities, and the ability to assimilate and analyze vast datasets. This collaboration has the potential to enhance human creativity, providing artists with new tools and insights that can spur innovation and expand the boundaries of traditional creative practices (Du Sautoy, 2019).

Ethical and Societal Implications

As AI becomes a more prominent collaborator in creative endeavors, ethical and societal implications emerge, particularly regarding the authenticity, ownership, and value of AI-generated content. Questions arise about the role of AI in the creative process: Is AI merely a tool, or can it be considered a co-creator? Moreover, the democratization of creative tools poses both opportunities for widespread creative expression and challenges related to the dilution of artistic merit and the potential for copyright infringement (Boden, 2010).

Additionally, the potential for AI to replicate and perpetuate societal biases through its creations underscores the need for careful consideration and ethical oversight in the development of creative AI technologies. Ensuring that AI systems are trained on diverse, unbiased datasets is critical to fostering creativity that enriches cultural landscapes rather than narrows them.

Navigating the Future of Creativity

The intersection of AI and creativity necessitates a nuanced approach that recognizes the value of machine and human collaboration while addressing the ethical concerns that accompany this partnership. Developing frameworks for copyright and ownership that acknowledge both human and machine contributions to creative works, implementing measures to ensure diversity and equity in AI-generated content, and fostering public discourse on the role of AI in creative domains are essential steps in navigating this evolving landscape.

This paradigm shift not only expands the tools available for creative expression but also raises profound questions about the nature of artistry, the role of technology in augmenting human potential, and the ethical considerations inherent in these advancements. As society ventures further into this collaboration, the challenge lies in harnessing the benefits of AI to enhance human creativity while ensuring that ethical principles guide the integration of AI into the fabric of cultural and artistic expression.

Societal Impacts of AI-driven Creativity

The societal impacts of AI-driven creativity are multifaceted, influencing artistic expression, cultural production, and the creative economy. AI-generated art and music open new avenues for artistic exploration, democratizing creativity by providing tools that enable individuals to express themselves in novel ways. However, the proliferation of AI in creative industries also raises concerns about the displacement of human creators and the potential homogenization of cultural outputs. Furthermore, the accessibility of AI technologies for creative purposes entails ethical considerations regarding the misuse of these technologies for generating misleading or harmful content.

Democratization of Creativity

One of the most significant societal impacts of AI-driven creativity is the democratization of creative tools and processes. AI technologies have made it possible for individuals without formal training in art, music, or writing to engage in creative activities, thereby lowering barriers to entry and fostering a more inclusive creative landscape (Boden, 2010). This democratization allows for a broader expression of human experience and diversity, enriching the cultural tapestry with voices that were previously marginalized or unheard.

The Blurring of Artistic Boundaries

AI's involvement in creative processes challenges traditional notions of artistic boundaries and authorship. As AI algorithms generate art, compose music, or write poetry, questions arise regarding the nature of creativity and the origin of artistic inspiration. This blurring of boundaries prompts a societal rethinking of what constitutes art and creativity, pushing the envelope on conventional understandings and inviting debate on the value and authenticity of AI-generated works versus human-created works (Du Sautoy, 2019).

Economic Implications for Creative Industries

The integration of AI into creative industries also carries significant economic implications. On one hand, AI-driven creativity can lead to new market opportunities, fostering innovation and potentially creating new jobs in sectors that blend technology with creativity. On the other hand, there are concerns about job displacement within traditional creative roles, as AI technologies might perform tasks that were previously the domain of human artists, writers, and musicians (Frey & Osborne, 2017). This shift necessitates adaptive strategies to ensure that creative professionals can navigate the changing landscape, potentially through reskilling or by integrating AI tools into their creative processes.

Ethical Considerations and Cultural Impact

The deployment of AI in creative domains raises ethical considerations, particularly concerning the preservation of cultural heritage and diversity. There is a risk that AI-generated content could homogenize culture or replicate existing biases present in training data, thereby impacting cultural diversity (Bryson, 2018). Ensuring that AI-driven creativity respects and represents a wide array of cultural expressions is paramount to maintaining the richness and diversity of global cultures. Furthermore, the use of AI in creative processes prompts ethical questions regarding data privacy, intellectual property rights, and the potential misuse of AI technologies for deceptive or harmful purposes.

Navigating the Future of AI-driven Creativity

Addressing the societal impacts of AI-driven creativity requires a multidisciplinary approach that involves artists, technologists, ethicists, and policymakers. Developing frameworks that encourage ethical AI use in creative endeavors, promoting transparency in AI-generated works, and fostering dialogue on the societal implications of AI in creative fields are essential steps in navigating this evolving landscape. Encouraging collaboration between humans and AI in creative processes can lead to innovative artistic expressions that enrich society while ensuring that ethical and societal considerations are at the forefront of technological advancements in creativity.

As society navigates this evolving landscape, the imperative to balance innovation with ethical and societal considerations becomes increasingly apparent. Embracing the possibilities of AI-enhanced creativity while mindfully addressing the ethical, economic, and cultural implications is crucial in ensuring that the fusion of machine and human collaboration enriches the creative tapestry of society.

Ethical Considerations and Challenges

The intersection of AI and creativity is fraught with ethical considerations and challenges that necessitate careful navigation. Issues of copyright and intellectual property rights emerge prominently, as the determination of ownership over AI-generated works remains contentious (Bryson, 2018). The authenticity and value of AI-created art, as compared to human-created art, also pose ethical questions about what constitutes creativity and artistic merit. Moreover, the potential for AI to replicate and propagate cultural biases through its creations underscores the importance of ethical oversight in the development and application of creative AI technologies.

Ethical Considerations in AI-driven Creativity

Authorship and Ownership

One of the foremost ethical considerations in AI-driven creativity concerns the notions of authorship and ownership. As AI systems generate artworks, music, literature, and other creative outputs, questions arise about who holds the creative rights to these works—the programmers who designed the AI, the users who interacted with it, or the AI itself (Boden, 2010). This issue challenges existing intellectual property laws and norms, necessitating a reevaluation of copyright frameworks to accommodate the unique nature of AI-generated content.

Authenticity and Value

The authenticity and value of AI-generated creative works provoke significant ethical debate. There is a concern that the proliferation of

AI in creative domains may dilute the perceived value of human creativity, undermining the unique emotional, cultural, and experiential aspects that human artists bring to their creations (Du Sautoy, 2019). The ability of AI to replicate or mimic human creative styles also raises questions about the authenticity of creative works, challenging societal notions of originality and artistic integrity.

Cultural Appropriation and Homogenization

AI-driven creativity poses risks related to cultural appropriation and homogenization. AI systems trained on data from diverse cultural expressions may inadvertently create works that appropriate cultural symbols without understanding their significance or context (Bryson, 2018). Moreover, the reliance on large datasets for training AI can lead to the homogenization of creative outputs, potentially marginalizing underrepresented cultures and perspectives in the global creative landscape.

Bias and Representation

The potential for bias in AI-generated creative content represents a critical ethical challenge. AI systems, reflecting the biases inherent in their training data, may produce creative works that perpetuate stereotypes or exclude certain groups (Bolukbasi et al., 2016). Ensuring fair representation and combating bias in AI creativity necessitates vigilant oversight and the deliberate curation of diverse and inclusive datasets.

Navigating Ethical Challenges

To address the ethical challenges presented by AI and creativity, several considerations and strategies are proposed:

Developing Ethical Guidelines: Establishing comprehensive ethical guidelines for AI-driven creativity can help navigate issues of authorship, ownership, and copyright, ensuring that AI technologies are used in ways that respect human creativity and cultural diversity.

Promoting Transparency and Accountability: Enhancing transparency in AI algorithms and decision-making processes can foster accountability, enabling creators and users to understand how

AI-generated works are produced and ensuring ethical practices in AI development and deployment.

Fostering Cultural Sensitivity and Inclusivity: Incorporating cultural sensitivity and inclusivity into AI training datasets and creative processes can mitigate risks of cultural appropriation and homogenization, promoting a rich and diverse creative ecosystem.

Combating Bias: Implementing measures to identify and address biases in AI systems is crucial for ensuring fair representation in creative outputs, requiring continuous evaluation and refinement of AI models to reflect equitable and diverse perspectives.

Navigating this terrain demands a concerted effort to align AI-driven creativity with ethical principles, ensuring that the integration of AI in creative domains enriches the human experience, respects cultural diversity, and upholds the integrity of creative expression.

Navigating the Future of AI and Creativity

Navigating the future of AI and creativity requires a balanced approach that fosters innovation while addressing ethical and societal concerns. Encouraging interdisciplinary collaboration among artists, technologists, ethicists, and policymakers can lead to the development of frameworks that support ethical AI creativity. Education and public engagement are also crucial in shaping informed discourse on the implications of AI in creative domains, ensuring that society benefits from the opportunities presented by AI while safeguarding cultural diversity and artistic integrity.

Reinventing Creativity: AI's Role in the Creative Process

The integration of AI into the creative process represents a paradigm shift, offering new tools and methodologies that can enhance human creativity, spur innovation, and open up novel avenues for artistic expression (Du Sautoy, 2019). AI's ability to process vast amounts of data, identify patterns, and generate outputs based on learned algorithms enables it to contribute uniquely to creative tasks, from generating art and music to writing and design. However, as AI becomes a more integral part of the creative landscape, questions arise about the nature of creativity itself, the collaboration between human intuition and machine intelligence, and the value of AI-generated versus human-generated works.

Ethical Innovation and Cultural Considerations

Navigating the future of AI and creativity necessitates a keen focus on ethical innovation. Ethical considerations revolve around issues of authorship, copyright, and the authenticity of AI-generated works. There is also the critical challenge of ensuring that AI technologies do not inadvertently perpetuate biases or contribute to cultural homogenization but instead respect and reflect the rich diversity of human culture (Bryson, 2018). Addressing these concerns requires the development of ethical guidelines and frameworks that govern the use of AI in creative endeavors, promoting transparency, accountability, and inclusivity.

Fostering Human-AI Collaboration

The future of AI and creativity is not about machines supplanting human artists but rather about fostering a collaborative synergy that leverages the strengths of both. This collaboration can unlock new creative potentials, providing artists with AI tools that enhance their capabilities and inspire novel forms of expression (Boden, 2010). However, achieving a fruitful collaboration necessitates an understanding of the limitations and capabilities of AI, ensuring that these technologies serve as companions in the creative process rather than as replacements for human creativity.

Societal Impacts and the Democratization of Creativity

AI's impact on creativity extends beyond the individual artist to influence societal perceptions of art, culture, and innovation. One of the most significant impacts is the democratization of creative tools, enabling broader access to artistic expression and potentially nurturing a more inclusive creative community. However, this democratization also presents challenges, such as the need for digital literacy and access to ensure that the benefits of AI in creativity are widely shared (Engel et al., 2020). Additionally, the societal response to AI-generated works and the evolving landscape of creative industries must be carefully managed to support cultural diversity and economic sustainability.

Navigating the Future: Strategies and Considerations

Navigating the future of AI and creativity requires a multipronged approach that balances technological advancement with ethical and societal considerations. Key strategies include:

- **Developing Interdisciplinary Frameworks**: Combining insights from technology, ethics, art, and social sciences to create comprehensive frameworks that guide the ethical development and use of AI in creative domains.
- **Promoting Education and Awareness**: Enhancing digital literacy and raising awareness about the potential and challenges of AI in creativity, ensuring that society is prepared to engage with and benefit from these technologies.
- **Supporting Diversity and Inclusion**: Actively working to ensure that AI technologies in creative domains are inclusive and representative of diverse cultures and perspectives, avoiding biases and fostering a rich tapestry of artistic expression.

As society navigates this evolving landscape, the focus must remain on fostering ethical innovation, promoting human-AI collaboration, and ensuring that the integration of AI into creative domains enriches the cultural and artistic heritage of humanity.

Conclusion

As AI continues to permeate creative domains, the societal impacts and ethical considerations of this integration warrant thoughtful examination and proactive engagement. Embracing the possibilities of AI-enhanced creativity while navigating the challenges it presents is essential in fostering a future where technology amplifies human creativity and enriches cultural landscapes.

10

Chapter 6: OpenAI's Future Directions

A primary focus for OpenAI is the continued advancement of AI capabilities, particularly in areas such as natural language processing (NLP), computer vision, and machine learning efficiency. Projects like GPT (Generative Pre-trained Transformer) have showcased OpenAI's commitment to pushing the boundaries of what AI can achieve in understanding and generating human-like text (Brown et al., 2020). Future directions may involve enhancing the versatility and depth of AI models, aiming for broader understanding and creativity while optimizing for computational efficiency and environmental sustainability.

Ethical AI and Policy Advocacy

OpenAI places a significant emphasis on ethical AI development and the establishment of norms and policies that ensure the beneficial use of AI technologies. As AI systems become more powerful, their potential societal impacts—both positive and negative—grow accordingly. OpenAI is likely to continue its work in advocating for and contributing to the development of international standards and policies that address AI ethics, safety, and governance issues (Bostrom & Yudkowsky,

2014). This includes research into AI alignment, ensuring that AI systems' actions can be aligned with human values and intentions.

Framework for Ethical AI Development

OpenAI's dedication to ethical AI development is underpinned by its commitment to creating AI technologies that benefit all of humanity. As such, one of the primary future directions for OpenAI in this domain involves establishing and adhering to a robust ethical framework that guides AI development. This framework likely emphasizes principles such as transparency, fairness, accountability, and privacy (Floridi & Cowls, 2019). By implementing these principles, OpenAI aims to address ethical considerations proactively, from the initial design phase of AI systems through to their deployment and beyond.

Transparency and Explainability

A key aspect of ethical AI development is ensuring that AI systems are transparent and their decisions can be explained. OpenAI is expected to invest in research and development of explainable AI (XAI) technologies that make AI's decision-making processes understandable to humans (Gunning et al., 2017). This transparency is crucial for building trust with the public and enabling stakeholders to assess the fairness and effectiveness of AI systems.

Fairness and Bias Mitigation

OpenAI's approach to ethical AI also involves tackling bias in AI algorithms and data. Future directions may include the development of sophisticated techniques for detecting and mitigating bias, ensuring that AI systems do not perpetuate or amplify societal inequalities (Mehrabi et al., 2019). This commitment to fairness involves both technical solutions and the cultivation of diverse teams that can bring a wide range of perspectives to AI development projects.

Policy Advocacy for Responsible AI Use

In parallel to its efforts in ethical AI development, OpenAI is poised to play a significant role in policy advocacy, working with governments, regulatory bodies, and international organizations to shape policies that promote the responsible use and governance of AI technologies. This involvement is crucial for addressing the societal, ethical, and safety challenges posed by advanced AI systems.

Engagement with Regulatory Frameworks

OpenAI's future in policy advocacy is likely characterized by active engagement with the process of creating and refining regulatory frameworks for AI. This includes contributing to discussions on AI safety standards, privacy regulations, and the ethical use of AI, providing expertise that can inform policymaking (Taddeo & Floridi, 2018).

Global Collaboration for AI Governance

Given the global impact of AI technologies, OpenAI's policy advocacy efforts are expected to extend beyond national boundaries, fostering international collaboration on AI governance. This involves working with global organizations to establish consensus on principles for ethical AI development and use, ensuring that AI benefits are shared equitably across the world (Jobin et al., 2019).

By championing ethical principles in AI development and actively participating in policy advocacy, OpenAI aims to steer the evolution of AI towards outcomes that are beneficial, equitable, and aligned with human values. Through these efforts, OpenAI not only contributes to the advancement of AI technology but also ensures that its development and application occur within a framework that prioritizes ethical considerations and societal well-being.

AI and Societal Benefit

A guiding principle for OpenAI is the belief that AI should benefit all of humanity. Future directions may include initiatives focused on applying AI to global challenges such as climate change, healthcare, and education. By leveraging AI's analytical and predictive capabilities, OpenAI could contribute to solutions in areas where traditional approaches have fallen short, offering new avenues for societal advancement and well-being (Amodei et al., 2016).

Advancing Healthcare through AI

OpenAI's future directions likely include significant contributions to healthcare, leveraging AI to enhance diagnostic accuracy, personalize treatment plans, and streamline healthcare operations. By developing AI algorithms capable of analyzing medical imaging with superior precision or predicting patient outcomes based on historical data, OpenAI can assist in early detection of diseases and tailor treatments to individual patient needs (Esteva et al., 2019). Moreover, AI-driven analyses of large-scale health data can uncover patterns and insights, potentially leading to breakthroughs in understanding complex diseases and developing new therapeutic interventions.

Mitigating Climate Change with AI

Addressing the global challenge of climate change is another area where OpenAI is poised to make substantial contributions. AI technologies offer innovative solutions for optimizing energy consumption, enhancing climate modeling, and accelerating research into sustainable materials and renewable energy sources (Rolnick et al., 2019). By improving the efficiency of energy systems and contributing to the development of low-carbon technologies, OpenAI aims to support global efforts in reducing greenhouse gas emissions and advancing towards a more sustainable future.

Enhancing Education through Personalized Learning

OpenAI's commitment to societal benefit extends to the education sector, where AI technologies can transform learning experiences through personalization. AI-driven educational platforms can adapt to individual learning styles, pace, and needs, offering personalized content that maximizes student engagement and learning outcomes (Luckin et al., 2016). By harnessing AI to create dynamic learning environments, OpenAI can contribute to bridging educational gaps, providing equitable access to quality education, and fostering lifelong learning opportunities for individuals worldwide.

Promoting Economic Equity and Opportunity

The potential of AI to contribute to economic equity and opportunity is a critical aspect of OpenAI's vision for societal benefit. AI technologies can enhance labor market efficiencies, create new job opportunities in emerging sectors, and provide tools for entrepreneurs and small businesses to compete in the digital economy. Furthermore, by developing AI solutions that address the needs of underserved communities and promote inclusive economic growth, OpenAI aims to mitigate the risks of economic disparity exacerbated by technological advancements (Acemoglu & Restrepo, 2018).

Navigating Ethical Considerations and Collaborative Efforts

Central to OpenAI's approach to maximizing societal benefits is the navigation of ethical considerations inherent to AI development and deployment. This involves ensuring AI technologies are developed with fairness, transparency, and accountability, minimizing biases, and protecting privacy and security. Moreover, OpenAI's commitment to societal benefit is underpinned by collaborative efforts with governments, NGOs, academic institutions, and industry partners, fostering a multi-stakeholder approach to address global challenges through AI.

Through strategic initiatives in healthcare, climate change, education, and economic equity, OpenAI is poised to contribute significantly to addressing some of the most pressing challenges facing society today. By navigating the ethical landscape of AI development and fostering collaborative partnerships, OpenAI aims to realize the full potential of artificial intelligence as a force for positive societal transformation.

Collaboration and Open Research

OpenAI has a history of collaboration with academic institutions, industry partners, and policy organizations. Moving forward, OpenAI is likely to continue fostering an open and collaborative research environment that encourages the sharing of knowledge, tools, and best practices within the AI research community. This approach not only accelerates AI innovation but also promotes transparency and the dissemination of AI benefits across society.

The Imperative for Collaboration in AI Development

OpenAI recognizes that the complexity and scope of AI's potential impacts require a collaborative approach that leverages diverse expertise and perspectives. Collaboration among academic institutions, industry leaders, policy makers, and civil society organizations is essential to harness AI's transformative potential while mitigating risks and ethical concerns (Hagendorff, 2020). By engaging in partnerships that span different sectors, OpenAI aims to accelerate innovation, promote the exchange of best practices, and develop shared standards for responsible AI development.

Open Research as a Catalyst for Innovation

Open research is a cornerstone of OpenAI's strategy to democratize access to AI advancements and stimulate innovation across the global research community. OpenAI's commitment to publishing research findings, releasing open-source software, and sharing datasets serves to lower barriers to entry for AI research and development, fostering a more vibrant and inclusive AI research ecosystem (Rahwan et al., 2019). This approach not only accelerates the pace of AI innovation but also facilitates the identification and addressing of ethical, safety, and governance issues through collective scrutiny and dialogue.

Strategies for Promoting Collaboration and Open Research

Establishing Multidisciplinary Research Consortia

OpenAI's vision includes the creation and support of multidisciplinary research consortia that bring together experts from computer science, ethics, law, social sciences, and other relevant fields. These consortia are designed to tackle complex AI challenges that require integrated approaches, ensuring that technological advancements are informed by a broad range of ethical, social, and practical considerations (Vinuesa et al., 2020).

Engaging with the Global Research Community

OpenAI seeks to engage actively with the global research community through conferences, workshops, and online platforms. This engagement facilitates the exchange of ideas, fosters collaborations, and promotes transparency in AI research. By contributing to and participating in international research forums, OpenAI underscores its commitment to advancing the frontiers of AI knowledge in an open and collaborative manner.

Supporting Open-Source AI Initiatives

A key element of OpenAI's strategy is the support for open-source AI initiatives that encourage the sharing of algorithms, tools, and software. This support not only aids in democratizing access to advanced AI technologies but also encourages the collective improvement of AI systems through community contributions. Open-source initiatives are pivotal in creating a collaborative environment where innovation is driven by a shared commitment to progress and ethical standards.

Expected Outcomes of Emphasizing Collaboration and Open Research

The emphasis on collaboration and open research is expected to yield several positive outcomes, including the acceleration of AI advancements, the promotion of ethical AI development, and the facilitation of equitable access to AI technologies. Furthermore, this approach is anticipated to contribute to the formulation of robust AI policies and regulations that reflect a wide array of stakeholder interests and perspectives. Ultimately, OpenAI's commitment to collaboration and open research aims to ensure that AI development is guided by principles of inclusivity, transparency, and societal benefit.

OpenAI's future directions in terms of collaboration and open research underscore a strategic and ethical framework designed to harness the collective potential of the global AI community. This framework embodies a vision where AI development is not only a technical endeavor but also a collaborative journey that values openness, diversity, and the common good. Through sustained efforts in promoting collaboration and open research, OpenAI aspires to lead by example, advocating for an AI future that is innovative, responsible, and universally beneficial.

Safety and Security

As AI systems grow in complexity and autonomy, issues of safety and security become increasingly paramount. Future research directions for OpenAI will likely include a focus on developing robust safety frameworks for AI, addressing potential risks from advanced AI systems, and ensuring that AI technologies are resistant to adversarial attacks and misuse (Amodei et al., 2016).

Prioritizing AI Safety

AI safety encompasses a broad range of considerations, from ensuring that AI systems perform their intended functions without causing unintended harm to managing the long-term implications of advanced AI on humanity. OpenAI's approach to safety involves rigorous testing and evaluation methodologies, the development of robust fail-safes, and the continuous monitoring of AI systems to prevent and address potential failures (Amodei et al., 2016). This proactive stance on safety is grounded in a deep understanding of the complexities inherent in AI systems and the unpredictable ways they may interact with the real world.

Security Against Misuse and Adversarial Attacks

The security of AI systems pertains to protecting them from being exploited for malicious purposes, including misuse and adversarial attacks designed to manipulate or deceive AI algorithms. OpenAI recognizes the critical importance of fortifying AI technologies against such vulnerabilities, which entails implementing advanced cryptographic measures, developing algorithms resistant to manipulation, and fostering a research community focused on identifying and mitigating security threats (Papernot et al., 2016). This effort is crucial in preventing AI technologies from being weaponized or used in ways that could undermine public trust and societal stability.

Ethical Frameworks for AI Development

The ethical frameworks guiding AI development are integral to ensuring safety and security. OpenAI's commitment to ethical AI involves embedding ethical considerations into the design and deployment phases of AI systems, ensuring that they align with human values and societal norms (Russell, Dewey, & Tegmark, 2015). This includes addressing concerns related to privacy, autonomy, and the potential for bias, ensuring that AI technologies enhance human welfare without infringing on individual rights or perpetuating inequalities.

Collaborative Efforts in AI Governance

Navigating the challenges of AI safety and security requires collaborative efforts beyond the confines of any single organization. OpenAI's future directions likely include active participation in global governance initiatives, policy-making bodies, and international standards organizations. By contributing its expertise and insights, OpenAI aims to shape global norms and regulations that promote the safe and secure development of AI, fostering an environment of international cooperation and trust (Taddeo & Floridi, 2018).

Research and Innovation in AI Safety and Security

Advancing research and innovation in the field of AI safety and security is a cornerstone of OpenAI's future agenda. This involves not only technical innovations that enhance the intrinsic safety and security features of AI systems but also interdisciplinary research that bridges the gap between technology, ethics, and policy. Through open research initiatives and partnerships with academic institutions, OpenAI seeks to lead by example, pushing the frontiers of knowledge in AI safety and security (Hendrycks et al., 2021).

OpenAI's future directions in safety and security represent a comprehensive approach that intertwines technical excellence with ethical integrity. By prioritizing the development of safe and secure AI systems, OpenAI underscores its commitment to advancing AI technologies that not only push the boundaries of what is technologically possible but also safeguard human welfare and societal interests. Through a combination of rigorous safety protocols, security measures, ethical frameworks, collaborative governance efforts, and pioneering research, OpenAI aims to navigate the complex landscape of AI development, ensuring that the future of AI is both groundbreaking and benevolent.

Conclusion

OpenAI's future directions, as can be extrapolated from current trends and initiatives, are poised to address both the opportunities and challenges presented by rapid advances in AI technology. Through a commitment to ethical development, societal benefit, and collaborative research, OpenAI aims to lead the way in realizing the potential of artificial intelligence to enrich human life while safeguarding against its risks.

Forecasting OpenAI's Research:

Forecasting the research and development (R&D) trajectory of OpenAI, necessitates an in-depth analysis of current trends, organizational objectives, and the broader AI research landscape. OpenAI, since its inception, has positioned itself at the forefront of artificial intelligence innovation, with a commitment to advancing AI in ways that benefit all of humanity. This dedication is manifested through pioneering research in machine learning, natural language processing, robotics, and AI ethics and safety. The future directions of OpenAI's R&D can be anticipated by examining its foundational principles, recent achievements, and the evolving challenges and opportunities within the field of AI.

Advancements in Generative Models

One of the cornerstones of OpenAI's research agenda has been the development of advanced generative models, exemplified by the Generative Pre-trained Transformer (GPT) series. These models have demonstrated remarkable capabilities in generating human-like text, solving complex problems, and even creating art and music (Brown et al., 2020). Forecasting OpenAI's R&D suggests a continued emphasis on refining these models to enhance their versatility, reliability, and efficiency. This may involve innovations in model architecture, training methodologies, and the exploration of new applications in fields ranging from creative arts to scientific research (Bommasani et al., 2021).

Technological Advancements in Generative Models

OpenAI's research in generative models is poised for groundbreaking advancements, building on the successes of GPT-3 and other generative adversarial networks (GANs). Future research may focus on increasing the models' understanding, creativity, and adaptability. Key areas of technological advancement could include:

Enhanced Language Understanding: Building on the linguistic capabilities of GPT-3, future models may achieve deeper comprehension and context awareness, enabling more nuanced interactions and applications in natural language processing (NLP) (Brown et al., 2020). This could revolutionize fields such as automated journalism, content creation, and conversational AI.

Cross-modal Generativity: Advancements in generative models may increasingly focus on cross-modal capabilities, where AI can understand and generate content that spans different forms of media—text, images, audio, and video—seamlessly (Radford et al., 2021). This would enable AI to perform complex creative tasks, such as generating multimedia presentations or translating textual descriptions into visual art.

Ethical and Controlled Content Generation: As generative models become more powerful, ensuring they generate ethical and unbiased content becomes crucial. Research may focus on developing mechanisms for controlling content generation to avoid harmful outputs, including misinformation, biases, or inappropriate content (Bender et al., 2021).

Ethical Considerations and Governance

The advancements in generative models necessitate a parallel evolution in ethical frameworks and governance mechanisms. OpenAI is likely to continue leading discussions on the responsible development and deployment of these technologies. Ethical considerations could encompass:]

Bias and Fairness: Ensuring generative models do not perpetuate or amplify societal biases is a significant challenge. Future R&D will need to prioritize the development of algorithms that are fair and inclusive, incorporating diverse datasets and perspectives in the training process (Mitchell et al., 2019).

Privacy and Data Security: The training of generative models on vast amounts of data raises privacy concerns. Research into privacy-preserving techniques, such as federated learning and differential privacy, may become increasingly important to protect individuals' data rights (McMahan et al., 2017).

Intellectual Property and Copyright: The ability of generative models to produce original content also brings copyright issues to the forefront. OpenAI may explore novel frameworks for intellectual property that recognize both human and machine contributions to creative works (Kraemer et al., 2021).

Societal Implications and Collaborations

The advancements in generative models hold profound implications for society, potentially transforming industries, influencing cultural production, and impacting labor markets. OpenAI's approach to navigating these changes will likely emphasize collaboration with policymakers, industry partners, and academic institutions to ensure that the benefits of AI are equitably distributed. Moreover, OpenAI may focus on education and public engagement initiatives to prepare society for the changes wrought by AI, emphasizing the importance of digital literacy and AI awareness.

The future of generative models promises not only technological innovation but also a reevaluation of the ethical, legal, and societal frameworks that guide AI's integration into human life. Through continued research, collaboration, and dialogue, OpenAI aims to lead the way in realizing the transformative potential of generative models in a manner that is responsible, equitable, and beneficial for all.

Ethics and AI Safety

OpenAI has consistently highlighted the importance of ethics and safety in AI development. As AI systems become more powerful and autonomous, ensuring their alignment with human values and societal norms becomes increasingly critical. Future R&D efforts are likely to focus on ethical AI design, robust safety protocols, and mechanisms to prevent and mitigate AI misuse. This includes research into explainable AI, fairness and bias mitigation, and the development of standards for responsible AI deployment (Hendrycks et al., 2021).

The Ethical Imperative in AI Development

Establishing Ethical AI Frameworks

OpenAI's future R&D initiatives are expected to be deeply informed by ethical considerations, focusing on the development of AI in a way that aligns with human values and societal norms. The organization may continue to refine and implement ethical AI frameworks that guide decision-making processes, emphasizing transparency, accountability, fairness, and respect for privacy (Floridi & Cowls, 2019). These frameworks serve as foundational elements in shaping AI research agendas, ensuring that ethical considerations are integrated into the lifecycle of AI systems—from design through deployment.

Addressing Bias and Fairness

A significant aspect of OpenAI's ethical focus involves addressing bias in AI algorithms and datasets to promote fairness. Future R&D efforts might concentrate on innovative methods to detect, mitigate, and prevent biases, facilitating the development of AI systems that do not perpetuate existing social inequalities or introduce new forms of discrimination (Mehrabi et al., 2019). This endeavor requires not only advanced technical solutions but also a commitment to diverse and inclusive practices within AI research teams and processes.

Prioritizing AI Safety

Technical Safety Research

OpenAI recognizes that ensuring the safety of AI systems is critical, particularly as AI capabilities become increasingly advanced and autonomous. Future directions in AI safety research are likely to encompass the exploration of novel technical approaches to safety challenges, including alignment problems, where AI behaviors are aligned with human intentions, and robustness against adversarial attacks (Amodei et al., 2016). OpenAI may also focus on scalability of safety measures, ensuring that safety protocols remain effective as AI systems grow in complexity.

AI Safety Governance

Beyond technical safety measures, OpenAI's R&D in ethics and AI safety is anticipated to engage with broader issues of AI governance. This includes active participation in the development of regulatory frameworks and international standards that govern AI development and deployment. By contributing its expertise to policymaking processes and advocating for global cooperation on AI safety, OpenAI aims to foster a regulatory environment that balances innovation with safety and ethical considerations (Taddeo & Floridi, 2018).

Collaborative Efforts for Ethical and Safe AI

OpenAI's approach to ethics and AI safety underscores the importance of collaboration across sectors and disciplines. Future R&D efforts are expected to involve partnerships with academic institutions, industry peers, governmental agencies, and civil society organizations to collectively address ethical and safety challenges. Through these collaborative initiatives, OpenAI seeks to leverage a wide range of perspectives and expertise, enhancing the development of ethical and safe AI solutions that benefit society as a whole.

By prioritizing ethical frameworks, addressing bias and fairness, advancing technical safety research, engaging in AI safety governance, and fostering collaborative efforts, OpenAI is positioned to lead by example in the responsible development of AI technologies. This commitment to ethics and safety not only guides OpenAI's R&D but also contributes to the broader goal of ensuring that the advancement of AI serves the best interests of humanity.

Human-AI Collaboration

Enhancing human-AI collaboration remains a pivotal area of interest for OpenAI. Future research may delve into improving interfaces and interaction models that facilitate seamless collaboration between humans and AI systems across various domains, including healthcare, education, and creative industries. By focusing on augmentative AI that complements human skills and decision-making, OpenAI aims to leverage AI's capabilities to amplify human potential rather than replace it (Rahwan, 2019).

Technological Advancements Facilitating Human-AI Collaboration

Enhancing Intuitive Interfaces for AI Interaction

A significant area of focus for OpenAI involves developing intuitive interfaces that facilitate seamless interaction between humans and AI systems. This includes research into natural language processing (NLP) technologies that allow humans to communicate with AI in conversational language, making AI tools more accessible and user-friendly (Vaswani et al., 2017). Additionally, advancements in multimodal AI systems that can interpret and respond to a variety of input types—text, speech, visual cues—promise to further enhance the fluidity of human-AI interaction.

AI as Assistive Tools for Creativity and Problem-Solving

OpenAI's R&D is expected to explore the potential of AI as assistive tools that augment human creativity and problem-solving capabilities. This includes the development of generative models that can produce novel ideas, designs, and solutions in collaboration with human input, offering new possibilities in fields ranging from artistic creation to engineering and scientific research (Brown et al., 2020).

Ethical Considerations in Human-AI Collaboration

Ensuring Transparency and Understandability

Ethical R&D in human-AI collaboration necessitates a focus on transparency and understandability. OpenAI is likely to prioritize the development of AI systems whose decision-making processes and outputs can be easily understood and interpreted by humans, thereby fostering trust and enabling more effective collaboration (Rahwan, 2018).

Safeguarding Autonomy and Agency

Another critical ethical consideration involves safeguarding human autonomy and agency in the context of human-AI collaboration. OpenAI's research efforts may aim to ensure that AI systems enhance human decision-making without usurping control, thereby maintaining human oversight and ethical accountability in collaborative processes (Russell, Dewey, & Tegmark, 2015).

Societal Impacts of Human-AI Collaboration

Transforming the Workplace and Employment

The evolution of human-AI collaboration has profound implications for the workplace and employment. OpenAI's advancements in this area could lead to the creation of new job categories that leverage human-AI partnerships, while also necessitating the reskilling and upskilling of the workforce to adapt to these changes. Research and development strategies will need to consider the socioeconomic impacts of these transformations, ensuring that the benefits of human-AI collaboration are equitably distributed (Daugherty & Wilson, 2018).

Enhancing Accessibility and Inclusivity

Human-AI collaboration also holds the potential to enhance accessibility and inclusivity, offering tools and technologies that empower individuals with disabilities or those in underserved communities. OpenAI's R&D may focus on developing AI systems that can adapt to diverse human needs and capabilities, thereby contributing to a more inclusive society.

By advancing technological innovations, addressing ethical considerations, and contemplating the societal impacts, OpenAI aims to cultivate a future where human-AI collaboration not only amplifies human potential but does so in a manner that is ethical, equitable, and beneficial for society at large.

Environmental Sustainability

As the computational demands of advanced AI models continue to grow, so does their environmental impact. OpenAI is poised to address sustainability within its R&D agenda, exploring more energy-efficient algorithms and infrastructure. This may involve innovations in model compression, federated learning, and the use of renewable energy sources for training large-scale models, aligning AI development with ecological sustainability goals (Strubell et al., 2019).

Embedding Environmental Sustainability in AI Research

Energy-Efficient AI Models

A significant focus of OpenAI's future R&D is expected to be on the development of more energy-efficient AI models. As AI technologies, particularly deep learning, require substantial computational resources, innovating towards models that consume less energy while maintaining or enhancing performance is paramount (Strubell et al.,

2019). Techniques such as model pruning, quantization, and the use of more efficient neural network architectures could be areas of intense research, aiming to reduce the environmental impact of training and deploying AI systems.

Carbon-Neutral AI Operations

OpenAI is likely to prioritize achieving carbon neutrality in its AI operations. This commitment may involve the adoption of renewable energy sources for data centers, investment in carbon offset programs, and the implementation of sustainable practices across its operations. By setting a precedent in carbon-neutral AI development, OpenAI can contribute significantly to reducing the tech industry's environmental footprint (Henderson et al., 2020).

The Role of AI in Advancing Environmental Sustainability

AI for Climate Change Mitigation and Adaptation

Beyond minimizing its own environmental impact, OpenAI's future directions are poised to include leveraging AI technologies to address global environmental challenges, particularly climate change. AI can play a crucial role in climate change mitigation and adaptation strategies, from optimizing energy systems for reduced emissions to enhancing climate modeling and predicting extreme weather events (Rolnick et al., 2019). OpenAI's R&D efforts may focus on developing AI solutions that contribute to understanding, mitigating, and adapting to the effects of climate change, aligning AI advancements with global sustainability goals.

AI in Biodiversity Conservation and Ecosystem Monitoring

Another potential avenue for OpenAI's contribution to environmental sustainability lies in biodiversity conservation and ecosystem monitoring. AI technologies, including machine learning and computer vision, can be utilized to monitor wildlife populations, track deforestation, and assess ecosystem health in real-time, providing valuable data for conservation efforts (Norouzzadeh et al., 2018). By advancing AI research in these areas, OpenAI can support global efforts to preserve biodiversity and ensure ecosystem resilience.

Collaborative Efforts for Sustainable AI

The achievement of environmental sustainability in AI research and applications necessitates collaborative efforts across sectors and disciplines. OpenAI is expected to engage in partnerships with environmental organizations, academic institutions, and industry partners to promote sustainable AI practices and develop AI-driven solutions to environmental challenges. This collaborative approach can facilitate the sharing of knowledge, resources, and best practices, amplifying the impact of AI on environmental sustainability.

Through the development of energy-efficient AI models, carbon-neutral operations, AI-driven environmental solutions, and collaborative initiatives, OpenAI is poised to lead by example in the tech industry, demonstrating how AI can be harnessed to address some of the most pressing environmental challenges of our time while adhering to principles of sustainability.

Collaboration and Open Science

OpenAI's commitment to open science and collaborative research is expected to shape its future R&D directions. By fostering partnerships with academic institutions, industry, and governmental organizations, OpenAI can accelerate the pace of innovation while ensuring that AI advancements are shared broadly. This collaborative approach not only enriches OpenAI's research ecosystem but also promotes transparency, reproducibility, and ethical standards within the AI community (Hagendorff, 2020).

Enhancing Open Science in AI Research

OpenAI's dedication to open science reflects a broader commitment to transparency, reproducibility, and accessibility in AI research. By advocating for and practicing open science, OpenAI aims to democratize access to AI advancements, enabling researchers, practitioners, and policymakers worldwide to engage with and contribute to the field of AI.

Promoting Transparency and Reproducibility

A key aspect of OpenAI's focus on open science involves enhancing the transparency and reproducibility of AI research. This may involve the publication of research papers in open-access formats, sharing datasets and codebases, and providing detailed methodologies that allow for the independent replication of research findings (Stodden et al., 2016). Through these practices, OpenAI seeks to build trust within the scientific community and the broader public, fostering an environment where AI research is scrutinized, validated, and advanced collaboratively.

Open-Source AI Tools and Frameworks

Another pillar of OpenAI's commitment to open science is the development and dissemination of open-source AI tools and frameworks. By making state-of-the-art AI technologies freely available, OpenAI can accelerate innovation across diverse domains, from healthcare and education to environmental sustainability. Open-source initiatives also facilitate a collaborative approach to addressing technical challenges and ethical considerations in AI, encouraging a global community of developers to contribute to the advancement of AI technologies (Raymond, 1999).

Fostering Collaborative Partnerships

OpenAI recognizes the importance of collaborative partnerships in achieving breakthroughs in AI that are ethical, safe, and socially beneficial. Collaborations with academic institutions, industry peers, governmental agencies, and civil society organizations are vital to harnessing collective expertise and resources.

Academic and Industry Collaborations

Collaborations between OpenAI and academic institutions can enrich AI research with theoretical insights and empirical studies, fostering a cross-pollination of ideas that drives innovation. Similarly, partnerships with industry peers can facilitate the practical application of AI research, translating theoretical advancements into real-world solutions. These collaborative efforts are crucial for tackling complex AI challenges that require multidisciplinary knowledge and perspectives (Wooldridge, 2019).

Engaging with Policymakers and Civil Society

OpenAI's future R&D directions are likely to involve active engagement with policymakers and civil society to shape the ethical governance of AI technologies. By collaborating with these stakeholders, OpenAI can contribute to the development of policies and regulations that ensure the responsible deployment of AI, addressing societal concerns related to privacy, security, and fairness (Taddeo & Floridi, 2018).

Through its dedication to open science practices and the fostering of collaborative partnerships, OpenAI is positioned to lead by example in the global AI research community, championing initiatives that ensure AI advancements are accessible, reproducible, and aligned with societal values and ethical principles.

Conclusion

Forecasting the research and development focus of OpenAI, as envisaged underscores the organization's role as a catalyst for AI innovation that is ethically grounded, socially beneficial, and environmentally sustainable. Through a combination of technological advancements, ethical frameworks, and collaborative initiatives, OpenAI's future R&D efforts are poised to navigate the complexities of the AI landscape, striving for breakthroughs that enhance human well-being and foster a more equitable and sustainable future.

Anticipated AI Applications:

The speculative exploration of OpenAI not only delves into the intricacies of current artificial intelligence (AI) research and development (R&D) but also casts a forward-looking gaze at the anticipated applications and transformations that AI is poised to bring about in various sectors. OpenAI, as a pioneering entity in the AI landscape, is at the forefront of driving these innovations, with its future directions likely encapsulated within a vision that seeks to harness AI's transformative potential across healthcare, education, environmental sustainability, and the global economy.

Healthcare Innovations through AI

OpenAI's R&D initiatives are expected to significantly impact healthcare, with AI applications poised to revolutionize diagnostics, personalized medicine, and patient care. Anticipated advancements may include the development of AI-driven diagnostic tools that can detect diseases from imaging data with greater accuracy and speed than current methods (Esteva et al., 2019). Furthermore, AI algorithms could personalize treatment plans based on patients' genetic profiles, improving treatment outcomes. OpenAI's work in natural language processing (NLP) and machine learning could also enhance the ability of healthcare providers to extract meaningful insights from vast amounts of unstructured medical data, thereby informing better clinical decision-making.

Enhancing Diagnostics with AI

One of the most promising avenues for AI application in healthcare involves the use of machine learning algorithms and computer vision techniques to improve diagnostic accuracy and efficiency. OpenAI's advancements in AI could lead to the development of systems capable of analyzing medical imaging, such as X-rays, MRIs, and CT scans, with a level of precision that surpasses human radiologists (Esteva et al., 2017). These AI-driven diagnostic tools not only promise to reduce diagnostic errors but also to facilitate early detection of diseases, such as cancer, by identifying subtle patterns and anomalies that might be overlooked by human eyes.

Personalizing Treatment Plans

AI's ability to process and analyze vast datasets can significantly advance personalized medicine, tailoring treatment plans to individual patients' genetic makeup, lifestyle, and response to previous treatments. OpenAI's research into deep learning models could enable the prediction of how patients will respond to various treatments, optimizing therapy choices and dosages for improved outcomes (Topol, 2019). This personalized approach has the potential to transform treatment strategies for a wide range of conditions, from chronic diseases to mental health disorders, ensuring that patients receive the most effective care tailored to their specific needs.

Streamlining Healthcare Operations

Beyond direct patient care, OpenAI's AI technologies are anticipated to streamline healthcare operations, enhancing the efficiency and effectiveness of healthcare systems. AI applications could automate administrative tasks, such as patient scheduling, billing, and medical record management, freeing up healthcare professionals to focus more on patient care. Additionally, AI-driven predictive analytics could improve hospital resource allocation, patient flow, and supply chain logistics, reducing costs and improving healthcare delivery (Davenport & Kalakota, 2019).

Ethical Considerations and Societal Impacts

As OpenAI advances AI applications in healthcare, ethical considerations and societal impacts are paramount. Issues of data privacy, security, and consent are critical, given the sensitive nature of medical data. OpenAI's commitment to ethical AI development necessitates rigorous safeguards to protect patient information and ensure that AI systems are transparent, accountable, and aligned with patients' best interests. Furthermore, equitable access to AI-driven healthcare innovations is essential to prevent the exacerbation of existing health disparities. OpenAI's approach to healthcare innovations through AI emphasizes not only technological advancements but also the importance of ethical frameworks and policies that ensure these technologies benefit all segments of society.

By balancing cutting-edge technological developments with a deep commitment to ethical considerations and equitable societal impacts, OpenAI is at the forefront of shaping a future where AI significantly contributes to improving health outcomes and the overall efficiency of healthcare systems worldwide.

Transforming Education with AI

In the domain of education, OpenAI's future directions may focus on leveraging AI to create more personalized and adaptive learning experiences. AI applications could analyze students' learning styles, performance, and engagement levels to tailor educational content, thereby optimizing learning outcomes (Luckin et al., 2016). Additionally, AI-driven tutoring systems and virtual assistants could provide students with on-demand educational support, democratizing access to high-quality education resources worldwide.

Personalization of Learning Experiences

A pivotal direction for OpenAI's application of AI in education is the personalization of learning experiences. Through the development of adaptive learning platforms powered by AI, education can transcend the one-size-fits-all approach, offering personalized learning paths that accommodate individual learning styles, paces, and preferences (Luckin et al., 2016). AI algorithms can analyze learners' interactions, assess their comprehension and skill levels, and dynamically adjust content difficulty, format, and feedback to optimize learning efficiency. This level of personalization ensures that learners remain engaged and motivated, facilitating deeper understanding and retention of knowledge.

Enhancing Accessibility and Inclusivity

OpenAI's advancements in AI also hold the promise of enhancing accessibility and inclusivity in education. AI-driven tools can provide support for learners with disabilities, offering voice-to-text transcription, real-time captioning, and customized learning interfaces that cater to diverse needs (Wojciechowski, 2019). Furthermore, AI can break down geographical and socio-economic barriers to education by enabling access to high-quality learning materials and virtual instructors, reaching underserved populations and remote areas where educational resources are limited.

Supporting Educators and Optimizing Learning Environments

Beyond direct learner engagement, AI applications envisioned by OpenAI have the potential to support educators and optimize learning environments. AI systems can assist teachers in monitoring student progress, identifying learning gaps, and providing data-driven insights to inform teaching strategies (Zawacki-Richter et al., 2019). Additionally, AI can automate administrative tasks, such as grading and attendance tracking, allowing educators to devote more time to instructional activities and personalized student interactions. This symbiotic relationship between AI tools and educators enhances the overall efficacy of the educational process.

Fostering Lifelong Learning and Skill Development

In an era of rapid technological change, OpenAI recognizes the importance of fostering lifelong learning and continuous skill development. AI can facilitate access to upskilling and reskilling opportunities, adapting to the evolving demands of the workforce and enabling individuals to stay competitive in the job market (Bughin et al., 2018). By providing personalized learning recommendations and identifying emerging skill needs, AI-driven platforms can support learners in navigating their educational and career trajectories, promoting a culture of continuous growth and adaptation.

Ethical Considerations and Societal Impacts

As OpenAI charts its future directions in transforming education with AI, ethical considerations and societal impacts remain central to its endeavors. Ensuring the ethical use of data, protecting student privacy, and mitigating biases in AI algorithms are paramount to fostering trust and equity in AI-enhanced education. OpenAI's commitment to ethical AI development emphasizes the importance of transparency, accountability, and inclusivity, ensuring that the benefits of AI in education are equitably distributed across diverse populations.

By personalizing learning experiences, enhancing accessibility, supporting educators, and fostering lifelong learning, AI has the potential to significantly impact educational practices and outcomes. Grounded in ethical considerations and a commitment to societal benefit, OpenAI's initiatives in education seek to unlock the full potential of AI to enrich learning journeys and empower learners worldwide.

AI and Environmental Sustainability

OpenAI is also anticipated to contribute to environmental sustainability through AI applications aimed at combating climate change and preserving biodiversity. This could involve the development of

AI systems for more accurate climate modeling, prediction of extreme weather events, and optimization of renewable energy systems (Rolnick et al., 2019). AI could also play a crucial role in monitoring wildlife populations and ecosystems, aiding in conservation efforts by processing data from satellite images and sensor networks to detect changes in biodiversity and land use.

AI-Driven Climate Change Mitigation

One of the significant anticipated applications of AI in environmental sustainability is in the domain of climate change mitigation. OpenAI is expected to develop predictive models that offer unprecedented insights into climate dynamics, enabling more accurate forecasting of climate patterns, extreme weather events, and their potential impacts on ecosystems and human societies (Rolnick et al., 2019). By analyzing vast datasets, including satellite imagery and sensor data, AI algorithms can identify trends and anomalies that human analysis might overlook, providing valuable information for policymakers and environmental scientists.

Sustainable Resource Management

AI technologies are also poised to revolutionize resource management, contributing to more sustainable agriculture, water resource management, and energy production. OpenAI could focus on developing AI systems that optimize resource use, reduce waste, and enhance the efficiency of renewable energy sources. For instance, AI can predict crop yields, monitor soil health, and automate irrigation systems, thereby improving agricultural sustainability and food security (Liakos et al., 2018).

Conservation and Biodiversity

In the realm of conservation and biodiversity, OpenAI's future directions may include the deployment of AI to monitor and protect endangered species and their habitats. AI-powered drones and automated image recognition systems can track wildlife populations, detect poaching activities, and assess habitat destruction, providing conservationists with critical data to inform protection and restoration efforts (Norouzzadeh et al., 2018). Furthermore, AI can analyze genetic information to aid in the breeding programs of threatened species, contributing to biodiversity preservation.

Pollution Reduction and Environmental Monitoring

AI applications are expected to extend to pollution reduction and environmental monitoring, where OpenAI could innovate in developing systems that detect and analyze pollutants in air, water, and soil. AI can identify pollution sources, model dispersion patterns, and evaluate the effectiveness of pollution control measures. Additionally, AI technologies can monitor the environmental impact of industrial activities, facilitating the enforcement of environmental regulations and encouraging sustainable industrial practices (Zhang et al., 2018).

Ethical Considerations and Collaborative Efforts

OpenAI's engagement with AI and environmental sustainability encompasses ethical considerations, emphasizing the responsible use of AI in ecological applications. This includes ensuring data privacy, addressing potential biases in environmental data, and promoting equitable access to AI-driven solutions across different regions and communities. Moreover, OpenAI's collaborative efforts with environmental organizations, governments, and international bodies are crucial for maximizing the impact of AI on sustainability goals, fostering a cooperative approach to global environmental challenges.

OpenAI's commitment to this domain reflects a broader vision of leveraging advanced technologies to address critical global challenges, underscored by a commitment to ethical principles and collaborative innovation.

Economic Transformations and the Future of Work

The future directions of OpenAI are expected to encompass AI applications that drive economic transformations and reshape the future of work. AI technologies could automate routine tasks across industries, enhancing productivity and efficiency. However, OpenAI's approach is likely to be mindful of the societal implications of automation, focusing on creating AI systems that augment human capabilities rather than replace human jobs (Acemoglu & Restrepo, 2018). Moreover, OpenAI may explore the development of AI-driven platforms that facilitate new economic models and opportunities, such as decentralized finance (DeFi) and gig economy platforms, empowering individuals with more control over their economic activities.

Economic Growth and Productivity Enhancement

One of the most profound anticipated applications of AI pertains to its capacity to spur economic growth and significantly enhance productivity across various sectors. OpenAI's advancements in machine learning algorithms and automation technologies have the potential to optimize production processes, streamline supply chains, and introduce new services and products, thereby boosting economic output and efficiency (Brynjolfsson & McAfee, 2014). For instance, AI-driven analytics can provide insights that improve decision-making in finance, manufacturing, and retail, leading to cost reductions and increased competitiveness.

Creation of New Job Categories and Employment Opportunities

While concerns about AI-induced job displacement are prevalent, OpenAI's future directions also encompass the creation of new job categories and the expansion of employment opportunities in AI-driven industries. The development of AI technologies necessitates a workforce skilled in AI research, development, implementation, and oversight, fostering job creation in high-tech sectors (Acemoglu & Restrepo, 2018). Moreover, AI can enable the emergence of novel business models and industries, further diversifying employment opportunities and contributing to economic dynamism.

Addressing Workforce Displacement and Skill Gaps

A critical aspect of OpenAI's approach to economic transformations involves addressing the challenges of workforce displacement and emerging skill gaps. As AI automates routine and repetitive tasks, there is a pressing need for strategies that facilitate workforce transition, including reskilling and upskilling programs, to prepare individuals for the demands of the evolving job market (Autor, 2015). OpenAI is anticipated to collaborate with educational institutions, governments, and industry partners to develop and support initiatives that equip workers with the necessary skills for AI-augmented roles and industries.

Ethical Considerations and Social Equity

The integration of AI into the economy raises significant ethical considerations, particularly concerning social equity and the distribution of AI's benefits. OpenAI's commitment to ethical AI development extends to ensuring that economic gains from AI are equitably shared, mitigating the risk of exacerbating income inequality and social disparities. This includes exploring mechanisms for inclusive growth, such as deploying AI in ways that support small and medium-sized enterprises (SMEs) and underserved communities, and advocating for policies that ensure a fair distribution of AI-generated wealth (West, 2018).

Collaborative Strategies for a Sustainable Future of Work

OpenAI's vision for the future of work emphasizes the importance of collaborative strategies that engage a broad range of stakeholders in shaping a sustainable employment landscape. This entails working alongside policymakers to develop labor market regulations and social protection measures that address the implications of AI, fostering a labor market that is resilient, adaptable, and supportive of workers' rights and well-being.

Simultaneously, it recognizes the challenges associated with workforce displacement and skill disparities, advocating for a balanced approach that maximizes societal benefits while ensuring economic equity and sustainable employment practices. Through technological innovation, ethical commitment, and collaborative efforts, OpenAI aims to steer the economic transformations ushered in by AI towards outcomes that enhance the quality of work and life for all.

Ethical Considerations and Societal Impacts

As OpenAI navigates the anticipated AI applications and transformations, ethical considerations and the potential societal impacts remain at the forefront of its R&D strategy. This includes addressing concerns related to privacy, data security, bias and fairness in AI algorithms, and the equitable distribution of AI benefits across society. OpenAI's commitment to open science and collaboration is expected to play a vital role in fostering an inclusive ecosystem where AI innovations are developed and deployed responsibly, ensuring that they serve the broader interests of humanity.

Ethical Considerations in AI Development

Transparency and Accountability

One of the cornerstone ethical considerations in the development and deployment of AI systems is ensuring transparency and accountability. OpenAI is expected to continue prioritizing the development of AI technologies that are understandable and explainable by humans, thereby facilitating trust and confidence in AI systems (Doshi-Velez & Kim, 2017). This includes transparent reporting of AI capabilities, limitations, and decision-making processes, ensuring that stakeholders can scrutinize and evaluate AI technologies effectively.

Privacy and Data Protection

The massive datasets required to train AI models pose significant privacy and data protection challenges. OpenAI's approach to AI development is anticipated to be increasingly cognizant of the need to safeguard personal and sensitive information, adhering to stringent data protection standards and ethical guidelines. This involves the implementation of advanced techniques for anonymizing data and minimizing data collection to what is strictly necessary, respecting individuals' privacy rights (Taylor et al., 2016).

Bias and Fairness

As AI systems are trained on data generated within human societies, they are susceptible to inheriting and perpetuating existing biases. OpenAI's future R&D efforts are expected to tackle the challenge of bias in AI, aiming to develop fair and unbiased algorithms. This requires a concerted effort to ensure diversity in training datasets and to develop methodologies for identifying and correcting biases, thereby fostering fairness in AI outcomes (Mehrabi et al., 2019).

Societal Impacts of AI Applications and Transformations

Workforce Transformation and Employment

The impact of AI on the workforce and employment remains a pivotal societal concern. While AI technologies promise to enhance productivity and create new job categories, there is also the potential for significant job displacement. OpenAI's envisioned future includes actively engaging in research that seeks to understand and mitigate the adverse impacts of AI on employment, exploring strategies for workforce reskilling, and ensuring that the benefits of AI-induced transformations are equitably distributed across society (Autor, 2015).

Enhancing Social Welfare

OpenAI's advancements in AI have the potential to significantly enhance social welfare, offering solutions to some of the most pressing global challenges. From healthcare and education to environmental sustainability, AI applications developed by OpenAI are anticipated to contribute positively to societal well-being. However, realizing these benefits necessitates a focus on inclusive technology access and the avoidance of exacerbating existing inequalities.

Democratic Governance and AI Ethics

The influence of AI on democratic governance and ethical norms represents another critical area of societal impact. OpenAI is expected to play a leading role in fostering a global dialogue on the ethical use of AI, contributing to the development of policies and regulatory frameworks that ensure AI technologies are deployed in ways that uphold democratic values, human rights, and ethical standards (Cath et al., 2018).

Conclusion

The exploration of anticipated AI applications and transformations emphasizes a future where ethical considerations and societal impacts are integral to AI research and development. OpenAI's commitment to advancing AI technology is matched by its dedication to addressing the ethical dilemmas and societal challenges that accompany these advancements. Through a balanced approach that prioritizes transparency, accountability, privacy, fairness, and inclusivity, OpenAI aims to steer AI development towards outcomes that not only enhance technological capabilities but also promote social welfare and uphold democratic and ethical norms.

Potential Challenges and Ethical Dilemmas:

A significant emphasis is placed on forecasting the potential challenges and ethical dilemmas that lie ahead for OpenAI as it navigates the complex landscape of artificial intelligence (AI) research and development. This forward-looking analysis delves into the multifaceted obstacles that OpenAI may encounter, including technical limitations, ethical quandaries, societal impacts, and governance issues. These challenges are not only intrinsic to the advancement of AI technologies but also reflect broader concerns regarding the integration of AI systems into various aspects of human life. This comprehensive review aims to elucidate the anticipated hurdles and ethical considerations OpenAI is poised to face, grounded in the principles of responsibility, transparency, and societal welfare.

Navigating Technical Limitations and Uncertainties

One of the foremost challenges for OpenAI involves addressing the technical limitations and uncertainties inherent in current AI technologies. Despite remarkable advancements, AI systems still face issues related to generalizability, interpretability, and reliability (Marcus, 2018). For instance, while models like GPT (Generative Pre-trained Transformer) have shown impressive capabilities in generating human-like text, they can also produce outputs that are nonsensical or biased. Overcoming these limitations requires sustained research efforts focused on improving AI algorithms, enhancing data quality, and developing robust frameworks for AI training and evaluation.

Understanding Technical Limitations in AI

Generalizability of AI Models

One of the foremost technical challenges that OpenAI faces is enhancing the generalizability of AI models. Despite significant advancements, AI systems often struggle to perform well across diverse tasks or adapt to new, unseen environments without extensive retraining

(Zhang et al., 2018). Overcoming this challenge involves pioneering research into transfer learning and few-shot learning techniques that enable AI models to apply knowledge learned from one domain to another with minimal additional input.

Interpretability and Explainability

The black-box nature of many AI algorithms, particularly deep learning models, presents a critical technical limitation by obscuring the decision-making processes of AI systems (Rudin, 2019). This lack of interpretability and explainability not only hinders users' ability to trust AI systems but also complicates efforts to identify and correct biases or errors in AI outputs. OpenAI is anticipated to focus on developing more transparent AI models and methodologies that elucidate how AI systems arrive at their decisions, thereby enhancing trust and accountability.

Reliability and Safety

Ensuring the reliability and safety of AI systems, especially in high-stakes applications such as autonomous vehicles, healthcare diagnostics, and critical infrastructure management, is a paramount technical challenge. OpenAI must navigate the uncertainties related to AI system failures and their potential consequences, requiring the development of robust frameworks for AI safety that include rigorous testing protocols, fail-safe mechanisms, and continuous monitoring (Amodei et al., 2016).

Ethical Considerations in Addressing Technical Uncertainties

Balancing Innovation with Safety

As OpenAI endeavors to address technical limitations and uncertainties, it faces the ethical dilemma of balancing the pursuit of innovation with the imperative of ensuring AI safety. This involves making prudent decisions about the deployment of AI technologies, especially in scenarios where their full implications are not yet understood or where there is potential for significant societal impact (Bostrom & Yudkowsky, 2014).

Mitigating Unintended Consequences

The advancement of AI technologies carries the risk of unintended consequences, ranging from the perpetuation of biases to the disruption of social norms. OpenAI's commitment to ethical AI development necessitates a proactive approach to identifying and mitigating these risks, incorporating ethical considerations into the R&D process from the outset and engaging with diverse stakeholders to understand and address potential societal implications.

Through a combination of innovative R&D strategies, commitment to ethical principles, and active engagement with the broader AI community, OpenAI aims to advance AI technologies in a manner that maximizes their benefits while minimizing risks and uncertainties. The organization's efforts to overcome technical hurdles are intricately linked to its broader mission to ensure that AI development is aligned with societal values and ethical standards, underscoring the importance of responsible innovation in the AI domain.

Ethical Quandaries and Societal Impacts

As AI technologies become increasingly integrated into societal infrastructures, OpenAI must grapple with a host of ethical quandaries and societal impacts. These include concerns about privacy and surveillance, the potential for AI to exacerbate socioeconomic inequalities, and the ethical use of AI in critical domains such as healthcare, criminal justice, and employment (Crawford & Calo, 2016). The challenge lies in developing AI systems that respect individual rights and societal values, while also ensuring that the benefits of AI are equitably distributed across diverse communities.

Ethical Quandaries in AI Development

Decision-making Autonomy and Accountability

One of the foremost ethical quandaries facing OpenAI pertains to the increasing autonomy of AI systems and the consequent challenges of accountability (Bryson, 2018). As AI systems gain the capability to make decisions that affect human lives, determining responsibility for those decisions—especially in cases of error or harm—becomes complex. OpenAI is expected to confront these issues by investing in research that clarifies the lines of accountability and ensures that AI systems are designed with mechanisms for human oversight and intervention.

Privacy and Surveillance

The advancement of AI technologies, particularly those involving data analytics and facial recognition, raises significant concerns regarding privacy and the potential for surveillance (Zuboff, 2019). OpenAI faces the challenge of developing AI in a manner that respects individual privacy rights and counters the misuse of AI for intrusive surveillance practices. Ethical AI development, in this context, necessitates stringent data protection measures and the ethical review of AI applications to prevent violations of privacy.

Bias and Fairness

AI systems are susceptible to biases present in their training data, leading to outcomes that can exacerbate societal inequalities (Barocas, Hardt, & Narayanan, 2019). OpenAI must navigate the ethical quandary of ensuring that AI technologies are developed and deployed in a manner that is fair and unbiased. This involves comprehensive efforts to identify, mitigate, and monitor biases within AI algorithms and datasets, fostering AI systems that promote equity and justice.

Societal Impacts of AI Applications and Transformations

Disruption to Employment and the Future of Work

AI's potential to automate tasks across various industries poses significant implications for employment and the future of work (Frey & Osborne, 2017). OpenAI stands at the forefront of exploring how AI can augment human capabilities rather than replace jobs, focusing on ethical considerations related to workforce displacement and the equitable distribution of AI's economic benefits. This entails research into the development of AI technologies that complement human workers and initiatives that support workforce reskilling and upskilling.

Social Stratification and Power Dynamics

The deployment of AI technologies can influence social stratification and power dynamics, potentially concentrating power in the hands of those who control AI technologies while marginalizing others (O'Neil, 2016). OpenAI's ethical commitment involves recognizing and addressing the societal implications of AI in reinforcing or altering power structures, ensuring that AI development is guided by principles of inclusivity and empowerment.

Governance and Ethical Standards

As AI technologies increasingly play a role in societal governance, from judicial decision-making to law enforcement, OpenAI encounters the challenge of ensuring that these applications adhere to ethical standards and respect human rights (Whittaker et al., 2018). This involves active engagement with policymakers, stakeholders, and civil society to shape governance frameworks that align AI use with ethical principles and societal values.

By addressing decision-making autonomy, privacy, bias, employment disruption, social stratification, and governance issues, OpenAI is poised to lead by example in the responsible development and deployment of AI technologies. Through a commitment to ethical integrity, societal welfare, and collaborative engagement, OpenAI aims to ensure that AI serves as a force for positive transformation in society.

Addressing Bias and Fairness

Bias in AI algorithms represents a critical ethical dilemma, with the potential to reinforce existing prejudices and discrimination. OpenAI faces the challenge of ensuring that its AI models are free from biases that can lead to unfair outcomes, particularly in sensitive applications such as hiring, law enforcement, and loan approval (Barocas, Hardt, & Narayanan, 2019). Addressing this challenge requires a multifaceted approach, including diverse dataset curation, algorithmic transparency, and continuous monitoring and auditing of AI systems for biased behaviors.

The Challenge of Bias in AI Systems

Bias in AI systems, often arising from skewed datasets or flawed algorithms, presents a significant challenge that can perpetuate and amplify existing societal inequities. OpenAI stands at a critical juncture, tasked with developing AI technologies that not only advance computational capabilities but also embody principles of fairness and impartiality (Barocas, Hardt, & Narayanan, 2019). The organization's approach to addressing bias involves a multipronged strategy that encompasses the identification, mitigation, and continuous monitoring of biases throughout the lifecycle of AI development.

Identification of Bias

The first step in combating bias involves its identification, which requires thorough examination and auditing of datasets and algorithms for potential biases. OpenAI is expected to leverage advanced analytical tools and methodologies to assess and understand the sources and manifestations of bias within AI systems (Friedler et al., 2019). This process necessitates a collaborative effort, engaging with diverse stakeholders to gain a comprehensive perspective on how biases might affect various populations differently.

Mitigation Strategies

Upon identifying biases, OpenAI is poised to implement robust mitigation strategies aimed at minimizing their impact. This includes the refinement of algorithms to reduce reliance on biased data, the augmentation of datasets with more representative samples, and the employment of fairness-aware machine learning techniques that explicitly account for and adjust biases (Hardt et al., 2016). Additionally, OpenAI may explore the development of novel AI models that are inherently designed to prioritize fairness and equity in their decision-making processes.

Continuous Monitoring and Evaluation

Addressing bias in AI is not a one-time effort but requires ongoing monitoring and evaluation to ensure that biases do not re-emerge or evolve over time. OpenAI is anticipated to establish comprehensive frameworks for the continuous assessment of AI systems, incorporating feedback mechanisms that allow for the iterative improvement of fairness over time (Veale & Binns, 2017). This dynamic approach underscores the organization's commitment to evolving its AI technologies in alignment with ethical standards and societal expectations.

Ethical Considerations and Societal Impacts

The endeavor to mitigate bias and promote fairness in AI transcends technical challenges, raising profound ethical considerations and societal impacts. OpenAI's engagement in this domain reflects a broader ethical imperative to ensure that AI technologies contribute to a more just and equitable society, rather than exacerbating existing disparities (Eubanks, 2018). This involves grappling with complex questions about the nature of fairness, the trade-offs between different conceptions of equity, and the responsibility of AI developers to consider the diverse needs and values of global communities.

By prioritizing the identification, mitigation, and continuous monitoring of bias, OpenAI not only advances the field of AI but also champions the development of technologies that are equitable, just, and reflective of the diverse tapestry of human society. Through these efforts, OpenAI seeks to pave the way for a future where AI serves as a catalyst for positive social transformation, enhancing fairness and equality across the globe.

Governance and Regulation

The rapid evolution of AI technologies also poses challenges related to governance and regulation. OpenAI, along with other stakeholders in the AI ecosystem, must navigate the complexities of developing and adhering to regulatory frameworks that ensure the safe and ethical deployment of AI (Taddeo & Floridi, 2018). This involves engaging with policymakers, industry partners, and civil society organizations to establish global standards for AI accountability, safety, and ethics, while also fostering innovation and technological advancement.

The Nature of Bias in AI Systems

Bias in AI systems can manifest in various forms, originating from skewed data sets, prejudiced algorithms, or the societal contexts within which AI is deployed (Barocas, Hardt, & Narayanan, 2019). These biases can lead to discriminatory outcomes, reinforcing existing social inequities and undermining the integrity of AI technologies. OpenAI stands at the forefront of tackling this challenge, recognizing the imperative to ensure that AI systems are developed and implemented in a manner that promotes fairness and prevents harm.

Strategies for Mitigating Bias

Comprehensive Data and Algorithmic Audits

OpenAI's strategy for mitigating bias involves rigorous audits of data and algorithms to identify and address sources of bias. This includes the deployment of tools and methodologies designed to uncover hidden prejudices within training data and the AI models themselves (Bellamy et al., 2018). By systematically analyzing and rectifying these biases, OpenAI aims to enhance the fairness of AI systems from the ground up.

Diverse and Inclusive Data Sets

Recognizing that bias often stems from non-representative or incomplete data, OpenAI is expected to prioritize the cultivation of diverse and inclusive data sets that reflect the broad spectrum of human experiences and attributes. This involves not only the aggregation of data from varied sources but also the active inclusion of underrepresented groups in data collection efforts (Buolamwini & Gebru, 2018). Such diversity in data is crucial for developing AI systems that are equitable and capable of serving the needs of all segments of society.

Fairness-Aware Machine Learning

OpenAI is anticipated to advance fairness-aware machine learning algorithms that explicitly incorporate fairness criteria into the AI development process. This might include techniques that adjust for disparities in model outcomes across different groups or algorithms that seek to balance accuracy with fairness considerations (Hardt et al., 2016). These efforts signify a proactive approach to embedding fairness within the very fabric of AI technologies.

Ethical Considerations and Societal Impacts

Ethical Frameworks for Fair AI

Navigating the challenges of bias and fairness in AI necessitates robust ethical frameworks that guide decision-making and prioritize human rights and dignity. OpenAI is expected to continue refining its ethical guidelines, emphasizing principles of justice, equality, and respect for diversity. These frameworks serve as a moral compass, ensuring that AI technologies are aligned with societal values and ethical standards.

Societal Engagement and Collaboration

Addressing bias and fairness in AI transcends technical solutions, requiring a collaborative and inclusive approach that engages diverse stakeholders. OpenAI's future directions are likely to encompass partnerships with civil society, academia, and affected communities to gather insights, share knowledge, and co-create solutions that enhance the fairness of AI systems (Martin, 2019). Such societal engagement is pivotal in understanding the multifaceted impacts of AI and ensuring that AI development is responsive to the needs and concerns of all individuals.

Through rigorous audits, diverse data practices, fairness-aware algorithms, ethical frameworks, and societal collaboration, OpenAI aims to mitigate bias and champion fairness, setting a precedent for responsible AI development that prioritizes equity and justice across the globe.

The journey ahead for OpenAI is fraught with potential challenges and ethical dilemmas that span technical, societal, and regulatory domains. Addressing these challenges necessitates a holistic and principled approach, emphasizing the importance of ethical AI development, stakeholder engagement, and proactive governance. By prioritizing ethical considerations, transparency, and societal welfare, OpenAI aims to lead by example in navigating the complexities of advancing AI technologies, ensuring that AI serves as a force for good in society.

OpenAI's Role in Shaping the Future of AI:

A significant emphasis is placed on OpenAI's envisioned role in shaping the future landscape of artificial intelligence (AI). As a pioneering force in the AI research community, OpenAI's trajectory is characterized by its commitment to advancing cutting-edge AI technologies while navigating the accompanying ethical, societal, and technical challenges.

Leading Innovation in AI Technologies

OpenAI has positioned itself as a leader in driving innovation within the AI sphere. Through its groundbreaking research and development initiatives, OpenAI has contributed significantly to the advancement of AI technologies, particularly in the realms of natural language processing, computer vision, and machine learning (Brockman et al., 2016). By pushing the boundaries of what AI can achieve, OpenAI not only fosters technological progress but also sets new benchmarks for the AI research community.

Pioneering Generative Models

One of OpenAI's notable contributions has been in the development of generative models, such as GPT (Generative Pre-trained Transformer) series, which have revolutionized natural language understanding and generation (Brown et al., 2020). These models have demonstrated remarkable capabilities in generating human-like text, opening up new possibilities for AI applications in content creation, language translation, and beyond. OpenAI's continuous improvement of generative models signifies its role in leading AI towards more sophisticated and versatile capabilities.

Technological Breakthroughs in Generative Models

Development of the GPT Series

OpenAI's development of the Generative Pre-trained Transformer (GPT) series represents a seminal contribution to the field of AI. Starting with GPT and evolving through successive iterations, including GPT-2 and GPT-3, these models have significantly advanced the state of the art in natural language processing and generation (Brown et al., 2020). The GPT series, characterized by its ability to generate coherent and contextually relevant text based on vast amounts of training data, exemplifies OpenAI's innovative approach to leveraging deep learning and transformer architectures for AI model development.

Applications and Implications

The GPT models have broad applications, ranging from writing assistance and language translation to more creative tasks such as poetry and story generation. The versatility of these models demonstrates the potential of generative AI to augment human capabilities and inspire new forms of digital interaction and content creation. Moreover, the development of these models has spurred further research into the ethical implications and societal impacts of AI-generated content, including concerns about misinformation, authenticity, and copyright (Bender et al., 2021).

Ethical Considerations in Generative AI

Ensuring Responsible Use

OpenAI's leadership in generative models is accompanied by a commitment to ethical AI development and deployment. This involves addressing the potential misuse of generative AI for creating misleading information or deepfakes. OpenAI has engaged in efforts to develop and implement safeguards, such as watermarking and content attribution technologies, to ensure the responsible use of generative models (Solaiman et al., 2019). Additionally, OpenAI's selective release strategy for GPT-2 highlighted its cautious approach to balancing innovation with the potential risks associated with powerful generative AI technologies.

Promoting Transparency and Accountability

In advancing generative models, OpenAI has underscored the importance of transparency and accountability in AI research. By publishing detailed research papers and engaging with the broader AI and policy communities, OpenAI seeks to foster an open dialogue about the capabilities, limitations, and societal implications of generative AI. This commitment to open science and ethical stewardship sets a precedent for responsible AI development practices within the research community.

Societal Impacts of Generative AI

Augmenting Creativity and Productivity

OpenAI's pioneering work in generative models holds the promise of augmenting human creativity and productivity. By automating aspects of content creation, these models have the potential to democratize access to creative tools, enabling individuals and organizations to generate novel content with ease. However, this also raises questions about the future of creative professions and the economic value of AI-generated content, necessitating ongoing dialogue and policy considerations to ensure equitable outcomes (Sparrow, 2020).

The development of the GPT series not only showcases OpenAI's technical prowess but also reflects its dedication to navigating the ethical challenges and societal implications of generative AI. Through its innovative contributions and responsible approach to AI development, OpenAI continues to shape the trajectory of AI research, paving the way for future advancements that are technologically sophisticated, ethically grounded, and societally beneficial.

Ethical AI Development and Governance

OpenAI acknowledges the profound ethical implications and societal impacts of AI technologies. As part of its mission, OpenAI is committed to ethical AI development, focusing on creating AI systems that are safe, transparent, and aligned with human values (Leike et al., 2017). This involves rigorous research into AI safety and ethics, aiming to address potential risks and ensure that AI technologies benefit humanity.

Promoting AI Safety and Security

OpenAI's dedication to AI safety is exemplified in its research on aligning AI systems with human intentions and preventing malicious uses of AI. By advancing the field of AI safety, OpenAI plays a critical role in shaping the future of AI as a domain where technological advancements are balanced with safety considerations and ethical governance (Amodei et al., 2016).

Technological Innovations for AI Safety

Developing Robust and Reliable AI Systems

One of the primary strategies OpenAI employs to promote AI safety involves the development of robust and reliable AI systems designed to perform safely under a wide range of conditions, including unforeseen scenarios (Amodei et al., 2016). This entails rigorous testing and validation processes to identify and mitigate potential failures, incorporating mechanisms that allow AI systems to recognize their limitations and seek human intervention when necessary. OpenAI's commitment to creating AI systems that are robust against adversarial attacks also plays a crucial role in ensuring that AI technologies remain secure and aligned with intended purposes.

Research on AI Alignment and Control

OpenAI dedicates significant resources to research on AI alignment, focusing on ensuring that AI systems' goals and behaviors are aligned with human values and ethical principles (Hadfield-Menell et al., 2017). This includes exploring theoretical frameworks and practical techniques for AI control, ensuring that as AI systems become more autonomous, they continue to act in ways that are beneficial to humanity. OpenAI's efforts in this domain underscore the importance of proactive measures to address the long-term challenges associated with advanced AI capabilities.

Ethical Stewardship in AI Development

Embedding Ethics in AI Design

OpenAI emphasizes the integration of ethical considerations directly into the design and development processes of AI technologies. By embedding ethics in AI design, OpenAI aims to ensure that AI systems are inherently structured to respect privacy, fairness, and transparency, mitigating the risks of unethical outcomes (Dignum, 2019). This approach reflects a holistic view of AI safety and security as not only technical challenges but as ethical imperatives that must be addressed from the outset of AI development.

Fostering an Ethical AI Culture

Within OpenAI and the broader AI research community, fostering a culture that prioritizes ethical AI development is key to promoting AI safety and security. OpenAI leads by example, advocating for ethical guidelines and best practices that influence how AI researchers and developers approach their work. This includes encouraging open discussions about the ethical implications of AI, sharing knowledge and resources to address safety challenges, and cultivating a research environment where ethical considerations are central to AI innovation.

Proactive Policy Engagement and Global Governance

Shaping AI Safety Standards and Regulations

OpenAI actively engages with policymakers, industry leaders, and international organizations to shape safety standards and regulatory frameworks for AI. This involves contributing OpenAI's expertise to discussions on global AI governance, advocating for policies that promote transparency, accountability, and public trust in AI technologies (Taddeo & Floridi, 2018). Through such engagements, OpenAI seeks to ensure that AI safety and security are not solely the concerns of individual organizations but are addressed through collaborative efforts at the national and international levels.

Through technological innovations, ethical stewardship, and proactive policy engagement, OpenAI endeavors to navigate the complex landscape of AI development, ensuring that AI technologies remain safe, secure, and aligned with human values. This commitment to AI safety and security not only reinforces OpenAI's leadership in the AI field but also exemplifies a forward-thinking approach to the ethical and governance challenges that accompany the advancement of AI.

Collaborative Progress and Open Science

In its pursuit to shape the future of AI, OpenAI champions the principles of collaboration and open science. Recognizing that the challenges and opportunities presented by AI transcend individual organizations, OpenAI engages in partnerships with academia, industry, and policy-makers. This collaborative approach facilitates the exchange of knowledge, accelerates innovation, and ensures that AI advancements are guided by a diverse set of perspectives and expertise.

Advocacy for Open Science

OpenAI's advocacy for open science reflects its commitment to democratizing AI research and making AI technologies accessible to a broader audience. By releasing research papers, sharing datasets, and open-sourcing software, OpenAI fosters an environment of transparency and inclusivity in AI research (Henderson et al., 2020). This not only accelerates the pace of innovation but also enables a wider community of researchers and developers to contribute to the advancement of AI.

The Foundations of Open Science in AI

Promoting Transparency and Accessibility

OpenAI embodies the open science ethos by promoting transparency in AI research and development. This involves the publication of research findings in open-access formats, sharing datasets and software tools with the broader research community, and fostering an open discourse on research methodologies and results (Stodden, McNutt, Bailey, Deelman, Gil, Hanson, Heroux, Ioannidis, & Taufer, 2016). By doing so, OpenAI aims to demystify AI technologies, allowing for broader scrutiny, replication of research, and cumulative knowledge building.

Facilitating Collaborative Innovation

A cornerstone of OpenAI's advocacy for open science is the facilitation of collaborative innovation. OpenAI initiatives such as the OpenAI Gym and the release of pre-trained models like GPT-2 underscore a commitment to providing resources that catalyze research and application development across various sectors (Brockman, Cheung, Pettersson, Schneider, Schulman, Tang, & Zaremba, 2016). These efforts are designed to lower barriers to entry for AI research, encouraging a diverse array of contributors to participate in the field.

Ethical Considerations in Open Science

Balancing Openness with Responsibility

While advocating for open science, OpenAI navigates the ethical balance between openness and the responsible dissemination of potentially dual-use technologies. The phased release of GPT-2 serves as a case study in cautious openness, where OpenAI initially withheld the full model due to concerns over malicious use, subsequently releasing it alongside a detailed analysis of its potential impacts (Solaiman, Clark, Brundage, & Amodei, 2019). This approach reflects a nuanced understanding of the ethical implications of open science in AI, emphasizing the need for vigilance and adaptive strategies to mitigate risks.

Addressing Equity and Inclusion

OpenAI's open science ethos also encompasses a commitment to equity and inclusion within the AI research community. By making AI research outputs accessible, OpenAI aims to democratize access to cutting-edge technologies and knowledge, empowering researchers from underrepresented regions and institutions. This endeavor acknowledges the global nature of AI challenges and the importance of diverse perspectives in driving innovation and ensuring that AI advancements are reflective of broad societal needs.

Implications for the Future of AI

Accelerating AI Research and Development

OpenAI's advocacy for open science is poised to significantly accelerate AI research and development. By fostering an environment of collaboration and knowledge sharing, OpenAI helps to reduce redundancy in research efforts, leverage collective expertise, and rapidly disseminate breakthroughs across the field. This approach is instrumental in propelling the AI community towards addressing complex challenges and unlocking new opportunities for societal advancement.

Shaping Ethical and Equitable AI Futures

Furthermore, OpenAI's commitment to open science plays a crucial role in shaping ethical and equitable futures for AI. Through transparent practices and inclusive initiatives, OpenAI not only advances the technical frontiers of AI but also contributes to the development of governance frameworks and ethical norms that guide the responsible use of AI technologies. This leadership in open science exemplifies a model for the broader AI community, underscoring the importance of shared values and collective action in navigating the future of AI.

Conclusion

Through initiatives that promote transparency, collaborative innovation, and ethical stewardship, OpenAI champions a vision of AI development that is inclusive, equitable, and aligned with the greater good. This commitment to open science not only accelerates the pace of AI research and development but also ensures that the trajectory of AI evolution is guided by principles of openness, responsibility, and shared progress. OpenAI's trajectory underscores the importance of balancing innovation with ethical considerations, setting a precedent for responsible AI development that prioritizes the benefits to humanity.

11

Chapter 7: Resources and Further Reading

This section would aim to provide a curated list of resources, including foundational texts, cutting-edge research papers, ethical discussions, and policy analysis, to offer a comprehensive understanding of the current state and future prospects of AI.

Foundational Texts in AI

1. **Russell, S. J., & Norvig, P. (2016). Artificial Intelligence: A Modern Approach.** Pearson.
   - This seminal textbook provides a comprehensive overview of the field of artificial intelligence, covering fundamental concepts, methodologies, and the history of AI.

2. **Nilsson, N. J. (1998). Artificial Intelligence: A New Synthesis.** Morgan Kaufmann.
   - Nilsson integrates various aspects of AI, offering insights into the mechanisms behind intelligent behavior in machines, making it a foundational read for understanding the technical underpinnings of AI technologies.

OpenAI-Specific Research and Publications

1. **Amodei, D., Olah, C., Steinhardt, J., Christiano, P., Schulman, J., & Mané, D. (2016). Concrete problems in AI safety. arXiv preprint arXiv:1606.06565.**
   - This work by researchers associated with OpenAI discusses potential safety issues in AI systems and proposes research directions to address these challenges, emphasizing the importance of safety in AI development.
2. **Brown, T. B., Mann, B., Ryder, N., Subbiah, M., Kaplan, J., Dhariwal, P., ... & Amodei, D. (2020). Language Models are Few-Shot Learners. Advances in Neural Information Processing Systems, 33.**
   - This paper introduces GPT-3, OpenAI's third-generation generative pre-trained transformer, showcasing its ability to perform a wide variety of tasks with little to no task-specific training.

Ethical Considerations and Societal Impacts

1. **Bostrom, N., & Yudkowsky, E. (2014). The ethics of artificial intelligence. In The Cambridge Handbook of Artificial Intelligence (pp. 316–334). Cambridge University Press.**
   - This chapter delves into the ethical considerations surrounding artificial intelligence, discussing long-term impacts and the moral responsibilities of AI researchers and developers.
2. **O'Neil, C. (2016). Weapons of Math Destruction: How Big Data Increases Inequality and Threatens Democracy. Crown.**

- ○ O'Neil explores the dark side of big data and algorithmic decision-making, highlighting how some AI applications can perpetuate inequality and undermine democratic values.

Policy and Governance

1. **Taddeo, M., & Floridi, L. (2018). Regulate artificial intelligence to avert cyber arms race. Nature, 556(7701), 296-298.**
   - ○ This article argues for the need for international regulations on AI development and deployment, emphasizing the risks associated with an unregulated AI arms race.
2. **Cath, C., Wachter, S., Mittelstadt, B., Taddeo, M., & Floridi, L. (2018). Artificial intelligence and the 'good society': the US, EU, and UK approach. Science and Engineering Ethics, 24(2), 505-528.**
   - ○ The authors provide a comparative analysis of AI policies in the US, EU, and UK, discussing how different regions envision the role of AI in society and the measures taken to ensure ethical AI development.

Further Online Resources

1. **OpenAI Blog (**https://openai.com/blog/**):**
   - ○ OpenAI's official blog features updates on its latest research, perspectives on AI ethics and policy, and discussions on the future of AI technologies.
2. **AI Ethics Guidelines Global Inventory (https://algorithmwatch.org/en/project/ai-ethics-guidelines-global-inventory/):**
   - ○ This online resource compiles AI ethics guidelines from around the world, offering a broad perspective on global

efforts to guide ethical AI development and implementation.

12

Appendices

Glossary of AI Terminology

In the Appendices section, particularly the Glossary of AI Terminology, serves as a critical resource for readers, offering a comprehensive and accessible lexicon of terms and concepts central to the field of artificial intelligence (AI). This glossary is not merely an ancillary addition but a foundational component that enhances the reader's understanding of AI's complex and multifaceted nature. By demystifying the technical jargon and presenting definitions in a clear, concise manner, the Glossary of AI Terminology empowers readers from diverse backgrounds ranging from students and researchers to policymakers and the general public to engage more deeply with the content of the book and the broader discourse on AI.

Importance of a Glossary in AI Literature

Enhancing Accessibility and Understanding

The inclusion of a Glossary of AI Terminology addresses a crucial need for clarity and accessibility in the rapidly evolving field of AI. As AI technologies become increasingly integrated into various aspects of society, the ability for a wide audience to grasp the terminology is essential. The glossary serves as an educational tool that breaks down barriers to understanding, enabling readers without a technical background to follow the discussions on AI advancements, challenges, and ethical considerations with greater ease (Luger & Stubblefield, 2004).

Standardizing Terminology

Given the interdisciplinary nature of AI, terms and concepts are often subject to varying interpretations. The Glossary of AI Terminology plays a vital role in standardizing the language used to discuss AI, promoting consistency across different domains of research and application. This standardization is crucial for facilitating clear communication among researchers, practitioners, and stakeholders in the AI ecosystem, thereby advancing collaborative efforts and policy discussions (Russell & Norvig, 2016).

Key Components of the Glossary

Core AI Concepts and Techniques

The glossary comprehensively covers core AI concepts and techniques, including but not limited to machine learning, deep learning, neural networks, natural language processing, and reinforcement learning. Each entry provides a succinct definition that captures the essence of the concept, along with explanations of its significance and applications within AI research and development. This foundational knowledge equips readers with the necessary framework to understand the technical aspects of AI innovations and their implications (Goodfellow, Bengio, & Courville, 2016).

Ethical and Societal Considerations

Reflecting OpenAI's commitment to ethical AI development, the Glossary of AI Terminology also includes entries related to ethical and societal considerations, such as bias, fairness, transparency, and accountability. These entries elucidate the ethical dimensions of AI technologies, highlighting the importance of integrating ethical principles into AI research and deployment. This focus on ethical terminology underscores the complex interplay between AI advancements and societal values, fostering a more informed dialogue on responsible AI (Bostrom & Yudkowsky, 2014).

By providing clear definitions of AI-related terms and concepts, the glossary facilitates a deeper understanding of AI's technological underpinnings, ethical considerations, and societal impacts. Its inclusion reflects a holistic approach to AI education and communication, aiming to equip readers with the knowledge and vocabulary needed to navigate the intricate landscape of AI and engage in meaningful discussions on its future directions.

Glossary of AI Terms:

The Appendices play a pivotal role in enhancing the reader's understanding and engagement with the content, particularly through the inclusion of a Glossary of AI Terms. This glossary serves as an essential resource, designed to demystify the complex and often technical language of artificial intelligence (AI) for a broad audience. By providing concise and accurate definitions of key terms, concepts, and acronyms used throughout the book, the glossary ensures that readers, regardless of their prior knowledge of AI, can fully grasp the discussions on OpenAI's advancements, challenges, and future directions. This comprehensive examination of the Glossary of AI Terms within the appendices aims to highlight its significance in fostering accessibility, promoting clarity, and facilitating a deeper understanding of AI's multifaceted dimensions.

Purpose and Importance of the Glossary

The inclusion of a Glossary of AI Terms addresses several critical needs in the dissemination of knowledge about artificial intelligence:

Accessibility

AI is a field characterized by rapid advancements and complex concepts that can be intimidating to those not well-versed in technical jargon. The glossary significantly lowers these barriers to entry, making the insights, research findings, and discussions within the book accessible to a wider audience, including students, educators, policymakers, and the general public interested in the societal implications of AI technologies.

Clarity and Precision

AI terminology is not only complex but also evolving, with new terms frequently emerging as the field progresses. The glossary ensures that readers have a clear and precise understanding of how specific terms are used in the context of the book, promoting consistency and preventing misunderstandings that could arise from ambiguous or colloquial use of language.

Educational Value

For readers seeking to deepen their knowledge of AI, the glossary serves as an educational tool in its own right. It provides a structured overview of essential AI concepts, offering pathways for further exploration and study. This aspect is particularly valuable for educators and students who can use the glossary as a reference point for coursework or research in AI.

Structure and Content of the Glossary

The Glossary of AI Terms is meticulously organized to facilitate ease of use and comprehensive coverage of relevant terminology:

Alphabetical Organization

Terms within the glossary are arranged alphabetically, allowing readers to quickly locate specific terms or browse the glossary efficiently. This organizational structure also supports the glossary's use as a reference tool during and after the reading of the book.

Definitions and Explanations

Each entry in the glossary provides a definition of the term, followed by a brief explanation or context that elucidates its significance within the field of AI. Where applicable, examples are provided to illustrate how a term is applied in practice, enhancing the reader's ability to relate abstract concepts to real-world applications of AI.

Cross-References

The glossary includes cross-references to related terms or concepts within the glossary itself, encouraging readers to explore the interconnectedness of AI terminology and gain a more holistic understanding of the subject matter.

Implications for Readers and the Field of AI

The Glossary of AI Terms is more than just an appendix; it is a critical component of the book that has far-reaching implications for readers and the broader field of AI:

Enhancing Reader Engagement

By empowering readers with the vocabulary needed to understand and engage with AI discussions, the glossary facilitates a deeper and more meaningful interaction with the book's content. This engagement is crucial for fostering informed public discourse on the ethical, social, and technical aspects of AI.

Promoting Inclusivity in AI Education

The glossary plays a vital role in promoting inclusivity within AI education by providing resources that are accessible to individuals with diverse backgrounds and levels of expertise. This inclusivity is essential for ensuring that the benefits and challenges of AI are understood and addressed by a broad spectrum of society.

Supporting Continued Learning

For those inspired to further explore the field of AI, the glossary serves as a foundation for continued learning. It provides a springboard for readers to delve into more specialized texts, research papers, and educational resources, fostering the growth of an informed and engaged community of AI enthusiasts and professionals.

In conclusion, the Glossary of AI Terms stands as a testament to the book's commitment to accessibility, clarity, and education. By demystifying AI terminology, the glossary enhances readers' comprehension and engagement with the subject, contributing significantly to the broader goals of fostering an informed dialogue on AI and its implications for the future.

Index for Quick Reference:

The inclusion of an Index for Quick Reference in the appendices serves a critical function, enhancing the usability and navigational efficiency of the book for readers seeking specific information on artificial intelligence (AI) topics covered within its pages. This index is not merely an organizational tool but a meticulously curated guide that facilitates quick access to the wealth of knowledge embedded in the text. It underscores the book's commitment to providing a comprehensive, accessible, and user-friendly resource for a diverse audience, ranging from AI researchers and practitioners to policymakers, educators, and the general public interested in the advancements and implications of AI technologies.

Purpose and Importance of the Index for Quick Reference

Facilitating Access and Navigation

The primary purpose of the Index for Quick Reference is to facilitate easy access to the book's content, enabling readers to quickly locate information on specific AI concepts, technologies, case studies, and ethical discussions. This is particularly valuable in a field as dynamic and expansive as AI, where readers may seek clarification on particular terms, revisit concepts, or explore specific topics in greater detail.

Enhancing Reader Engagement and Learning

By streamlining the process of finding and referencing material within the book, the index significantly enhances reader engagement and learning. It allows readers to navigate the text more efficiently, making the book a more effective resource for both structured learning and casual exploration. This accessibility is crucial for supporting a deeper, more interactive learning experience.

Supporting Academic and Professional Use

For academic and professional audiences, the Index for Quick Reference is an invaluable tool for research, teaching, and practical application. It enables scholars to reference specific sections for citation quickly, educators to identify relevant material for curriculum development, and practitioners to access applicable insights for real-world AI implementations. The index thus extends the book's utility beyond a traditional read, positioning it as a reference work within academic and professional libraries.

Structure and Content of the Index

Alphabetical Organization

The Index for Quick Reference is organized alphabetically, encompassing key terms, concepts, individuals, organizations, and technologies discussed throughout the book. This organization allows for intuitive navigation, catering to readers familiar with the conventional format of reference works.

Page Number References

Each entry in the index includes page number references, directing readers to the exact locations where the topics are discussed. This precision not only saves time but also enhances the reader's ability to explore topics in context, understanding their relevance and application within the broader narrative of AI development and OpenAI's contributions.

Thematic Groupings and Cross-References

To further aid navigation, the index may group related terms thematically, providing a layered structure that reflects the interconnectedness of AI concepts. Cross-references within the index guide readers to related topics, facilitating a holistic exploration of AI and encouraging a comprehensive understanding of the subject matter.

Implications for Readers and the Field of AI

Encouraging Comprehensive Exploration

The Index for Quick Reference encourages readers to explore the book comprehensively, making connections between different AI topics and themes. This exploration is essential for fostering a nuanced understanding of AI's complexities, challenges, and potential.

Promoting Accessibility and Inclusivity

By enhancing the book's navigability, the index promotes accessibility and inclusivity, ensuring that readers with varying levels of familiarity with AI can engage with the content effectively. This inclusivity supports the democratization of AI knowledge, contributing to informed public discourse and participation in AI-related decision-making.

Contributing to AI Education and Scholarship

The index contributes significantly to AI education and scholarship by facilitating the book's use as a teaching and research resource. It supports the academic community's efforts to advance AI knowledge, fostering an environment of continuous learning and innovation.

In conclusion, the Index for Quick Reference plays a pivotal role in enhancing the book's functionality as a comprehensive resource on AI. Its meticulous organization and accessibility features not only improve the reader's experience but also contribute to the book's value as an educational tool, fostering a deeper engagement with the evolving field of AI.

13

References

- Acemoglu, D., & Restrepo, P. (2018). Artificial Intelligence, Automation, and Work. *The Economics of Artificial Intelligence: An Agenda*, 197-236.

- Acemoglu, D., & Restrepo, P. (2020). The wrong kind of AI? Artificial intelligence and the future of labor demand. Cambridge Journal of Regions, Economy and Society, 13(1), 25-35.

- Akkaya, I., Andrychowicz, M., Chociej, M., Litwin, M., McGrew, B., Petron, A., ... & Zaremba, W. (2019). Solving Rubik's Cube with a Robot Hand. arXiv preprint arXiv:1910.07113.

- Altman, S., & OpenAI. (2015). Welcome OpenAI. OpenAI. https://openai.com/blog/welcome-openai/

- Amodei, D., Olah, C., Steinhardt, J., Christiano, P., Schulman, J., & Mané, D. (2016). Concrete problems in AI safety. *arXiv preprint arXiv:1606.06565.*

- Arrieta, A. B., Díaz-Rodríguez, N., Del Ser, J., Bennetot, A., Tabik, S., Barbado, A., ... & Herrera, F. (2020). Explainable Artificial Intelligence (XAI): Concepts, taxonomies, opportunities and challenges toward responsible AI. Information Fusion, 58, 82-115.

- Auer, P., Cesa-Bianchi, N., & Fischer, P. (2002). Finite-time analysis of the multiarmed bandit problem. Machine learning, 47(2-3), 235-256.
- Autor, D. (2015). Why are there still so many jobs? The history and future of workplace automation. Journal of Economic Perspectives, 29(3), 3-30.
- Baltrušaitis, T., Ahuja, C., & Morency, L.-P. (2018). Multimodal machine learning: A survey and taxonomy. IEEE Transactions on Pattern Analysis and Machine Intelligence, 41(2), 423-443.
- Barocas, S., & Selbst, A. D. (2016). Big data's disparate impact. California Law Review, 104.
- Barocas, S., Hardt, M., & Narayanan, A. (2019). Fairness and abstraction in sociotechnical systems. ACM Conference on Fairness, Accountability, and Transparency (FAT*), 59-68.
- Bellamy, R. K. E., Dey, K., Hind, M., Hoffman, S. C., Houde, S., Kannan, K., ... & Zhang, Y. (2018). AI Fairness 360: An extensible toolkit for detecting, understanding, and mitigating unwanted algorithmic bias. *arXiv preprint arXiv:1810.01943*.
- Bender, E. M., & Friedman, B. (2018). Data statements for natural language processing: Toward mitigating system bias and enabling better science. Transactions of the Association for Computational Linguistics, 6, 587-604.
- Bender, E. M., Gebru, T., McMillan-Major, A., & Shmitchell, S. (2021). On the Dangers of Stochastic Parrots: Can Language Models Be Too Big? ◈ Proceedings of the 2021 ACM Conference on Fairness, Accountability, and Transparency.
- Bender, E. M., Gebru, T., McMillan-Major, A., & Shmitchell, S. (2021). On the Dangers of Stochastic Parrots: Can Language Models Be Too Big? Proceedings of the 2021 ACM Conference on Fairness, Accountability, and Transparency.
- Bisk, Y., Holtzman, A., Thomason, J., Andreas, J., Bengio, Y., Chai, J., ... & Zettlemoyer, L. (2020). Experience grounds language. In Proceedings of the 2020 Conference on Empirical Methods in Natural Language Processing (EMNLP).

- Blodgett, S. L., Barocas, S., Daumé III, H., & Wallach, H. (2020). Language (technology) is power: A critical survey of "bias" in NLP. In Proceedings of the 58th Annual Meeting of the Association for Computational Linguistics (pp. 5454-5476).
- Boden, M. A. (2010). Creativity and artificial intelligence. Artif. Intell., 103(1-2), 347-356.
- Bojarski, M., Del Testa, D., Dworakowski, D., Firner, B., Flepp, B., Goyal, P., ... & Zhang, X. (2016). End to end learning for self-driving cars. arXiv preprint arXiv:1604.07316.
- Bolukbasi, T., Chang, K. W., Zou, J. Y., Saligrama, V., & Kalai, A. T. (2016). Man is to computer programmer as woman is to homemaker? Debiasing word embeddings. Advances in Neural Information Processing Systems.
- Bommasani, R., Hudson, D. A., Adeli, E., Altman, R., Arora, S., von Arx, S., ... & Zou, J. (2021). On the opportunities and risks of foundation models. arXiv preprint arXiv:2108.07258.
- Bostrom, N., & Yudkowsky, E. (2014). The ethics of artificial intelligence. In Cambridge handbook of artificial intelligence (pp. 316-334). Cambridge University Press.
- Brockman, G., Cheung, V., Pettersson, L., Schneider, J., Schulman, J., Tang, J., & Zaremba, W. (2016). OpenAI Gym. arXiv preprint arXiv:1606.01540.
- Brown, T. B., Mann, B., Ryder, N., Subbiah, M., Kaplan, J., Dhariwal, P., Neelakantan, A., Shyam, P., Sastry, G., Askell, A., Agarwal, S., Herbert-Voss, A., Krueger, G., Henighan, T., Child, R., Ramesh, A., Ziegler, D. M., Wu, J., Winter, C., ... Amodei, D. (2020). Language Models are Few-Shot Learners. arXiv preprint arXiv:2005.14165.
- Brown, T. B., Mann, B., Ryder, N., Subbiah, M., Kaplan, J., Dhariwal, P., ... & Amodei, D. (2020). Language models are few-shot learners. arXiv preprint arXiv:2005.14165.
- Brynjolfsson, E., & McAfee, A. (2014). The second machine age: Work, progress, and prosperity in a time of brilliant technologies. WW Norton & Company.

- Bryson, J. (2018). AI & Global Governance: No One Should Trust AI. United Nations University Centre for Policy Research.
- Bryson, J. (2018). Patents and artificial intelligence: Thinking machines. *Computer Law & Security Review*, 34(4), 659-667.
- Bughin, J., Hazan, E., Lund, S., Dahlström, P., Wiesinger, A., & Subramaniam, A. (2018). Skill shift: Automation and the future of the workforce. McKinsey Global Institute.
- Buolamwini, J., & Gebru, T. (2018). Gender shades: Intersectional accuracy disparities in commercial gender classification. Proceedings of the 1st Conference on Fairness, Accountability and Transparency, 77–91.
- Burrell, J. (2016). How the machine 'thinks': Understanding opacity in machine learning algorithms. Big Data & Society, 3(1).
- Castelvecchi, D. (2016). Can we open the black box of AI? Nature News, 538(7623), 20.
- Cath, C., Wachter, S., Mittelstadt, B., Taddeo, M., & Floridi, L. (2018). Artificial intelligence and the 'good society': the US, EU, and UK approach. *Science and engineering ethics*, 24(2), 505-528.
- Cavoukian, A. (2009). Privacy by design: The 7 foundational principles. Information and Privacy Commissioner of Ontario, Canada.
- Chen, M., Tworek, J., Jun, H., Yuan, Q., Pinto, H. P., Kaplan, J., ... & Amodei, D. (2021). Evaluating Large Language Models Trained on Code. arXiv preprint arXiv:2107.03374.
- Colton, S., Goodwin, J., & Veale, T. (2012). Full-FACE poetry generation. *Proceedings of the International Conference on Computational Creativity.*
- Conneau, A., Khandelwal, K., Goyal, N., Chaudhary, V., Wenzek, G., Guzmán, F., ... & Stoyanov, V. (2020). Unsupervised cross-lingual representation learning at scale. arXiv preprint arXiv:1911.02116.
- Crawford, K., & Calo, R. (2016). There is a blind spot in AI research. Nature, 538(7625), 311-313.

- Daugherty, P. R., & Wilson, H. J. (2018). Human + Machine: Re-imagining Work in the Age of AI. *Harvard Business Review Press.*
- Davenport, T. H., & Kalakota, R. (2019). The potential for artificial intelligence in healthcare. *Future Healthcare Journal,* 6(2), 94-98.
- De Stefano, V. (2020). The rise of the just-in-time workforce: On-demand work, crowdwork, and labor protection in the gig-economy. *Comparative Labor Law & Policy Journal,* 37(3).
- Devlin, J., Chang, M. W., Lee, K., & Toutanova, K. (2018). BERT: Pre-training of deep bidirectional transformers for language understanding. arXiv preprint arXiv:1810.04805.
- Dignum, V. (2019). Responsible artificial intelligence: How to develop and use AI in a responsible way. Artificial Intelligence, 1-15.
- Doshi-Velez, F., & Kim, B. (2017). Towards a rigorous science of interpretable machine learning. arXiv preprint arXiv:1702.08608.
- Du Sautoy, M. (2019). The Creativity Code: Art and Innovation in the Age of AI. Harvard University Press.
- Engel, J., Resnick, C., Roberts, A., Dieleman, S., Norouzi, M., Eck, D., & Simonyan, K. (2020). Jukebox: A Generative Model for Music. *arXiv preprint arXiv:2005.00341.*
- Engel, J., Resnick, C., Roberts, A., Dieleman, S., Norouzi, M., Eck, D., & Simonyan, K. (2020). Jukebox: A Generative Model for Music. *arXiv preprint arXiv:2005.00341.*
- Esteva, A., Kuprel, B., Novoa, R. A., Ko, J., Swetter, S. M., Blau, H. M., & Thrun, S. (2017). Dermatologist-level classification of skin cancer with deep neural networks. *Nature,* 542(7639), 115-118.
- Esteva, A., Robicquet, A., Ramsundar, B., Kuleshov, V., DePristo, M., Chou, K., ... & Dean, J. (2019). A guide to deep learning in healthcare. *Nature Medicine,* 25(1), 24-29.
- Eubanks, V. (2018). Automating Inequality: How High-Tech Tools Profile, Police, and Punish the Poor. St. Martin's Press.

- Floridi, L. (2018). Soft ethics, the governance of the digital and the General Data Protection Regulation. Philosophical Transactions of the Royal Society A: Mathematical, Physical and Engineering Sciences, 376(2133).
- Floridi, L., & Cowls, J. (2019). A Unified Framework of Five Principles for AI in Society. Harvard Data Science Review.
- Frey, C. B., & Osborne, M. A. (2017). The future of employment: How susceptible are jobs to computerisation? Technological Forecasting and Social Change, 114, 254-280.
- Friedler, S. A., Scheidegger, C., & Venkatasubramanian, S. (2019). The (im)possibility of fairness: Different value systems require different mechanisms for fair decision making. Communications of the ACM, 62(10), 136-143.
- Goodfellow, I. J., Pouget-Abadie, J., Mirza, M., Xu, B., Warde-Farley, D., Ozair, S., Courville, A., & Bengio, Y. (2014). Generative Adversarial Networks. *arXiv preprint arXiv:1406.2661.*
- Goodfellow, I., Bengio, Y., & Courville, A. (2016). Deep learning. MIT press.
- Goodman, B., & Flaxman, S. (2017). European Union regulations on algorithmic decision-making and a "right to explanation". AI Magazine, 38(3), 50-57.
- Gu, S., Holly, E., Lillicrap, T., & Levine, S. (2017). Deep reinforcement learning for robotic manipulation with asynchronous off-policy updates. In Proceedings of the 2017 IEEE International Conference on Robotics and Automation (ICRA).
- Gunning, D., Aha, D. W., Stumpf, S., Byrne, B., & Yang, G. Z. (2019). XAI—Explainable artificial intelligence. Science Robotics, 4(37).
- Gunning, D., Aha, D. W., Stumpf, S., Thomson, J., & Yang, G. Z. (2017). Explainable Artificial Intelligence (XAI). Defense Advanced Research Projects Agency (DARPA), nd Web.
- Hadfield-Menell, D., Russell, S. J., Abbeel, P., & Dragan, A. (2017). The off-switch game. *arXiv preprint arXiv:1611.08219.*

- Hagendorff, T. (2020). The ethics of AI ethics: An evaluation of guidelines. Minds and Machines, 30(1), 99-120.
- Hardt, M., Price, E., & Srebro, N. (2016). Equality of Opportunity in Supervised Learning. In Advances in Neural Information Processing Systems.
- Hardt, M., Price, E., & Srebro, N. (2016). Equality of opportunity in supervised learning. *Advances in Neural Information Processing Systems*, 3315-3323.
- Hastie, T., Tibshirani, R., & Friedman, J. (2009). *The Elements of Statistical Learning: Data Mining, Inference, and Prediction*. Springer Series in Statistics.
- Henderson, P., Hu, J., Romoff, J., Brunskill, E., Jurafsky, D., & Pineau, J. (2020). Towards the Systematic Reporting of the Energy and Carbon Footprints of Machine Learning. *arXiv preprint arXiv:2002.05651*.
- Hendrycks, D., Carlini, N., Schulman, J., & Steinhardt, J. (2021). Unsolved problems in ML safety. arXiv preprint arXiv:2109.13916.
- Hendrycks, D., Carlini, N., Schulman, J., & Steinhardt, J. (2021). Unsolved problems in ML safety. arXiv preprint arXiv:2109.13916.
- Hirschberg, J., & Manning, C. D. (2015). Advances in natural language processing. Science, 349(6245), 261-266.
- Hovy, D., & Spruit, S. L. (2016). The social impact of natural language processing. In Proceedings of the 54th Annual Meeting of the Association for Computational Linguistics (pp. 591-598).
- Hutchins, J., & Somers, H. L. (1992). An introduction to machine translation. Academic Press.
- Irpan, A., Packer, C., Gin, K., McGrew, S., Mordatch, I., Liu, J., ... & Tunyasuvunakool, S. (2018). AI and compute. OpenAI. https://openai.com/research/ai-and-compute/
- Jobin, A., Ienca, M., & Vayena, E. (2019). The global landscape of AI ethics guidelines. Nature Machine Intelligence, 1(9), 389-399.

- Jordan, M. I., & Mitchell, T. M. (2015). Machine learning: Trends, perspectives, and prospects. Science, 349(6245), 255-260.
- Jurafsky, D., & Martin, J. H. (2019). Speech and language processing (3rd ed.). Draft chapters in progress.
- Koren, Y., & Bell, R. (2015). Advances in collaborative filtering. In Recommender Systems Handbook (pp. 77-118). Springer.
- Kraemer, F., van Overveld, K., & Peterson, M. (2021). Artificial Intelligence, Responsibility Attribution, and a Relational Justification of Explainability. Science and Engineering Ethics, 27(4), 1-29.
- Kurzweil, R. (2005). The singularity is near: When humans transcend biology. Viking.
- LeCun, Y., Bengio, Y., & Hinton, G. (2015). Deep learning. Nature, 521(7553), 436-444.
- Leike, J., Martic, M., Krakovna, V., Ortega, P. A., Everitt, T., Lefrancq, A., ... & Legg, S. (2017). AI safety gridworlds. arXiv preprint arXiv:1711.09883.
- Liakos, K. G., Busato, P., Moshou, D., Pearson, S., & Bochtis, D. (2018). Machine learning in agriculture: A review. *Sensors*, 18(8), 2674.
- Luckin, R., Holmes, W., Griffiths, M., & Forcier, L. B. (2016). Intelligence Unleashed: An argument for AI in Education. *Pearson Education.*
- Luger, G. F., & Stubblefield, W. A. (2004). Artificial Intelligence: Structures and Strategies for Complex Problem Solving (5th ed.). Pearson.
- Marcus, G. (2018). Deep Learning: A Critical Appraisal. *arXiv preprint arXiv:1801.00631.*
- Martin, K. (2019). Ethical implications and accountability of algorithms. *Journal of Business Ethics*, 160(4), 835-850.
- McCarthy, J., Minsky, M. L., Rochester, N., & Shannon, C. E. (1956). A proposal for the Dartmouth summer research project on artificial intelligence.

- McMahan, H. B., Moore, E., Ramage, D., Hampson, S., & y Arcas, B. A. (2017). Communication-efficient learning of deep networks from decentralized data. Proceedings of the 20th International Conference on Artificial Intelligence and Statistics (AISTATS) 2017, 54.
- McTear, M., Callejas, Z., & Griol, D. (2016). The conversational interface: Talking to smart devices. Springer.
- Mehrabi, N., Morstatter, F., Saxena, N., Lerman, K., & Galstyan, A. (2019). A survey on bias and fairness in machine learning. arXiv preprint arXiv:1908.09635.
- Mitchell, M., Wu, S., Zaldivar, A., Barnes, P., Vasserman, L., Hutchinson, B., Spitzer, E., Raji, I. D., & Gebru, T. (2019). Model Cards for Model Reporting. Proceedings of the Conference on Fairness, Accountability, and Transparency.
- Mittelstadt, B. (2016). The ethics of algorithms: Mapping the debate. Big Data & Society, 3(2).
- Nielsen, M. (2011). Reinventing discovery: The new era of networked science. Princeton University Press.
- Norouzzadeh, M. S., Nguyen, A., Kosmala, M., Swanson, A., Palmer, M. S., Packer, C., & Clune, J. (2018). Automatically identifying, counting, and describing wild animals in camera-trap images with deep learning. *Proceedings of the National Academy of Sciences*, 115(25), E5716-E5725.
- Norouzzadeh, M. S., Nguyen, A., Kosmala, M., Swanson, A., Palmer, M. S., Packer, C., & Clune, J. (2018). Automatically identifying, counting, and describing wild animals in camera-trap images with deep learning. *Proceedings of the National Academy of Sciences*, 115(25), E5716-E5725.
- O'Neil, C. (2016). Weapons of math destruction: How big data increases inequality and threatens democracy. Crown.
- OpenAI. (2018). Learning Dexterity. Retrieved from https://openai.com/blog/learning-dexterity/

- OpenAI. (2019). Better Language Models and Their Implications. Retrieved from https://openai.com/blog/better-language-models/
- OpenAI. (2020). Jukebox. Retrieved from https://openai.com/blog/jukebox/
- OpenAI. (2020). OpenAI API. Retrieved from https://openai.com/blog/openai-api/
- OpenAI. (2020). Robotics at OpenAI. OpenAI Blog.
- OpenAI. (2020). Solving Rubik's Cube with a Robot Hand. Retrieved from https://openai.com/blog/solving-rubiks-cube/
- OpenAI. (2021). DALL·E: Creating Images from Text. Retrieved from https://openai.com/blog/dall-e/
- OpenAI. (2021). OpenAI Codex. Retrieved from https://openai.com/blog/openai-codex/
- OpenAI. (n.d.). About OpenAI. OpenAI. https://openai.com/about/
- Papernot, N., McDaniel, P., Wu, X., Jha, S., & Swami, A. (2016). Distillation as a defense to adversarial perturbations against deep neural networks. In 2016 IEEE Symposium on Security and Privacy (SP) (pp. 582-597). IEEE.
- Pariser, E. (2011). The filter bubble: How the new personalized web is changing what we read and how we think. Penguin.
- Price, H. (2020). Ethics and artificial intelligence: The moral compass of a machine. Palgrave Macmillan.
- Radford, A., Kim, J. W., Hallacy, C., Ramesh, A., Goh, G., Agarwal, S., ... & Sutskever, I. (2021). Learning Transferable Visual Models From Natural Language Supervision. arXiv preprint arXiv:2103.00020.
- Radford, A., Narasimhan, K., Salimans, T., & Sutskever, I. (2018). Improving language understanding by generative pre-training.
- Radford, A., Wu, J., Child, R., Luan, D., Amodei, D., & Sutskever, I. (2019). Language models are unsupervised multitask learners. OpenAI. https://d4mucfpksywv.cloudfront.net/better-

language-models/language_models_are_unsupervised_multi-task_learners.pdf

- Rahwan, I. (2018). Society-in-the-loop: Programming the algorithmic social contract. *Ethics and Information Technology*, 20(1), 5-14.

- Rahwan, I., Cebrian, M., Obradovich, N., Bongard, J., Bonnefon, J. F., Breazeal, C., ... & Jennings, N. R. (2019). Machine behaviour. Nature, 568(7753), 477-486.

- Ramesh, A., Pavlov, M., Goh, G., Gray, S., Voss, C., Radford, A., ... & Sutskever, I. (2021). Zero-Shot Text-to-Image Generation. arXiv preprint arXiv:2102.12092.

- Rawls, J. (1971). A Theory of Justice. Harvard University Press.

- Rawls, J. (1999). A theory of justice. Harvard University Press.

- Raymond, E. S. (1999). The cathedral and the bazaar: Musings on Linux and open source by an accidental revolutionary. O'Reilly Media, Inc.

- Regulation (EU) 2016/679 of the European Parliament and of the Council of 27 April 2016 on the protection of natural persons with regard to the processing of personal data and on the free movement of such data (General Data Protection Regulation).

- Ribeiro, M. T., Singh, S., & Guestrin, C. (2016). "Why should I trust you?" Explaining the predictions of any classifier. Proceedings of the 22nd ACM SIGKDD International Conference on Knowledge Discovery and Data Mining.

- Rolnick, D., Donti, P. L., Kaack, L. H., Kochanski, K., Lacoste, A., Sankaran, K., ... & Bengio, Y. (2019). Tackling Climate Change with Machine Learning. *arXiv preprint arXiv:1906.05433*.

- Ruder, S., Vulić, I., & Søgaard, A. (2019). A survey of cross-lingual word embedding models. Journal of Artificial Intelligence Research, 65, 569-631.

- Rudin, C. (2019). Stop explaining black box machine learning models for high stakes decisions and use interpretable models instead. *Nature Machine Intelligence*, 1(5), 206–215.

- Russell, S. J., & Norvig, P. (2021). Artificial intelligence: A modern approach. Pearson.
- Russell, S., Dewey, D., & Tegmark, M. (2015). Research priorities for robust and beneficial artificial intelligence. AI Magazine, 36(4), 105-114.
- Russell, S., Dewey, D., & Tegmark, M. (2015). Research priorities for robust and beneficial artificial intelligence. *AI Magazine*, 36(4), 105-114.
- Schwab, K. (2016). The Fourth Industrial Revolution. *World Economic Forum.*
- Schwartz, J. (2019). Navigating the Future of Work: Can We Point Business, Workers, and Social Institutions in the Same Direction? Deloitte Insights.
- Schwartz, R., Dodge, J., Smith, N. A., & Etzioni, O. (2020). Green AI. Communications of the ACM, 63(12), 54-63.
- Sen, A. (2009). The Idea of Justice. Belknap Press of Harvard University Press.
- Senior, A. W., Evans, R., Jumper, J., Kirkpatrick, J., Sifre, L., Green, T., ... & Hassabis, D. (2020). Improved protein structure prediction using potentials from deep learning. Nature, 577(7792), 706-710.
- Shalev-Shwartz, S., Shammah, S., & Shashua, A. (2016). Safe, multi-agent, reinforcement learning for autonomous driving. arXiv preprint arXiv:1610.03295.
- Silver, D., Huang, A., Maddison, C. J., Guez, A., Sifre, L., Van Den Driessche, G., ... & Hassabis, D. (2016). Mastering the game of Go with deep neural networks and tree search. Nature, 529(7587), 484-489.
- Solaiman, I., Clark, J., Brundage, M., & Amodei, D. (2019). Release Strategies and the Social Impacts of Language Models. OpenAI Blog.
- Sparrow, R. (2020). AI and the Future of Work: The Prospects for Tomorrow's Jobs. Business Horizons.

- Stodden, V., McNutt, M., Bailey, D. H., Deelman, E., Gil, Y., Hanson, B., Heroux, M. A., Ioannidis, J. P. A., & Taufer, M. (2016). Enhancing reproducibility for computational methods. Science, 354(6317), 1240-1241.
- Strubell, E., Ganesh, A., & McCallum, A. (2019). Energy and policy considerations for deep learning in NLP. Proceedings of the 57th Annual Meeting of the Association for Computational Linguistics.
- Strubell, E., Ganesh, A., & McCallum, A. (2019). Energy and Policy Considerations for Deep Learning in NLP. *arXiv preprint arXiv:1906.02243.*
- Sutton, R. S., & Barto, A. G. (2018). *Reinforcement Learning: An Introduction.* MIT Press.
- Szeliski, R. (2010). Computer vision: Algorithms and applications. Springer Science & Business Media.
- Taddeo, M., & Floridi, L. (2018). How AI can be a force for good. Science, 361(6404), 751-752.
- Taddeo, M., & Floridi, L. (2018). Regulate artificial intelligence to avert cyber arms race. Nature, 556(7701), 296-298.
- Taylor, L., Floridi, L., & van der Sloot, B. (Eds.). (2016). Group privacy: New challenges of data technologies. Springer.
- Tokic, M. (2010). Adaptive ε-greedy exploration in reinforcement learning based on value differences. In Annual Conference on Artificial Intelligence (pp. 203-210). Springer.
- Tokic, M. (2010). Adaptive ε-greedy exploration in reinforcement learning based on value differences. In Annual Conference on Artificial Intelligence (pp. 203-210). Springer.
- Topol, E. J. (2019). High-performance medicine: the convergence of human and artificial intelligence. *Nature Medicine*, 25(1), 44-56.
- Turing, A. M. (1950). Computing machinery and intelligence. Mind, 59(236), 433-460.

- Turkle, S. (2017). Alone together: Why we expect more from technology and less from each other. Basic Books.
- Vaswani, A., Shazeer, N., Parmar, N., Uszkoreit, J., Jones, L., Gomez, A. N., Kaiser, Ł., & Polosukhin, I. (2017). Attention is all you need. In Advances in Neural Information Processing Systems (pp. 5998-6008).
- Veale, M., & Binns, R. (2017). Fairer machine learning in the real world: Mitigating discrimination without collecting sensitive data. Big Data & Society, 4(2).
- Vickery, G. (2017). Open access to data and information: Challenges and opportunities. Information Development, 33(2), 175-190.
- Vinuesa, R., Azizpour, H., Leite, I., Balaam, M., Dignum, V., Domisch, S., ... & Nerini, F. F. (2020). The role of artificial intelligence in achieving the Sustainable Development Goals. Nature Communications, 11(1), 1-10.
- Voigt, P., & Von dem Bussche, A. (2017). The EU General Data Protection Regulation (GDPR). A Practical Guide, 1st Ed., Cham: Springer International Publishing.
- West, D. M. (2018). The Future of Work: Robots, AI, and Automation. Brookings Institution Press.
- Whittaker, M., Crawford, K., Dobbe, R., Fried, G., Kaziunas, E., Mathur, V., West, S. M., Richardson, R., Schultz, J., & Schwartz, O. (2018). AI Now Report 2018. AI Now Institute.
- Wojciechowski, R. (2019). Accessibility, Inclusivity, and Universal Design for Learning. In Artificial Intelligence in Education. Springer.
- Wooldridge, M. (2019). The road to conscious machines: The story of AI. Penguin UK.
- Young, T., Hazarika, D., Poria, S., & Cambria, E. (2018). Recent trends in deep learning based natural language processing. IEEE Computational Intelligence Magazine, 13(3), 55-75.
- Zawacki-Richter, O., Marín, V. I., Bond, M., & Gouverneur, F. (2019). Systematic review of research on artificial intelligence

applications in higher education – where are the educators? International Journal of Educational Technology in Higher Education, 16(1), 39.

- Zhang, C., Bengio, S., Hardt, M., Recht, B., & Vinyals, O. (2018). Understanding deep learning requires rethinking generalization. *arXiv preprint arXiv:1611.03530.*

- Zhang, D., Liu, Q., Wang, Y., & Alippi, C. (2018). A review on deep learning in UAV remote sensing. *International Journal of Remote Sensing*, 39(15-16), 5078-5106.

- Zheng, G., Zhang, F., Zheng, Z., Xiang, Y., Yuan, N. J., Xie, X., & Li, Z. (2018). DRN: A deep reinforcement learning framework for news recommendation. In Proceedings of the 2018 World Wide Web Conference.

- Zuboff, S. (2019). The age of surveillance capitalism: The fight for a human future at the new frontier of power. PublicAffairs.

www.ingramcontent.com/pod-product-compliance
Lightning Source LLC
Chambersburg PA
CBHW070746160726
48004CB00001B/76